# ANGRY
# KIDS

*Also by Richard Berry*

Haven't We Gone through This Before?

# ANGRY KIDS

Understanding
and Managing
the Emotions
That Control
Them

DR. RICHARD L. BERRY

Fleming H. Revell
A Division of Baker Book House Co
Grand Rapids, Michigan 49516

© 2001 by Richard L. Berry

Published by Fleming H. Revell
a division of Baker Book House Company
P.O. Box 6287, Grand Rapids, MI 49516-6287

Printed in the United States of America

**Library of Congress Cataloging-in-Publication Data**

Berry, Richard L., 1950–
 Angry kids : understanding and managing the emotions that control them /
Richard L. Berry.
  p.  cm.
 Includes bibliographical references.
 ISBN 0-8007-5757-2
 1. Anger in children. 2. Anger in children—Case studies. 3. Anger in adolescence.
4. Anger in adolescence—Case studies. 5. Child rearing. I. Title.
BF723.A4 B47  2001
694'.64—dc21                               2001019789

*32530 60562 7841*

Unless otherwise indicated, Scripture is taken from the HOLY BIBLE, NEW INTERNATIONAL VERSION®. NIV®. Copyright© 1973, 1978, 1984 by International Bible Society. Used by permission of Zondervan Publishing House. All rights reserved.

For current information about all releases from Baker Book House, visit our web site:
http://www.bakerbooks.com

To:

The angry children and adolescents and their concerned parents. Thanks for courageously sharing your family story and working hard to change it.

The wonderful staff at Youth Alternatives who care every day about kids. It's a privilege to work with you.

# Contents

# Acknowledgments

A project like this isn't done in isolation. Thanks to:

- Alona Geist and Mary Suggs for making the manuscript readable.
- Bonnie Berry, Brian Berry, Mike Berry, and Melissa Berry for reading, critiquing, and encouraging.
- Pat Stoehrmann, Bob and Jill Jensen, Martha Thein, and Denise Martin for reading and correcting at crucial times.
- The wonderful people at Fleming Revell, especially Bill Petersen, Jennifer Leep, Karen Steele, and Sheila Ingram.

# Introduction

*Roots of Your Child's Anger*

Why is he so angry, and what can I do about it? You've thought a lot about these questions and still don't have any answers. Today was the last straw. He came home, slammed the screen door, stomped through the house, and went to his room. Shortly after you heard his door slam shut, there was a loud smack. When you went to investigate, you found he had punched a hole in his bedroom wall. It's hard to keep calm, but you realized last weekend that losing your cool doesn't accomplish anything.

"Why are you so angry? Don't you know what you are doing isn't okay? It's going to get you into a lot of trouble. Let's talk about this. Why are you so angry?"

"It's none of your business. Get out of my room!"

After a long pause you say, "I'm not leaving until we get this figured out. You can't keep going on like this. What's the matter?"

He responds with a shrug of the shoulders and an "I don't know."

"Come on, you must have some idea why you're so mad."

"I don't want to do the stuff I do, but I just get so mad I can't stop myself. I'm sorry for punching the hole in the wall. I don't want to talk about it now. Can we talk later?" (What he really means is "not now—not ever.")

Even though your child is a very angry person, you still love him. You're concerned about him, his behavior, and the possible consequences he and others may suffer if he doesn't learn to control himself. It would help if you knew why he is mad, but you have no idea.

Out of frustration you think, What he needs is a good spanking. Generally this isn't a good option, particularly as children reach junior high age. Physical altercations usually produce more aggression and hostility, not less. So what are you supposed to do?

To develop a positive approach to dealing with your child's anger, you must discover the root of it. When concerned parents call for help with their child's behavior, I have them consider four root causes of anger. Your child may be angry because of his life experiences, his lack of problem-solving skills, his lack of self-control, or his success in using anger to get what he wants. While any one of these root causes may be the main contributor to his anger, probably all four play a part and should be addressed. This book will help you identify the causes for your child's anger. Other help provided here includes:

- *Explanation of typical patterns of behavior* associated with specific events that generate anger.
- *Guidelines* for differentiating parental responsibilities and child responsibilities. You don't have to be responsible for everything! Focusing on your responsibilities allows you to step out of negative parent-child interactions.
- *Practical parental plans.* These plans provide you with specific points to follow in dealing with the root causes of your child's anger.
- *Cue cards* that actually tell you what to say to your angry child.
- *Appendices* that summarize vital information.

# Part 1

# Dealing with Life Experiences

Your child may have experienced situations that would cause anyone in his position to be angry. Over the years of working with angry children, I've learned to check for these eight causes of childhood anger: abuse (physical or sexual), divorce, blended family, parental favoritism, parental abandonment, losses, parental alcoholism or drug use, or being overindulged.

Let's begin by examining these eight issues that we know create anger in children. Be careful not to prematurely dismiss them because you think they don't apply to your child. Examine the behavioral and relational characteristics provided in the following chapters and compare them to your child's behavior. You may find indications that one of these issues is contributing to your child's anger. By directly addressing these concerns, you will be able to help lessen your child's anger.

# 1

# Physical and Sexual Abuse

## Eric: A Physically Abused Child

Eric, a fourteen-year-old boy with blond hair and a contagious smile, was brought in for counseling so he could learn to control his temper. His mother, Barbara, reported, "Eric is extremely defiant and nothing is ever his fault. He's so angry that I'm afraid he's going to hurt his younger stepbrother." Bob (second stepdad) was a nice man and did care about Eric. Even so, Eric often pushed his stepdad beyond the limits of his patience. Eric was very angry at him and showed it by secretly breaking things Bob valued. After discovering his broken possessions, Bob felt justified in spanking Eric—nothing else appeared to work. Barbara knew something had to be done, but she worried about the increasing number of physical altercations between Bob and Eric.

Bob wanted Barbara to take a firmer hand with her son, but she just couldn't. She felt extremely guilty about the physical abuse Eric had experienced at the hands of her previous husband, Tim. When Barbara and Tim disagreed, Tim would hit her, causing Eric to step in to protect his mother. Tim would then turn his anger on Eric. During one of those times, he broke Eric's wrist.

Because of the abuse and all they had gone through together, Eric and his mom interacted more like peers than mother and son, and Eric was never able to talk about his anger toward his mom for her lack of protection and poor marital choices. Because he couldn't deal with the anger, Eric channeled it to the person in the dad's role. The tension in the home continued to escalate, finally resulting in Eric's placement in a group home to work on his temper.

## Katie: A Sexually Abused Child

Katie, a precocious junior high student, currently has no use for school. Last year she made the honor roll, but she now has all Ds except for one F. Katie looks and acts much older than her thirteen years. When she and her parents came in for counseling, she rarely made eye contact with me and certainly didn't want to talk to me or her parents. The only thing she said was an extremely angry statement toward her parents for not allowing her to go to an out-of-town concert with her seventeen-year-old boyfriend.

The parents appeared to have the right balance between loving their daughter and setting firm limits on her unacceptable behavior. Katie's actions just didn't make sense given her history and her parents' presentation of the situation. After an intense session in which the parents expressed their love and great confusion about her behavior, Katie broke down and told them she had been raped earlier in the year by one of her classmates after a volleyball game. She chose not to tell them because she was so embarrassed and ashamed. She knew they would be disappointed in her.

Fortunately for Katie, her parents were very responsive to her pain. Even though they were disappointed and hurt, they understood her apprehension in telling them. They chose to focus on helping her, not condemning her or calling her names. Katie was visibly relieved to have her parents' support. At her request, I arranged for Katie to meet with a female therapist. While Katie worked in the individual counseling, we continued the family sessions to reestablish trust and develop a plan for getting Katie's life back on track. She made excellent progress, brought up her grades, and became the "old Katie" her parents so much enjoyed.

# Abuse Generates Anger

Physical and sexual abuse are difficult to work through because they involve so many issues, each generating more anger. Pain is inflicted. Safety is compromised. Trust is broken. Power is abused. Fear is heightened. All of these limit the abused person's ability to cope, creating a sense of hopelessness, frustration, and anger. Typically the abused person believes there is *nothing* she can do to help the situation. Could abuse be an underlying reason for your child's anger?

## *Typical Responses to Abuse*

Children may respond to physical abuse in the following behavioral or relational ways:

### Physical Abuse

| Behavioral Responses | Relational Responses |
|---|---|
| Making up stories to explain bruises or marks | Having great difficulty trusting others |
| Flinching in response to sudden movements | Not allowing others to get too close |
| Having startle response to loud noises or unexpected occurrences | Not sharing feelings or significant thoughts |
| Scanning environment for possible sources of trouble—hypervigilant | Having superficial relationships due to their anger and lack of trust |
| Finding safety in knowing situation and environment, not from knowing or being with significant others | Violating others' space or boundaries |
| Having a high need to be in control at all times | |
| Unwilling to obey those in authority | |
| Being defiant, even when cooperation would be beneficial | |
| Erupting over small things | |
| Being mean to pets or smaller children | |
| Avoiding contact with people | |
| Sabotaging their own success, believing they don't deserve to be successful | |
| Resisting talking about their concerns | |
| Running away from home | |

## Sexual Abuse

| Behavioral Responses | Relational Responses |
| --- | --- |
| Engaging in precocious sexual activity or language | Having high need to be in control of the relationship |
| Acting much younger or older than their age | Reversing roles with their mother or having poor relationship with their mother |
| "Dating" older boys | Having poor peer relationships |
| Coping by being flirtatious or seductive | Distrusting of those in authority |
| Being fearful of being left alone with certain people | Receiving special favors: material possessions, privileges, exemptions from punishment |
| Not feeling good about themselves | Having trouble trusting others |
| Being uncomfortable with their body and their body image | Choosing negative relationships involving sex, drugs, acting out |
| Being hostile, angry, and disobedient to those in authority | Having sexualized relationships—sex is focal point of many relationships |
| Showing feelings in a sexual, delinquent, or aggressive way | Not respecting boundaries or limits, violating personal space of others |
| Taking dangerous risks: self-destructive, perhaps suicidal | |
| Acting depressed (listless, weight fluctuation, sleep problems, no energy) | |
| Running away from home | |
| Retreating into fantasy life | |
| Using drugs as a way to escape | |
| Having bladder problems, bed wetting, infections, sexually transmitted diseases | |
| Being cruel to animals | |
| Starting fires | |

The more of these signs you see, the more likely that your child has been physically or sexually abused.

Abused children may deal with their anger in several ways:

*Expressing it indirectly in a passive/aggressive manner.* Because children in abusive situations don't feel safe expressing their anger directly, they disguise it and express it indirectly. They learn to get even while minimizing the probability of getting caught and being in trouble.

Eric couldn't talk about his anger with Mom or Bob. Mom couldn't tolerate the anger and the distance it created in their relationship. Because of his experience with Tim, Eric couldn't risk a direct confrontation with Bob, so he got back at Bob by breaking his possessions and lying about it.

Katie wasn't able to directly express her anger because of her guilt and shame. To do so would mean others would find out about the rape.

*Being mean and hurting those who are younger or smaller—pets included.* From their experiences, abused children may learn to vent their frustrations on those who can't directly and effectively retaliate. Eric unloaded his anger on his younger stepbrother. Unfortunately this also created more antagonism with Bob. Abused children often vent their anger on pets. How does the family pet act around your child? Does it seem frightened?

*Picking fights—about anything.* Abused children get tired of the abuse and eventually decide they don't have to take it anymore. Driven by anger, they begin testing their strength by setting up confrontations (often physical ones). Typically this occurs during adolescence when they target the person who abused them or a person in a similar role. Eric's growth spurt caused him to wonder how much longer Bob could control him. Their physical confrontations proved that the two were pretty evenly matched, encouraging Eric to push even harder to have his way.

*Using anger to get what they want.* Anger works. If abused children have seen someone use anger and abusive behavior to get what he/she wanted, it becomes a viable option for them to use. Because of the anger generated by the abuse, physical and sexual abuse victims may use their anger to get what they want.

*Directing anger toward those people who should have protected them.* Believing they should have been better protected, some children direct all of their anger toward the nonabusive parent. This helps them deal with their anger, while minimizing the danger of a strong and painful response from the abusive parent. Many children, however, are hesitant to vent anger toward the nonabusive parent because they don't want to risk losing that relationship. This was the main reason Eric could never talk about his anger toward his mother. The anger toward the nonabusive parent probably won't be expressed until the environment is stable and secure. While it is hard for the parent to hear, the child needs to express her anger for the lack of reasonable protection.

*Directing it toward themselves.* The perpetrator usually tells the child that she (the child) is wrong, the problem, and the bad person. Believing what she's told, she thinks she deserves to be punished and must feel bad about herself. Punishing herself is viewed as a way of penance. Directing anger inward may cause her to become self-destructive, depressed, and perhaps suicidal. Katie dealt with her anger by focusing it on herself. Her behavior evoked anger and disappointment from her parents, exactly what she thought she would receive from them if they knew about the rape. Believing she was at fault, she acted in a way that ensured her punishment.

*Directing it toward the perpetrator.* An abused child typically doesn't openly direct his anger toward the perpetrator because of possible repercussions she or someone she loves may suffer. However, if the rule in the house has been "might makes right," when the child goes through a growth spurt and is as big or bigger than the abuser, she is then more likely to vent her anger on the perpetrator.

 *Parental Plan*

The plan for assisting your child to deal with the abuse and her anger depends on who did the abuse. Whether *you* did the abuse or it was done by *another person,* you have a key role in helping your child cope. As she successfully works through the abuse issues, her anger will subside.

### Plan A: If You Were Abusive

*Take responsibility for your actions.* You gain nothing by minimizing the harm you have done. Admitting that what you did was wrong and apologizing are the first steps in repairing the relationship. Given the right (or wrong) circumstances, almost anyone is capable of overreacting and hurting his/her child. Your child certainly may have had a part in pushing you to the limit, but minimizing your actions and blaming it on her encourages her to take a similar stance of blame and avoidance.

*Make a commitment that the abuse won't reoccur.* You can take charge of the situation by not allowing the abuse to occur again. Abusive situations inflict great damage on the parent-child relationship. Do whatever you need to do to keep from abusing: Take a time out,

> ### A Parent's Cue Card
>
> *"There is no excuse for what I did. I was wrong and I'm sorry I hurt you."*

leave, go for a walk, get help, include someone in a tough conversation so it doesn't escalate. Most decisions and conflicts can be put on hold while you regain your composure. Don't drink alcohol, which lowers your ability to control your actions. Don't allow your child to push you to a breaking point.

> ### A Parent's Cue Card
>
> *"What happened hurt our relationship. Because I care about you, I'm going to make sure this will not happen again. When things start to get out of hand, I will call a 'time-out.' At that point, I need you to go to your room and I'll go to mine for fifteen minutes. This will allow me to cool down."*

*Provide a safe environment.* After an abusive episode, it's best to refrain from any type of physical discipline because it will be frightening for your child and may allow you to be more physical than you want to be. Until your child feels safe, she won't feel comfortable being with you or talking with you. If you keep your temper under control, over time her trust in you will return.

If your child doesn't believe she can safely express her thoughts and feelings, she won't share them. Reassure her that you won't lose control and that you want to communicate with her. Listening is key.

Don't try to rationalize or justify what you did. What your child needs is simply an opportunity to say what she needs to say. Setting the ground rules and the place to talk may reassure your child she will be safe and will be heard.

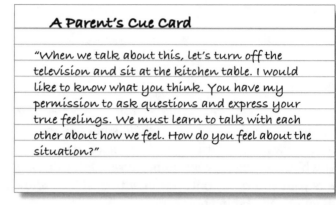

### A Parent's Cue Card

"When we talk about this, let's turn off the television and sit at the kitchen table. I would like to know what you think. You have my permission to ask questions and express your true feelings. We must learn to talk with each other about how we feel. How do you feel about the situation?"

*Find new ways to discipline.* Eliminating physical force from the consequence list doesn't make you impotent in responding to misbehavior. Often, the *certainty* of the punishment has more impact on changing the child's behavior than does the severity. Focus on what you can do to hold your child accountable. Don't interfere with the natural consequences associated with an action. For example, your child should pay her speeding ticket, not you. Use "If-then" statements for situations under your control.

*Take away his threat of turning you in for abuse.* If your child uses the threat of an abuse report to get what he wants, he will continue to

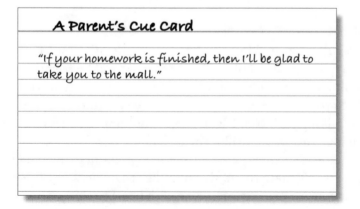

### A Parent's Cue Card

"If your homework is finished, then I'll be glad to take you to the mall."

use it until it no longer works. If you are threatened, offer to make the call yourself.

**A Parent's Cue Card**

"If you think this is abuse, I will call Family Services and we will talk with them together about this situation and how we should handle it. You talk first and then I'll give them my perspective."

*Find time to do fun things together.* Positive time must occur to shift the focus of the relationship away from the abuse. Be willing to do something she likes to do. All you can do is offer. It is up to her to accept or refuse.

**A Parent's Cue Card**

"Let's do something fun this weekend. You mentioned a movie you'd like to see. Let's go on Saturday afternoon."

### Plan B: If Another Person Was Abusive

*Provide safety and support.* The first step in dealing with an abusive situation is to make sure your child is safe and protected. To do this, you may need to call the police, go to a safe house, move to another location, or limit contact with the abuser. Before any progress can be made, safety must be assured.

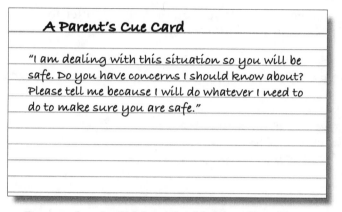

*Reassure her she did the right thing by telling.* To ensure the child's silence, the abuser usually threatens harm to her or other family members or otherwise points out the negative repercussions of her telling. Your child may have had to overcome huge barriers to confide in you. Reinforce that she did the right thing.

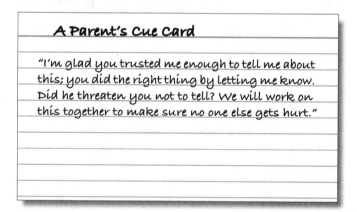

*Reinforce that it wasn't her fault.* In an attempt to control, the abuser repeatedly advises the child that she is at fault: "You are the reason these things occur." He wouldn't do what he does if it were not for the fact that she causes him to do it. Because of this tactic, it is important to also repeatedly emphasize that she isn't at fault.

*Identify her strengths and empower her.* At the time of the abuse there may have been little or nothing she could have done. This belief or mind-set that she could do nothing often gets carried over to other times and situations. She then believes she can't do anything *now*

> ### A Parent's Cue Card
>
> "Let's be clear about this. What happened wasn't your fault. You are not to blame. He is the one with the problem and he needs to work it out. What he did wasn't okay. It wasn't your fault. Do you believe that? If you don't, let's talk about why you think it might have been your fault."

about her life circumstances. Having this conversation gives you an opportunity to help her see she has power and control over her life. Focusing on how she is now bigger, stronger, wiser, or faster can help your child feel more secure.

> ### A Parent's Cue Card
>
> "Sometimes when people have been abused, they believe that because they couldn't do anything about it at the time, they are helpless to do anything about their life now. I'd like to know how you have changed since it occurred. How have you changed?"

*Encourage her to talk about her feelings.* She may need your support to specifically identify such feelings as sadness, anger, hurt, humiliation, shame, embarrassment, or guilt. When a child understands how she feels, she is able to look more objectively at the thoughts and beliefs behind the feelings. She may indeed feel guilty, but identifying and talking about why she feels guilty will allow her to work through the guilt, determining if she did anything that warrants her guilty feelings.

Abuse can inflict great damage on an adolescent's sense of her self—of who she is. Because of sexual abuse, the adolescent may be-

lieve she is "damaged goods" and lock onto the script that all she deserves in life is to be a mistreated sexual object.

Finding a balance between always talking about the abuse or never
talking about it will help your child heal. Focusing on the trauma and
awfulness of the situation may cause your child to believe it was
worse than it really was. Avoiding talking about it or minimizing the
significance of the event causes her to keep her thoughts and feelings
to herself. Be aware of times she may need to talk about these issues,
always reinforcing her ability to cope.

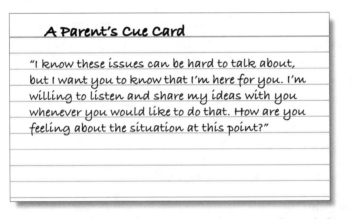

### A Parent's Cue Card

"I know these issues can be hard to talk about,
but I want you to know that I'm here for you. I'm
willing to listen and share my ideas with you
whenever you would like to do that. How are you
feeling about the situation at this point?"

*Be aware of the need to reexamine these issues.* Sexual abuse victims typically need to rethink what the abuse means to them when they move
on to different developmental stages or deeper levels of intimacy.
How does the abuse influence what she thinks about dating? Is she
ready to deal with the closeness, the possibility of physical contact,
the sexual pressures? Does she expect to be treated properly, or will
she accept any kind of male attention? Can she set firm limits and
have them respected? Dealing with these concerns will allow her to
have a healthy male-female relationship.

A boy who has been sexually abused by another male may have a
real concern that the experience makes him a homosexual. You need
to reassure your child that isn't true.

*Teach how normal relationships work.* Kids may believe that physical
or sexual abuse is normal. They may not know any families where
abuse doesn't happen. They don't realize that people aren't abused
in healthy relationships.

---

### A Parent's Cue Card

"I've heard your friends talking a lot more about boys. Do you remember when we last talked and how I said the abuse might influence the way you feel about certain situations? Having a boyfriend may be one of those situations. How do you feel about going out? Do you think you are ready for a relationship?"

---

### A Parent's Cue Card

"Sometimes when the abuser is a man, guys can mistakenly think that the experience makes them gay. This isn't true, but a lot of guys worry about it. Have you ever wondered about that?"

---

### A Parent's Cue Card

"Even though this has happened, I know Dad still loves you and doesn't want to do these things. He needs help. People don't hit others as a way of solving problems."

Or . . .

"People have the right to determine for themselves what is done to their bodies."

Help your children set appropriate boundaries for themselves. Talking about what is healthy and normal will help them make better choices in their relationships.

If your child has experienced abuse, there will be long-term repercussions that she will have to deal with. Helping her see that she wasn't at fault and that she has strength to successfully cope with the abuse will greatly reduce her anger. If she's unable to cope successfully, get her in to see a counselor who works with sexual abuse.

## Recommended Books

Jill Murray. *But I Love Him: Protecting Your Teen Daughter from Controlling, Abusive Dating Relationships*. New York: HarperCollins, 2000.
Mic Hunter. *Abused Boys: The Neglected Victims of Sexual Abuse*. New York: Fawcett Columbine, 1990.

# 2

# Divorce

## Jessie and John: Children of Divorce

Lee and Linda have a thirteen-year-old daughter, Jessie, and a seven-year-old son, John. As a precocious redheaded eighth grader, Jessie is quick to say what she thinks and has a strong sense of fairness. In contrast, John is quiet and shy. Even though he doesn't talk much, he pays close attention to what happens in his family.

In many divorces there is a specific identifiable event or reason that causes the divorce (affair, death of child, domestic violence, child abuse, alcoholism, financial problems, invalidation of one's feelings and thoughts), but Lee and Linda just gradually grew apart. They stopped doing things together, they pursued different interests, and Lee's job required him to be out of town several days a month. When problems occurred with the children, Linda liked to sit down and talk with the kids about the situation and come up with a plan—just like her folks did with her. She rarely used physical punishment. Lee wasn't as severe with the children as his dad was with him, but he meant to be clear and firm with his punishment. "If it is to help, it must hurt" was his guideline.

Things were quieter and calmer when Lee was out of town. On returning home he tried to reconnect and reinvolve himself with his family by imposing harsher penalties for the children's misbehavior, irritating both the children and Linda. So when Lee was home, he and Linda frequently fought about the children. They finally decided to divorce.

Linda told Jessie and John about the divorce plans. While the announcement to actually divorce surprised the children, they knew their parents weren't getting along very well. They had heard them argue, and the family time they used to enjoy had all but stopped.

The court gave the parents joint custody, with the children being placed with Mom. Jessie was very angry about losing her dad. Even though they fought about privileges, they were close and she really missed spending time with him. Jessie's grades dropped, which contributed to the conflict she and her mom experienced. Nothing Linda did was ever good enough. When Jessie returned from Dad's, it would take three to four days before she could utter even a neutral statement to her mother. She was angry at Mom for requiring a large child support payment. She felt sorry for Dad because he had to live in a small, dark, sparsely furnished apartment, while they still had the house. Dad asked Jessie to talk to Mom about lowering the amount he had to pay. When Mom refused, Jessie became even more angry about the money Mom spent on herself, yelling: "The money is supposed to be used for us kids." Jessie demanded to have her share of the money Dad paid. When Linda wouldn't give it to her, Jessie threatened to go live with Dad. Linda tried to hold her tongue, but she thought Jessie needed to know she wasn't the only one to blame and proceeded to list Dad's faults and misdeeds that led to the divorce.

John looked forward to the contact with Dad but didn't miss it that much when the visits were canceled. He was closer to Mom and was content with her attention. He worried about her and frequently asked if she needed a hug, which he was glad to supply. Linda was moved by his affection, which usually caused her to cry. At those times she would talk with John about her anguish over the situation.

When Linda came to me for help, I encouraged her not to interfere with the relationship Jessie had with her father and to keep the negative thoughts about Lee to herself. Because Mom did that, it helped Jessie identify more clearly why she was mad: She couldn't see Dad, and Mom wasn't doing anything about it. When Dad agreed to come to my office and meet with Jessie and me, Jessie's demeanor brightened. When Dad understood how hurt Jessie was when their time together was cancelled and how much she needed him, he made their regular contact a priority. This also had a positive impact on the relationship between Mom and Jessie.

## Divorce Generates Anger

The divorce itself and the changes brought about by the divorce may be causing your child's anger. Divorce generates anger because:

- There is nothing the children can do about it.
- The children have many adjustments to make. They feel it's unfair. They complain about missing a parent, having to choose sides, lacking money or other resources, and changing schools, routine, or activities.
- They lose a parent or parental contact in some form, which may be a significant loss for them.
- They are pulled from both directions and can't make one parent happy without hurting the other one. This causes loyalty problems for them.
- Some parents make their child into a confidant, junior parent, or pseudo-spouse. This causes the child to be jealous and angry if he loses the role to the new person the parent begins to date.

Children suffer the most and become very angry when parents:

- Constantly fight.
- Use the children as pawns in their fights.
- Lobby for the children to be on their side.
- Expect them to be spies, messengers, or snitches.
- Draw out the litigation. (Research shows a direct correlation between length of litigation and the deterioration of the child's mental health.)
- Put the other parent down.
- Expect 100 percent loyalty to only one parent.

Could your divorce be an underlying reason for your child's anger?

## Typical Responses to Divorce

Depending on their age, children may respond to divorce in the following behavioral or relational ways:

| Behavioral Responses | Relational Responses |
|---|---|
| Regressing to earlier ways of acting: sucking their thumbs, not controlling bowel or bladder, talking baby talk | Trying to get parents back together |
| | Slanting conversations so both parents believe they really want to be with each parent and are unhappy with the other parent |
| Having trouble separating from a parent, e.g., at day care | |
| Being anxious about how basic needs will be met | Dividing up so that at least one child is more committed to each parent |
| Getting sick, losing appetite, complaining of aches and pains | Putting one parent on a pedestal and giving no credit to the non-favored parent |
| Having trouble sleeping, nightmares | Fighting with those who are loyal to the other parent |
| Playing more aggressively | |
| Disobeying, being uncooperative, acting up to get negative attention or punishment | "Parenting" the emotionally distraught parent |
| Achieving less in school, letting grades drop, cutting school, or getting into trouble with the law | Assuming the role of the absent parent |
| | Looking to peers for support and help |
| Withdrawing emotionally/physically | Unwilling to share thoughts or feelings about the situation |
| Escaping by using drugs, being sexually active | |
| Acting sad, angry, depressed, or even suicidal | |
| Being angry at one or both parents | |
| Trying to be perfect | |

If you have divorced and your child's behavior and relationships are consistent with these signs, it's quite likely he is struggling with issues concerning the divorce.

In general, children who struggle with the divorce deal with their anger in the following ways:

*Acting out their anger rather than talking about it.* People, including children, have two basic choices in what they can do with their anger: Show others they are angry or talk about their anger. When children believe their anger isn't heard or taken seriously, they often choose to stop talking about their feelings and to act in a way that releases their anger. By not doing homework and allowing her grades to fall, Jessie showed her mom how angry she was and how little control her mother had over her.

*Withdrawing.* Some parents lobby for and expect their child's total loyalty, not allowing allegiance to the other parent. When parents take this stance, their child has no acceptable way of dealing with his affection for and loyalty to both parents. So, instead of deciding between the two, he withdraws emotionally from a no-win situation.

*Blaming.* He may blame the parent with whom he feels more secure. While both parents have responsibility, the child is apt to be more critical of the person who hasn't already left. Expressing dissatisfaction or anger toward the absent parent may push that parent even further away.

*Taking sides.* Especially in stepfamilies and families with more than two children, side taking usually occurs. The children align themselves so each parent has at least one child on his/her side.

*Threatening to go live with the other parent.* This angry and helpless message often comes when your child is extremely frustrated with you and your rules or when he feels sorry for the other parent. This threat can cause you, the custodial parent, much distress. After calming down, listen to your child's concerns. You don't have to change your mind about your limits, but you do need to understand. If you can, empathize with his thoughts and feelings concerning the other parent. It doesn't mean the problems are your fault, nor that you need to do something about them, but if you give in to your child's threat just to keep him from leaving, he has gained the power to effectively blackmail you the next time he wants something. Jessie used "I'll go live with Dad" as a way to make Mom give her some of the child-support money. Fortunately it didn't work and they talked through their anger. They negotiated the problem rather than the relationship.

 ## *Parental Plan*

### Provide Appropriate Information

*Tell your children about the impending divorce only when it is absolutely certain.* The announcement will upset them, so wait until you are sure before you talk to them. It works best when both parents tell all of the children together the reasons for the divorce and the plans for separating. Everyone is then operating on the same information. Children don't need to know all the intimate details, but certainly let them know they weren't the cause of the divorce. Allow plenty of time so they can emotionally deal with the announcement—not five minutes before they have to go to school or work.

*Reassure your children they didn't cause the divorce.* The perceptions of children usually contain magical-type thinking. If they ever wished a parent to be gone when they were angry, they may now think they caused him/her to leave.

### A Parent's Cue Card

"We've decided we no longer want to be married to each other, so we are getting a divorce. The reason for the divorce has nothing to do with you kids. You didn't do anything to cause this divorce. As you know, we have been fighting and can't reach any kind of an agreement. We both still love all of you and you are not to blame for our split. We simply can't live together any longer and we need to separate. Do you want to ask us any questions?"

*Provide pertinent information regarding changes, moves, school, contact with the other parent, location of favorite toys.* If they know what is happening and what to expect, children's anxieties and fears will greatly decrease. Explain to them which parent will move out, how the children will maintain contact with that parent, where they will live, whether they will have food and shelter, and how their lives will be once the divorce is final.

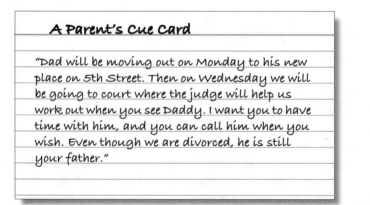

### A Parent's Cue Card

"Dad will be moving out on Monday to his new place on 5th Street. Then on Wednesday we will be going to court where the judge will help us work out when you see Daddy. I want you to have time with him, and you can call him when you wish. Even though we are divorced, he is still your father."

> "We will be staying in this house. You will still be going to the same school and riding the same bus. We will go to the same church. You will be able to continue on with your soccer and music lessons. Spot will live with us, and Tiger will live with Dad. Do you have any questions you would like to ask? . . . When you think of other questions, please feel free to ask me. I want you to know all you can about what will be happening."

*Encourage your children to ask questions.* Most children have questions but refrain from asking because they don't want to upset either parent. Encourage them by asking a question for them. This may help them ask one of their own.

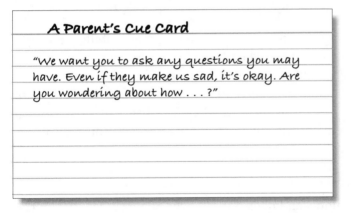

### A Parent's Cue Card

"We want you to ask any questions you may have. Even if they make us sad, it's okay. Are you wondering about how . . . ?"

### Minimize Changes When Possible

If parents make decisions that consistently minimize the impact of the divorce, fewer adjustments by the children need to be made. Try to keep the children:

- In the same residence if possible.
- In the same school. If you have to move, try to find a place in the same school district so they don't lose their old friends and have to adjust to a new school.

- In the same activities at church, home, school.
- In contact with relatives and extended family on both maternal and paternal sides.
- Together, avoiding another loss.

Find a routine that works and stick with it. Baris and Garrity make the following recommendations.[1]

| Age of Child | Recommendations |
|---|---|
| Infancy to 2½ years | Nonresidential parent has short, frequent visits; overnights are not recommended. |
| 2½ years to 5 years | Gradually extend visitation time; implement one overnight per week up to a maximum of three per week toward the end of this time frame. |
| 6 years to 8 years | The child visits from one to three days weekly with noncustodial parent. A full week at each parent's house may be phased in toward the end of this time frame. |

Beyond eight years of age, children have greater ability to adapt. However, frequent shifting of children between parents can be very disruptive. There is usually an adjustment period lasting twenty-four to seventy-two hours after changing households. So if you alternate your child every two to three days, they are always in a transitional state. Set up a schedule that allows for some flexibility but also allows them to settle in.

### Maximize Time and Connection with Each Parent

As parents, moms and dads don't do the same things. When the child is with Mom, the parenting that Dad provides is unavailable, and vice versa. It is therefore crucial for both parents to continue their positive involvement with their children.

A research team reported in the *American Journal of Orthopsychiatry* that when children had continued contact with both parents who had separated, there was significant positive impact.

In summary, 30 percent of the children in the present study experienced a marked decrease in their academic performance following parental separation, and this was evident three years later. Access to both parents seemed to be the most protective factor, in that it was associated with better academic adjustment.[2]

They also concluded:

Moreover, data revealed that noncustodial parents (mostly fathers) were very influential in their children's development. These data also support the interpretation that the more time a child spends with the noncustodial parent the better the overall adjustment of the child.[3]

A positive, nurturing relationship with their fathers helped girls value their femininity.

At the time of the marital separation, when (as is typical) father leaves the family home and becomes progressively less involved with his children over the ensuing years, it appears that young girls experience the emotional loss of father egocentrically as a rejection of them. . . . The continued lack of involvement is experienced as an ongoing rejection by him. Many girls attribute this rejection to their not being pretty enough, affectionate enough, athletic enough, or smart enough to please father and engage him in regular, frequent contacts. . . . Without this regular source of nourishment, a girl's sense of being valued as a female does not seem to thrive.[4]

For your children, you should establish a situation "where the children feel they have reasonable and comfortable access to each parent in his or her new family situation."[5] Determine the amount of time to be spent at each residence based on the percentage of physical care that has been provided by each parent. If Mom has provided 80 percent of the physical care, it would be more of a loss and certainly not maximizing the relationship with each parent to have the children live with Dad 80 percent of the time.[6] "Very young children should have short, frequent visits with their nonresidential parent because they—appropriately—become anxious when they are away from their primary caretaker for too long."[7]

When making arrangements for the children following the divorce, consider the importance of parental connections and how they've been previously made.

*Make regular contact with your child (if you are the noncustodial parent).* Because it's hard to say good-bye at the end of the visit, many non-

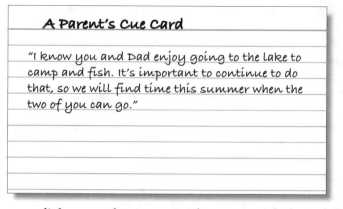

A Parent's Cue Card

"I know you and Dad enjoy going to the lake to camp and fish. It's important to continue to do that, so we will find time this summer when the two of you can go."

custodial parents begin to avoid contact with their children. Contact with your child is vital, so don't fade from the picture. Regular and predictable contact is preferred over several visits followed by a large gap with no contact. When everything is changing, your child needs to count on you and the predictability of your interactions. This helps him feel more secure. He needs to hear from you in some way (call, card, letter, gift) on his birthday, Christmas, and other special occasions. These are times when he gauges his importance to you by your response.

A Parent's Cue Card

"I want to see you and be with you, so I am planning to get together with you every Sunday. I'm putting the date on my calendar and you can count on it."

*Don't use visitation as a weapon.* This is a hard one, especially if the noncustodial parent isn't paying child support. Withholding visitation takes away the opportunity for your child to develop and benefit from his relationship with the other parent and sets you up to be blamed. If the other parent doesn't follow through with seeing your child, that parent should be accountable for her decision, not you. Allowing reasonable visitation with the other parent, provided safety issues aren't a concern, always helps your child adjust to the divorce and minimizes its negative impact. If necessary, reassure your child that he will be able to see the other parent.

---

### A Parent's Cue Card

*"It is really important to me that you continue to see your mother, even though she isn't living with us. She is still your mother and I know she loves you. Because you need to see her and she needs to see you, we will make arrangements for you to stay with her every other weekend and see her on Wednesday evenings."*

---

*Periodically reassess the visitation situation.* This means keeping flexible so your child's developmental needs can be addressed. "Although there is individual variation, most children's developmental needs change within an age frame of two and a half to three years. This means that approximately every two to three years the arrangements may become antiquated and need to be revised."[8]

#### Avoid the Necessity of Choosing Sides

Although you and your spouse are divorcing each other, your child is not divorcing either parent. No matter who is right or who is wrong, he will feel uncomfortable being forced to choose a side. *Don't put your child in a position where he must choose one parent over the other.* Doing so will cause loyalty problems for him. Also, threatening him with never seeing you or his siblings if he chooses to live with the other parent is extremely destructive to your child and your relationship with him.

*Encourage your child to be honest.* Your child will be tempted to slant each conversation he has with you in a positive way to avoid hurting your feelings, *and* he will do the same with his other parent. Each parent may then believe that he/she is the better parent and the child would be happier living with him/her. The child is not really giving

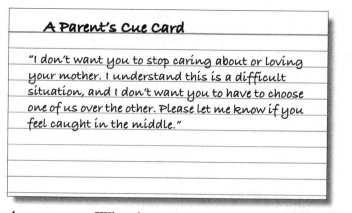

**A Parent's Cue Card**

"I don't want you to stop caring about or loving your mother. I understand this is a difficult situation, and I don't want you to have to choose one of us over the other. Please let me know if you feel caught in the middle."

that message. What he is saying is: "I don't want to hurt either of you, so I say things in a way that will make you both feel better."

**A Parent's Cue Card**

"I really want to know what you are thinking and feeling. It doesn't do us any good if you tell your mother and me both what you think we want to hear. It will be a lot easier for all of us if you simply tell us honestly how you feel. It might hurt a bit at first, but we want you to be honest with us."

*Don't entice or manipulate the child to want to live with you by offering large gifts, special privileges, or extravagant vacations.* You may not believe it, but what children want most from their parents is to spend some enjoyable time with them. Sure, you can buy them things, and if that is all you offer, they will take the things. *But it isn't what they want.* Spend time with them instead.

*Keep negative thoughts about the other parent to yourself.* If you call your ex-spouse lazy when she isn't there to speak up for herself, out of loyalty your child will probably step in and defend her. The more your child verbally supports your ex-spouse's behavior, the more likely it becomes that he will believe it. Because this isn't the direction you want things to go, don't bad-mouth the other parent.

> ### A Parent's Cue Card
>
> "Your mom and I may not agree on everything, but she is entitled to her opinion, just as I am to mine. I prefer not to hear the things she may say about me, and I'm not going to say negative things to you about her. I know she is still your mom and you still love her."

*Don't pump your child for usable information about the other parent.* Your child doesn't want to be a snitch or a spy, so don't ask questions to obtain information about what your ex-spouse is doing or how she is conducting her life (dating, drinking, and so on). Inquiring about how your child got along during the visit is acceptable. Also don't pull your child into your fights, forcing him to take sides. Because he can't please both of you at the same time, he is caught in a no-win situation.

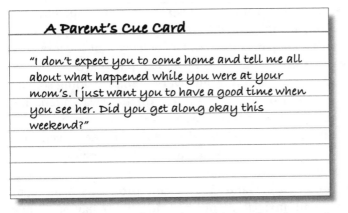

> ### A Parent's Cue Card
>
> "I don't expect you to come home and tell me all about what happened while you were at your mom's. I just want you to have a good time when you see her. Did you get along okay this weekend?"

If he chooses to tell you about his weekend experiences, please listen, because what he offers is important to him.

### Resolve Differences

Resolving issues with your ex-spouse as quickly as you can promotes a return to stability and reduces the number of fights and conflict within the family. Either spouse may be so angry that he/she chooses to seek revenge. This is extremely counterproductive not only for the children but also for both spouses. Some people pour more energy into a negative relationship with an ex-spouse than they put into their relationship while they were married. The key principle here is: *What receives energy grows.* Resolving issues without going to court or involving your child in the court process is very beneficial.

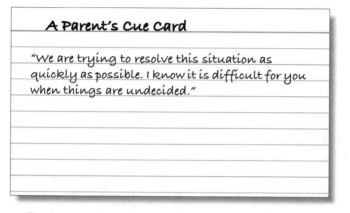

A Parent's Cue Card

"We are trying to resolve this situation as quickly as possible. I know it is difficult for you when things are undecided."

*Don't try to control or punish your ex-spouse.* You hurt. Everything you worked for is being pulled from your grasp. You say to yourself, "If I could only hang on, I might be able to stop this from happening." You may believe that exerting more control will prevent the loss, separation, or divorce from happening, so you manipulate, you threaten, you verbally intimidate, you physically overwhelm. By doing so, you will end up pushing your spouse and children further away, alienating those who were once sympathetic to your side, and creating great fear and animosity in your ex-spouse. You could even be served with a restraining order and perhaps spend time in jail. Pursuing control as a means of stopping the divorce and the accompanying losses usually makes the losses bigger and creates new problems. Face your losses. Deal with your anxieties. Control your own behavior. When you reach a point where you have shifted gears and no longer see control as the way to fix things, you might communicate to your spouse and children.

*Focus energy on things you can control.* Trying to control things that are out of your control will only frustrate you and make matters worse. You can't control what your ex-spouse chooses to do when

---

### A Parent's Cue Card

"You are all very important to me and it really hurts to think about losing you. I know in the past I've dealt with these hurts by trying to force you to do what I wanted you to do. I now see it doesn't work. I've pushed you further away and caused more harm. I'm sorry."

---

your child is with her. If you can't control a situation, find a way to turn it loose and move on.

*Reach for the goal of resolution, not exact fairness for each parent.* Making everything exactly equal, demanding every minute of your scheduled time with your children, and refusing to be flexible usually create more anger and more difficulties for your children. If you are acting with the best interests of your children at heart, they will know that. *As they grow older, count on their acting consistently with the way you have acted.*

### Make Parent/Child Boundaries Clear

Because you lost your spouse and are in emotional pain, it is natural to look for someone who understands and can be supportive. Your child is clearly aware of the situation and may try to comfort or even "parent" you. Making him into your confidant blurs the parent-child boundaries, perhaps to the point where you and your child become peers. This can be difficult for your child as he may feel overly responsible for you. Your child isn't an adult and shouldn't be expected to carry adult responsibilities. He will need his energy to cope with his own adjustments. Also, if at some point you choose to remarry, he will have difficulty giving up his "adult status," causing additional conflict with the new stepparent. Find adults who can support you and meet your needs for companionship. Build a support system for yourself. Going through a divorce is painful and lonely. Don't do it by yourself.

*Retain reasonable rules and expectations for your children.* Your sympathy, guilt, or exhaustion may cause you to think about lightening

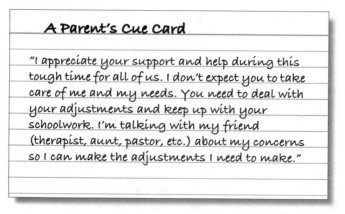

### A Parent's Cue Card

"I appreciate your support and help during this tough time for all of us. I don't expect you to take care of me and my needs. You need to deal with your adjustments and keep up with your schoolwork. I'm talking with my friend (therapist, aunt, pastor, etc.) about my concerns so I can make the adjustments I need to make."

your expectations of your child, especially if your ex-spouse drops all of her expectations and creates a party atmosphere when your child is with her. (She may take that approach as a way of winning his loyalty.) Now is not the time to feel sorry for your child or allow him to do things you normally wouldn't condone. Your reasonable expectations should remain the same through good times and bad times. Dropping your expectations creates confusion about the legitimacy of the rules. Keep things as stable as possible, providing your child with the security he needs to cope with the other changes.

### A Parent's Cue Card

"Your mother needs to make the rules at her house, and I will make the ones at my house. My house rules and expectations haven't changed even though your mother and I are divorced. I still expect you to . . ."

### Tend to Your Own Needs

*Deal with your loss, anger, sadness, and guilt from losing your marriage.* Dealing with your feelings and the reasons for the divorce is essential. Avoiding these issues, drinking, or finding someone new to fill the void in your life are all good ways to ensure a repeat of the same problems that caused the divorce. Take time to deal with your feelings before dating. Seek counseling if needed.

*Invest your time and energy in building your new life.* Because your energy is greatly limited at this time, invest it wisely in your new life, not in trying to get even or control your ex-spouse's life.

*Take care of yourself.* Do positive things to nurture yourself. Taking the time for these is important. You could spend an afternoon at the library, get some extra rest, soak in the tub, paint, write, take a walk on the beach or in the mountains. Do things that feel good but don't cause more long-term problems. Things like excessive spending, doing drugs, getting involved in sexual relationships, and other ways of escaping may immediately feel good but in the long run will contribute to the problems you have to manage.

*Attend a divorce recovery group.* Many of these groups are available throughout the country. Find one that addresses your parental and adult concerns as well as your child's issues. To find one in your community, contact your pastor, counselor, or local mental health center.

Every divorce will have a negative impact on the children involved but that impact can be mitigated by parents who put the best interests of their children first. Focus on making the changes in the child's life as painless as possible and be sensitive to your child's feelings and need to talk.

## Recommended Books

Judith Wallerstein, Julia Lewis, and Sandra Blakeslee. *The Unexpected Legacy of Divorce.* New York: Hyperion, 2000.

Jeenie Gordon. *If My Parents Are Getting Divorced, Why Am I the One Who Hurts?* Grand Rapids: Zondervan, 1993.

# 3

# Blended Family

## Brittany and Dustin: Children of a Blended Family

Dustin's mom, Cindy, married Brittany's dad, Dave. Everyone thought it was a "match made in heaven."

Dustin's dad was killed in an automobile accident six years ago when Dustin was eight years old. Dustin adjusted to the tragic loss rather well but is a bit overindulged by his mother. She feels sorry for him because he doesn't have anyone who will play ball with him or do other "guy things." Cindy is a capable single parent but looks forward to having a male influence for her son and being able to share some of the difficult parental decisions. Dustin and his mother live in a small, neatly kept apartment.

Brittany's parents divorced about a year ago (when she was eleven years old) with custody being awarded to Dave. To ensure she wouldn't "be bothered with any parental duties," her mother left Wyoming. Mom called on Brittany's birthday, but that has been the only contact. Brittany really misses her mother. Dave, a carpenter, needs help supervising Brittany. Since her mother left, Brittany's grades have dropped, she hangs out with a marginal group at her school, and she has strange scratch marks on her arms. Little things seem to bother her and she's quite moody. Dad and Brittany live in a large house that is often messy because neither of them takes time to do regular cleaning.

Cindy and Dave dated for about three months before deciding to get married. It pleased the parents that Dustin and Brittany seemed to get along with each other. Dustin and Cindy were glad to move into Dave's big house after living in their small apartment.

Cindy stays at home and so monitors the children's homework. Even though this has created tension between her and Brittany, Brittany's grades are coming up! Dave sometimes thinks Cindy is too hard on Brittany and makes too many allowances for Dustin, but he doesn't say anything because it seems to be working.

About six months after the wedding, however, Cindy and Brittany had a major confrontation, with Brittany accusing Cindy of trying to change everything in their home and Cindy accusing Brittany of not doing her fair share of the housework. She snapped at Brittany, "Perhaps if you had helped out your mother a bit, she would still be around."

Brittany's feelings about her mom were still quite tender, so Cindy's comments really stung. Brittany angrily yelled back, "You don't know anything about me and my mom, so just shut up!" With that she ran to her room and slammed the door.

Cindy immediately felt terrible about her comment. She waited about fifteen minutes and went to Brittany's room to apologize. She knocked on the door twice. There was no response. After waiting a few moments, she opened the door. Brittany was sitting on her bed, making small cuts on her arm with a razor blade. Cindy was shocked. How did things get this bad?

## Blending Families Generates Anger

Adults may view a remarriage as an "addition" of another parent to provide for the family. However, children view it as another loss: They lose their parent to the stepparent. Note the differences (given below) to which children must adjust as they go through the family-structure changes brought about by divorce and remarriage.

### Biological Parents in Relative Harmony
#### Child Lives with Both Parents

| Parental Relationship | Parent-Child Bond | Child's Privileges | Child's Power |
|---|---|---|---|
| Loving and supportive with differences being resolved. Child feels safe and secure. | Positive and supportive with adequate parental attention. Clear parent-child boundaries. | May have many or few privileges. | Uses personal power to get personal needs met. |

## Biological Parents Who Are Divorcing
### Child Lives with Both Parents

| Parental Relationship | Parent-Child Bond | Child's Privileges | Child's Power |
| --- | --- | --- | --- |
| Tense, under pressure, with increasing conflict. Child feels tense, scared, and worried about her parents. | Initially may be quite strong, but as the marital tension increases, less time and energy are available for the child. Child feels left out. | Privileges may increase as parents have less parenting energy and less time to monitor expectations. | Child may feel powerless as the marriage crumbles and she can't do anything about it. |

## Divorced Parents Who Live Separately
### Child Lives with One Parent at a Time

| Parental Relationship | Parent-Child Bond | Child's Privileges | Child's Power |
| --- | --- | --- | --- |
| May still be tense, but there usually aren't daily fights or problems. Child often feels relieved not to have parents fighting all of the time. She focuses on adjusting to changes. | At this point, the child often feels very close to her custodial parent. They lean on each other to cope with the divorce. Parent-child boundaries may fade, promoting the child in status to a junior parent or pseudo-spouse. | Because the parent feels sorry for the child, she's often granted many privileges with few expectations. | As a junior parent or pseudo-spouse, the child has the most power she has ever experienced. The mother may say, "We argue more like sisters than mom and daughter." |

## Remarried Parents
### Child Lives with One Biological Parent and a Stepparent

| Parental Relationship | Parent-Child Bond | Child's Privileges | Child's Power |
| --- | --- | --- | --- |
| Biological parents may still fight. Newly formed marital bond is susceptible to pressure. Child may feel overwhelmed by all of the adjustments, angry about the losses, displaced by new people in her family structure. | Parent has to balance time between his children and his new spouse. The child may feel left out or less important than the new spouse. Parent-child boundaries are sharpened, returning her to a "child status." | Fewer privileges are granted, and expectations are increased. The child needs to behave herself and do her part to make the new family work. | She loses power, no longer having the parent's ear. She's expected to return to being "just a kid." The new stepparent assumes the child's preferred position of closeness to the biological parent. |

While there are exceptions, the following graph shows how the child's privileges and power, as well as the parental expectations, usually change as the family moves through the four different forms.

### Family Form Comparisons

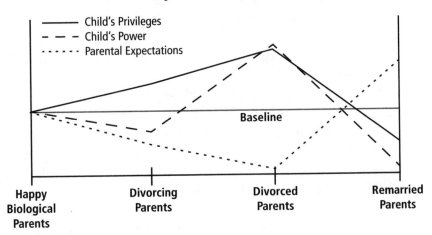

If we use the Happy Biological Family as the baseline, we see the child has gained power and privileges by the time her parents are divorced. But when her custodial parent remarries, she ends up with significantly fewer privileges, less power, and more parental expectations. This all occurs in the context of losing contact and closeness with her biological parent. This is why she is so angry.

So a remarriage and the blending of families can create anger for children because of:

*Lost hope.* The child loses hope her biological parents will reunite. Her loss becomes a permanent one and she may not be ready to move on to a new family configuration. Dustin knew his dad was not coming back, and he had a considerable amount of time to adjust to that fact before Cindy remarried. Even though Brittany initially liked Cindy, she hadn't given up the hope that Mom would return. Cindy was an okay friend for dad, but Brittany wasn't interested in having her in the mom role.

*All the losses.* The child has less contact with one parent, less income, and less emotional support. When her parent remarried, she may have had to move and change schools, resulting in fewer friends. She loses privileges and certain role benefits. She also loses her parent to the new stepparent, and perhaps to stepsiblings as well.

*Loyalty conflicts.* The child can't live with both Mom and Dad at the same time and it's very hard to please both of them. Children become quite upset when one parent bad-mouths the other, or uses them as snitches, spies, or message carriers.

*Changes without their control or influence.* These changes may include where the child lives, who lives with her, how the family now operates, where she fits in, how she gets along with the stepsiblings, and who makes the parental decisions. She must adjust to the new parent, new rules, and new people in the home. Although Brittany knew how hard Dustin worked for his grades, she still resented the comparisons that were often made. She had always been number one. Being number two wasn't fun.

*Authority and discipline problems.* Whom does the new stepparent have authority to discipline? As should be expected, children dislike feeling blamed for everything that goes wrong in a blended family and having expectations, consequences, and rewards that are not consistent for all of the children in the home. They may believe their stepsiblings receive more attention and material things but do less work. They don't like having their space invaded by the newcomers. Brittany was angry that Dad had turned over the disciplining to Cindy, who seemed to hold her accountable for everything but would grant huge favors to her son. From Brittany's perspective things were far from fair.

*Lack of power to achieve their desires.* Children in blended families can't do all they want to do because there are now more people to consider when decisions are made. The child loses power when the parent marries the stepparent.

*Having to move between two households.* It's hard for children to move and not have their belongings in one place. Transitions are difficult.

Could the blending of families be an underlying reason for your child's anger?

# Typical Responses to Blending Families

Because getting married (like getting divorced) changes the basic form of the family, your child's behavior may be similar to those behaviors listed in the divorce chapter. Depending on their age, children may respond to the blending of families in the following behavioral or relational ways:

| Behavioral Responses | Relational Responses |
| --- | --- |
| Regressing to younger ways of acting to gain attention or express anger | Purposely creating tension in relationships |
| | Distancing themselves and withdrawing emotionally |
| | Shunning or ignoring other family members |
| Getting sick, losing their appetite, or complaining about aches and pains | Avoiding any contact with others |
| | Venting their anger on other people in their lives—teachers, those in authority |
| Numbing their feelings through drugs, alcohol, or cutting themselves | Intentionally hurting others' feelings |
| | Fighting with those associated with the stepparent |
| | Sabotaging positive interactions |
| Allowing grades to drop and avoiding responsibility | Engaging in power struggles |
| | Looking to peers for support and help |
| Threatening to go live with the other parent | Being hateful to the custodial parent: He is to blame for their problems |
| Looking out only for their own interests | Defending absent biological parent |
| | Hurting or snubbing other siblings and stepsiblings |
| Jockeying for position/roles in the stepfamily | Blaming the stepparent for problems |
| | Being uncooperative, particularly with the stepparent |
| Withdrawing, leaving the house at every chance | Being rude, defiant, and disobedient to the stepparent |
| | Trying to drive the stepparent out of the house |

If you have a blended family and your child's behavior and relationships are consistent with these signs, it's quite likely she's struggling with issues concerning the stepfamily.

Children often express their anger about the remarriage in the same way they did about the divorce. In general, they may:

- Act out their anger rather than talking about it (yelling, pouting, going on sit-down strike, hurting others, hurting themselves).
- Withdraw.
- Blame.
- Take sides.
- Threaten to go live with the other parent.

When parents are fighting and divorce becomes an option to end the tension, children can often hang on until the divorce is final. They can see there is an ending point where things should get better. If they are in a stepfamily, the end (which they usually can't see) is when they move out of the house. This time frame is simply too long to endure. If the child believes she's lost the advocate she used to have in her parent because the parent has now sided with the new spouse, she may feel that she needs to fend for herself. She may try once or twice to let her parent know what bothers her, but if the words fall on deaf ears, she quickly withdraws and quits trying.

Once children reach this point, they may become seriously depressed. Suicide, drugs, and cutting themselves may become options to avoid the emotional pain, distract themselves, get a high, feel alive, or gain attention. Once they reach this point, they need assistance—counseling, medication, and even hospitalization.

## *Parental Plan*

### *Deal with the Changes*

*Take time to grieve the losses and changes associated with the divorce.* Take time yourself, and give your child time and opportunity to grieve her losses (living with both parents, daily contact, hugs when wanted, and so on). If she hasn't adjusted to the changes, she can't attach to someone new. She must let go of the old before she can take hold of the new. This may be difficult if, as was the case with Brittany, one parent is absent from the child's life and does not maintain regular contact. You will find it beneficial to put your life on hold temporarily to help your child through the grieving process. If you date and marry too quickly, it is guaranteed that your child will reject your new spouse, setting the family on a rocky road.

> If remarriage occurs in a short space of time after the death or divorce, it is likely that the mourning and grief are not yet over for the children, and as a result the children are not prepared to accept new adults into their lives. If the new partner is presented as a replace-

ment for the lost parent, the resentment and grief are particularly acute.[1]

Family researchers have identified the best predictor of stepfamily happiness to be the quality of the relationship that develops between the stepparent and children. . . . The next most important factor in stepfamily adjustment, as in any family, is the strength and quality of the couples' bond.[2]

One of the reasons parents may move too quickly to remarry is because things appear to be going well. Parents easily believe: *If my child and my soon-to-be new spouse get along before the marriage, they will continue to get along after the marriage.* Things change. The main reason for this is that through the marriage the friend becomes a parent, an authority figure. The child then needs to relate to him and develop a relationship on a parent-child basis. Unresolved divorce and loss issues for the parent, stepparent, and child will then emerge, causing difficulties with the blending of the new family.

*Share your feelings and listen, listen, listen to your child.* Sharing your feelings and dealing with your losses helps your child do the same. If you don't grieve the losses but quickly remarry to fill the void in your life, you've put yourself and your children on a course to repeat your previous patterns and mistakes. Take plenty of time to talk with your child and really listen to her.

### Be Realistic in Your Stepfamily Expectations

Stepfamilies are very different from nuclear families. If you transfer your nuclear family expectations to your stepfamily, you will be disappointed and angry and feel like a failure. Because the two family units are very different, they can't be treated the same.

Parents usually have some of the following expectations for their blended family:

- We will all get along and be happy now because of the positive changes.
- We will support and care about each other.
- It will be easy to love each other.
- We can make the transition quickly and easily into a blended family.

- Because I'm not trying to "replace" their biological parent, the kids will like me and we will get along.
- I can show the children that stepmothers don't have to be wicked.

You and your family need to make your expectations known.

---

**A Parent's Cue Card**

"I know there have been a lot of changes, and we all have certain expectations about how things are going to go from here. Let's sit down together and list the expectations we have of ourselves and each other. Who wants to start?"

---

Being aware of how stepfamilies are different from nuclear families may help you be more realistic in your expectations. Review the following chart as you discuss expectations.

| First Family | Blended Family |
| --- | --- |
| There is no previous marriage. | Problems may exist from the first marriage, and relational concerns may not have been addressed. *Implications.* Deal with the issues rather than avoid them and have them well under control before starting a new relationship. |
| There are no previous commitments to another family and children. | The blended family is born from a loss. *Implications.* Take time to think and deal with your emotions regarding the loss of your marriage. Don't numb the pain by finding a new person. |
| The family naturally has high levels of commitment and cohesion. | Parents are committed, but all family members may not share that commitment. *Implications.* Maintain special times with your biological children as well as building "family time." Find ways to make positive connections with each other. |

Affection and sexuality are not issues for the family to deal with.

Affection and sexuality become family issues.
*Implications.* Use discretion in displaying affection. Reinforce privacy and boundaries.

Family roles and rules develop over time, with changes occurring relatively slowly, allowing ample time to adjust.

Creation of the family is instantaneous, allowing little or no time to adjust to major changes. Current roles may undergo significant changes.
*Implications.* With input from children, parents need to develop clear, practical rules and consequences that apply to all family members. Talk about roles and family jobs. What do family members like? What makes them feel uncomfortable?

Parental roles are clear.

Roles are confusing, and there are negative connotations of stepparents.
*Implications.* Go slowly in developing your stepparent role. Make a positive connection with stepchildren. Don't start with being a strict disciplinarian.

The couple bond is older than the parent-child bond.

Parent-child bond predates couple bond, which can create loyalty problems for all family members.
*Implications.* Honor the parent-child bond, being careful not to create loyalty problems. Elicit input from the children when appropriate, giving them a "buy in."

Only two adults occupy the parental roles.

Up to four adults may perform parental duties.
*Implications.* Confusion may develop, so be clear and as consistent as possible with your expectations. Don't try to control what happens in the other home.

Both biological parents are in the same home. There are fewer hindrances to working out their differences.

Biological parents aren't in same home but both still need to have a say in what occurs. More people now have a voice in the child's business.
*Implications.* Develop a businesslike relationship with ex-spouse so you can make decisions together based on what's best for your child. Don't use your child to punish or control your ex-spouse.

Children are expected and encouraged to be loyal to both parents.

Children must remain loyal to both biological parents while getting along with the new stepparent.
*Implications.* Don't talk negatively about the other parent or force the relationship with the new stepparent.

The number of people in the family gradually increases, allowing people time to develop a relationship.

Instant relationships are formed with a ceremony, sometimes without input or the blessing of those involved in the new relationships.

*Implications.* Step-relationships initially lack depth because they have not had time to develop. They may break down under stress. Nurture all the relationships within the new family.

Encourage your child to have a positive relationship with her stepparent, but don't expect family unity and harmony to be achieved within a few months. Instant intimacy doesn't happen. It often takes two to three years for adjustments to be made and relationships to develop.

### Minimize Changes and Additional Losses

*Try to keep the children in the same school.* Particularly if you need more bedrooms, your children will understand the need to move to a larger house. However, disrupting both their living situation and their school makes it harder for them to adjust to their new family and makes it more likely they will blame the new spouse for all of the trouble.

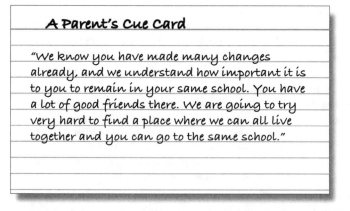

**A Parent's Cue Card**

"We know you have made many changes already, and we understand how important it is to you to remain in your same school. You have a lot of good friends there. We are going to try very hard to find a place where we can all live together and you can go to the same school."

If you must move and also have your children change schools, allow them as much input as possible on the choice of a new house or apartment. Part of the difficulty for children is in not having much control over what happens in their lives. Give them a vote when you can.

*Maintain the usual activities if possible.* When a child's activities remain pretty much the same, there is a sense of continuity and stability. She is able to count on doing the things she has enjoyed in the past.

*Provide substitute roles or jobs when practical.* Because Dustin was the only other person in the house prior to the marriage, he typically took out the trash, cleared the evening dishes from the table, and checked in with Mom to make sure she had had a good day. After the marriage, everyone in the family was fine with Dustin doing the trash. Brittany's job was to clear the supper dishes, so Dustin didn't mind at all giving up that job. However, he didn't like it when Dave took over his job of caring for Mom. Dustin felt replaced and didn't like it. Cindy quickly recognized Dustin's jealousy and took time to have Dustin care for her before Dave arrived home. When Dave would then show concern, it was acceptable because Dustin had already done his job.

### Spend Special Individual Time with Your Biological Child

*Schedule a regular time to be with your biological child and keep it a priority.* If your child "loses" you to the new stepparent, she may feel that she has no parents left at home who pay attention to her and her needs. This loss can cause great resentment, resulting in a very uncooperative child.

Take time to be with your child and reassure her of your care and love. If you don't spend some time with her, she will be angry with you but will blame the stepparent, creating even more tension in their relationship. The sureness and regularity of this contact are generally more important than the frequency. If you can spend only a couple of hours with her alone every two weeks, then set that up. But whatever you establish, make sure you keep it a priority. If she isn't reassured of your love and concern, she isn't likely to be cooperative with family time.

*Don't include the stepparent in your individual time.* Be sure that your new spouse understands that the goal is not to exclude him/her, but to show your child she is still important to you. If your spouse also has biological children living in the home, he/she could meet with those children while you meet with yours. Filling your child's need for attention will make it easier for her to allow you special time with your spouse and should have priority over trying to unite the family with family time.

---

### A Parent's Cue Card

*"I know we've gone through a lot of changes, but our relationship is still very important to me. I want to stay caught up with what's going on in your life, so I would like to make sure we get together every other Thursday evening to talk. Will that work for you?"*

---

*Avoid the Need to Choose Sides*

When divorcing, don't put your child in a position where she must choose one parent over the other one. When blending families, don't put your child in a position where she must choose a stepparent over her biological parent. Follow this "Don't List" to help minimize conflict between your child and the stepparent.

- Don't ask your child to choose or like the stepparent over the biological parent.
- Don't make her call the stepparent Mom or Dad. It's fine if she chooses to do that, but don't force her. Determine together what level of affection feels comfortable and settle on a name that works for both stepparent and child (first name or nickname, for example).
- Don't bad-mouth the other parent (no matter how deserving) and then list the great qualities of the stepparent. Your child can't be grateful for the stepparent's qualities and must minimize them.
- Don't tell your child she doesn't have to listen to or obey her other biological parent's new spouse.

*Clarify and Enforce Parental Rules*

*Stop feeling sorry for your child.* Because divorced parents tend to feel sorry for their children, they lighten their expectations of them.

Base your rules and guidelines for acceptable behavior on your principles, not your sympathy.

*Parent and stepparent need to clarify, agree upon, and apply reasonable rules, expectations, and consequences to all the children in the home.* Because many stepchildren already feel they've lost out, they are extremely sensitive to favoritism. If parents impose the rules and consequences in a subjective manner, children will focus on the inequity rather than on their own choices and responsibility. It's better to go light on the rules and consequences so they can be comfortably applied to each child in the home. As I said earlier, for changing behavior, the certainty of the consequence is usually more important than the severity of the punishment.

Tom and Adrienne Frydenger's book *Stepfamily Problems: How to Solve Them* lists seven principles for coparenting:[3]

*Principle 1:* Develop a discipline plan with your mate using the techniques of a team builder.
*Principle 2:* Do not defect from the discipline plan.
*Principle 3:* If you don't want your mate to be too harsh with your children, don't be too lenient with them.
*Principle 4:* If you don't want your mate to be too lenient with his or her children, don't be too harsh with them.
*Principle 5:* When the biological parent is reprimanding or pointing something out to his or her children, the stepparent should not interject.
*Principle 6:* When the stepparent is reprimanding his or her stepchildren, the biological parent can interject, but should not undermine the stepparent's discipline.
*Principle 7:* Always remember that your mate's children are precious to him or her. When you speak ill of the cub or attack the cub, you can be sure the bear will come after you.

If you as parents aren't working together, you can't hold your children accountable for their actions.

*Initially have the biological parent make the bulk of the discipline decisions, allowing the stepparent time to develop a positive relationship.* This also helps prevent fighting over discipline.

*Inform your children of the stepparent's authority and jurisdiction.* Some biological parents expect the stepparent to have the same authority and jurisdiction as they do. If the parent doesn't convey this expectation to both the stepparent and the child, the stepparent may be hesitant to intervene and the child may be quite resistant to obeying the stepparent. "I don't have to obey you because you are not my real parent." But if the biological parent has been clear, the stepparent may respond with: "That's true, I'm not your biological parent, but I am an adult in the house and your father gave me authority to deal with this situation." It's crucial that the biological parent back up the stepparent. If that isn't possible, then the parents aren't on the same page and need to renegotiate their expectations, rules, and consequences.

---

### A Parent's Cue Card

"I know it's sometimes difficult to listen to your stepmother. However, I want you to know that when I'm gone, she has my full authority to deal with any problem. I want you to obey her just like you would obey me. Do you have any problems doing that? If so, let's talk about them."

---

### Seek Input from the Children

*Elicit the children's opinions and pay attention to them.* One of the major complaints from stepchildren is that they have no say in what happens to them. Many have given up trying to talk with either biological or stepparent because "they don't listen and nothing changes anyway." Asking for their input and using their ideas gives them a way to feel like a co-molder of the family. If they have no input, they have no "buy in" to making the family work.

After you ask, make sure you stop talking and listen!

*Help your children distinguish between those things they can do something about and those they must accept.* The family is not a democracy. As parents, you are in charge of the direction of your family and children. But children must know that their input is always welcome and that some things are negotiable while others are not. Be clear with your children on the nonnegotiable issues. Don't give the children the

---

**A Parent's Cue Card**

"We are in the process of trying to make some decisions about... It would be helpful if we knew what you were thinking. What ideas do you have for us?"

---

idea your mind can be changed, when it cannot. Make this a slogan in your home:

Input is always welcome. Some things are negotiable.

*Involve the children in solving family conflicts.* Conflicts will occur as the two families join together. Gayle Peterson described it as follows:

> If the joining of two individuals in marriage is comparable to blending two different cultures, as many a family therapist has suggested, then the joining of two individuals with histories of past marriages, divorce and children must be the joining of two different galaxies.[4]

This meshing of the two galaxies can take a toll on the couple's relationship. Talk with each other about what's occurring.

Successfully blending two families is possible, but it takes time, patience, compassion, and realistic expectations. You may feel pulled in several directions as you try to meet the needs of a new spouse, your children, and your stepchildren. Honest communication is essential and will help you through difficult times.

## Recommended Books

Tom and Adrienne Frydenger. *Stepfamily Problems: How to Solve Them.* Grand Rapids: Revell, 1991.
James Bray and John Kelly. *Stepfamilies.* New York: Broadway Books, 1998.

# 4

# Parental Favoritism

## Tom: A Favored Child

Toni, a divorced mother, brought her sixteen-year-old, Tom, and her fourteen-year-old, Tyler, in for counseling because of the intense anger between the two of them. She worried about leaving them home alone because things often escalated into a physical confrontation. Last week she took Tyler to the emergency room for six stitches in the back of his head. Tom became angry when Tyler took one of his CDs. So as Tyler ran from the room, Tom threw a flower vase and hit him in the back of the head. Tyler immediately called Toni and told her what happened. She had to leave work and take him to the hospital. On a good day, Toni receives about five calls at work—one of the boys complaining about the other one. The stitches were the last straw, so she called to make a counseling appointment.

In meeting with the family it was immediately clear that the boys really hated each other. They focused on what they perceived to be the problem—the other brother—and weren't particularly interested in finding a solution. Blame was the name of the game. How did things get this intense? Toni helped me understand their situation. Tom Sr., the boys' father, was very close to Tom. They carried the same name, liked the same things (hunting and fishing), had similar personality styles, and even looked a lot alike. Because of these similarities, Dad clearly favored Tom and avoided time with Tyler because he was so "quiet and sensitive." Tom and Dad often took hunting trips together. Tyler wasn't invited because "he didn't like the killing part." Dad bought Tom a hunting rifle when he was fourteen years old. Even though Tyler didn't particularly like the hunting, he looked forward to turning fourteen so he could get a rifle from Dad as well. The rifle had become a symbol of Dad's love and approval. When Tyler turned fourteen, there was no rifle, no gift, no card, and no call.

When Tyler didn't receive the rifle, he shifted from trying to please Dad to win his favor to actively hating him. Tyler decided if Dad wouldn't give him his fair share, he would just take it for himself—from Tom. The fight over the CD occurred because Tyler was taking one of Tom's birthday CDs he'd received from Dad. Tyler thought this was fair because Tom had received two and he hadn't received any.

The father's favoritism was not a secret and was probably the main reason Toni divorced Tom. She tried constantly to make up for the gross inequities by doing more for Tyler than she did for Tom.

## Favoritism Generates Anger

Favoritism generates anger in the nonfavored siblings for several reasons:

*"It's not fair!"* The favored sibling receives the best the parent has to offer (extra privileges and attention) not because of his hard work, but because of his special relationship with the parent. The other siblings get the "parental leftovers." They resent the star's special gifts and often do something to destroy them.

*The nonfavored child feels that the parent doesn't understand him.* He feels misunderstood because the parent doesn't listen to him as he does the special child.

*The parent isn't doing anything to correct the unfair situation.* The non-favored child has asked the parent to make things more equal, but nothing happens. The child becomes quite frustrated when his requests produce no tangible results.

*The children can't do anything to correct the situation.* If the nonfavored siblings band together to get even, they are reprimanded for ganging up on their brother. The parent then feels sorry for him and gives him even more attention and possessions.

*The nonfavored siblings believe they can't do anything to become a favored child.* Typically the favoritism is based on something the other siblings can't change, like birth order, sex, athletic or artistic ability, or basic personality style. This increases their frustration because they are stuck in a situation they can't fix.

*They don't have the kind of relationship they desire with the parent.* They would like to have the close relationship they see between the parent and the favored child. They are jealous of that closeness.

*The favored child reports bad things to the parent about the other siblings and becomes quite arrogant about his position.* He uses his position with the parent to tell on his siblings and to put them in a bad light.

Could favoritism be an underlying reason for your child's anger?

## Typical Responses to Favoritism

Children may respond to favoritism in the following behavioral or relational ways:

| Behavioral Responses | Relational Responses |
|---|---|
| Emulating favored child as a way of obtaining parent's affection or attention | Wanting a positive and accepting relationship with the parent who shows the favoritism |
| Acting nicer so the parent will like them more | Being angry with the favored sibling, increasing sibling rivalry |
| Working harder to please the parent | |
| Trying to show the parent things are unfair | Seeking a special relationship with the parent who doesn't show the favoritism |
| Talking with the parent about the unfair situation | |
| Trying to make things even | Opposing anything the other side is for |
| Giving up because they can't fix the situation | Ganging up with other siblings to show the favored one he isn't in control |
| Getting in considerable trouble to make their parent pay attention to them | Being loyal to the ideas and people on their side |
| Running away from home to escape or to get the parent's attention | Avoiding contact with the unfair parent |
| Refusing to help the favored sibling | Wanting to disown the unfair parent |
| Talking badly about the favored sibling | Wanting to get even with the favored sibling and unfair parent |
| Setting up the favored sibling for trouble | |
| Destroying the favored sibling's things | Trying to connect with a group of people with whom they feel special and wanted, e.g., gang affiliation |
| Trying to get rid of the favored sibling | |
| Doing things to gain power, e.g., gang affiliation | Treating the favored sibling poorly, fighting |

If there is a possibility that favoritism is occurring in your family and your child's behavior and relationships are consistent with these signs, it's quite likely he's struggling with issues concerning favoritism.

In general, children who struggle with favoritism deal with their anger by:

*Focusing anger on the favored child.* The siblings may fear that if they go to the parent and confront her for unfairness, it may push the parent even further away. It's much safer to dump their anger on the favored sibling. This can be done by actually hurting the sibling or ruining her possessions. Those special gifts given as evidence of the favoritism are apt to be prime targets.

*Trying to get rid of the sibling.* If they can get rid of the favored sibling, they think they will have more of their parents' attention and good will.

*Looking for ways to get their share.* They want to get something to make things more equitable.

*Being deceitful.* Because they believe their anger toward Mom can't be directly expressed, they do deceitful things to get back at her.

*Doing nothing.* If the siblings don't think they can do anything to improve their situation, they give up. They stop trying to make things better and become very uncooperative.

## Parental Plan

### Pay Attention to Claims of Favoritism

Parental favoritism stirs strong emotional responses. Your child can talk with you about his concerns and feelings or he can act on them, creating more tension among your children. If the former is your preference, encourage him to come to you to talk.

*Make sure your affection, resources, and attention are equitably distributed.* (Things don't have to be exactly even, just reasonable.) Sometimes I hear from parents: "We're so tired of going to counseling appointments, probation meetings, and school conferences for our child." When this occurs, I'm reminded that kids will extract their "due share" of goods and attention from their parents. The choice

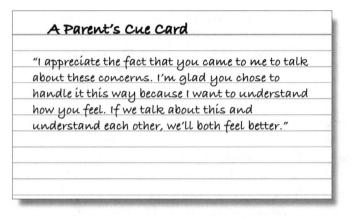

**A Parent's Cue Card**

"I appreciate the fact that you came to me to talk
about these concerns. I'm glad you chose to
handle it this way because I want to understand
how you feel. If we talk about this and
understand each other, we'll both feel better."

we need to make is not whether they will get our attention; rather, what kind of attention we will give them. If it seems you are caught in a cycle of meetings and repair-type activities, take the offensive! Begin to give positive attention. This won't fix everything, but it will definitely help.

Children have tunnel vision. You may have given them considerable love, attention, and privileges yesterday, but if you say no today, they'll claim you never let them do anything. Writing things down on the calendar will help remind them of what they did get.

### Validate Your Child's Perceptions

*Listen to your child's perceptions and try to understand that this is the way he sees the situation.* His perceptions may be accurate or inaccurate, just like yours. Nevertheless, it is his perspective and he is entitled to it, just as you are to yours. Putting him down or calling him "stupid" or a "liar" won't be helpful. Your job is not to judge his perceptions for accuracy but to understand them. Ask questions to clarify what he *sees* and how it *feels* to him. Once you understand his point of view, and have communicated that to him, you can then determine whose perceptions may be more accurate. Feeding back to him what you heard helps clarify what he really thinks.

### Deal with His Concerns

*Develop a plan to address the concerns of both the favored child and his siblings.* If you see from your child's concerns that you need to make

---

### A Parent's Cue Card

"So concerning curfew, you believe that I allow your brother to stay out as long as he wishes, but I lower your curfew for every little infraction of the rules. You don't think this is fair and it makes you very angry. Did I understand what you said? How would you like for things to be?"

---

changes, please do so! He may have some specific requests that will help the situation. Use them if you can.

You don't have to agree with him, but you do need to take his perceptions seriously. Scheduling a time to reevaluate the situation in a week or ten days will help him see you are thinking about his input.

---

### A Parent's Cue Card

"I'm glad you came to me and I think I understand your concerns. I would like to watch these interactions for a while with your input in mind. Let's get together and talk again on Wednesday of next week. By then I will have watched how things go and will be better able to let you know what I can do to help make this better for all of us."

---

### *Deal Fairly with All the Children*

Children usually understand the connection between privileges and responsibilities. Problems arise, however, when a slightly younger sibling, who does his chores and has good grades, has significantly less freedom than his older brother, who doesn't do chores and is flunking several classes. If this is the way you match privileges with responsibilities, you can expect to have great turmoil in your family. Setting up an equitable structure, with consistent expectations, rewards, and consequences, that applies to all of the children will greatly reduce the amount of sibling tension. Consider the following checklist to see if your structure is helping or hindering.

### Home Structure

Check the following statements that describe the way things work in your home.

1. Privileges are based on performance (greater responsibility equals greater privileges).
2. As parents, we agree on the rules and consequences.
3. Rules, expectations, and consequences are clear. (Everyone knows what they are.)
4. We apply the rules and consequences consistently with each child.
5. As parents, we support each other and don't undermine the other parent's authority.
6. One parent is too soft on one child or all the children.
7. One parent is too harsh on one child or all the children.
8. Your spouse treats his/her biological children differently but claims equal treatment of all the children (if you live in a blended family).
9. Either or both parents spend considerable time refereeing the children's fights.
10. We foster competition among the children.

If you checked any of items 1–5, you are heading in the right direction. Pat yourself on the back. Good work! Read over the ones you didn't check and begin working on them. If you checked any of items 6–10, you are headed for more trouble. Review these so you can make changes.

*Hold all family members accountable.* Earlier in the chapter we discussed the cycle of favoritism that may develop in a family. It's easy to jump into the cycle and respond to what's occurring at any given moment. If you do that without considering the bigger picture, you may inadvertently perpetuate the negative sequence.

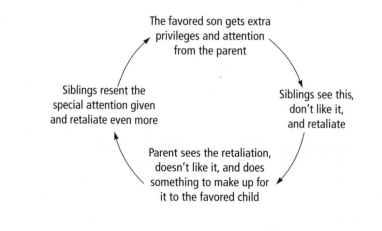

Parents often see the siblings ganging up on the favored child and expect them to stop. But don't forget that the actions from one side influence the response from the other side. It's imperative that you hold all children accountable for their actions. Otherwise you are caught in an ever-escalating situation in which one side is upping the ante to get even for what was done to them.

### Affirm Your Love

When I talk with some parents, it's clear that they love their children, but when I talk with their children, I discover they don't feel it. This is truly unfortunate.

*Help your children see how you communicate your love to them.* Do your children see, understand, and appreciate the things you do to show your love for them? If they don't, now is the time to do two things:

1. Remind them of the things you already do to show them your love. Help them see how you communicate love (your love language).
2. Understand the way they feel love. Speak (talk and act) to them in the way they feel love (their love language).

If your love language is buying something special and your child's language is a warm hug with an "I'm very proud of you" statement, buying him something won't make him feel loved. Asking your child for help is fine:

---

### A Parent's Cue Card

*"Sometimes I'm not sure you really feel how much I love you. It's hard for me to tell you. Is there something I could do that would let you know how much I love you?"*

---

*Indicate ways the nonfavored siblings could also gain your approval and blessing.* Sometimes the siblings see favoritism when it is really a reward connected to good behavior. If, for example, some of your children aren't getting a later curfew because they are always late, make clear the reason for their earlier curfew:

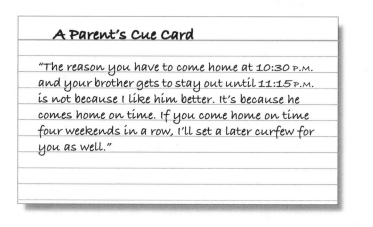

### A Parent's Cue Card

"The reason you have to come home at 10:30 P.M. and your brother gets to stay out until 11:15 P.M. is not because I like him better. It's because he comes home on time. If you come home on time four weekends in a row, I'll set a later curfew for you as well."

### Find Things to Like in Nonfavored Siblings

You raised each of your children in the same home with the same basic rules. How could they be so different? Because they are, it means you will naturally click more with one than another. Some combinations of children and parents produce sparks and conflicts. Some children are just easier to manage than others.

Even though children differ greatly, they all have similar wants and needs. They want their parents to:

- Value them as individuals.
- Take time to enjoy them.
- Encourage them to find their strengths.
- Be patient with their shortcomings.
- Love them for who they are, not always for what they do (or don't do).
- Be proud of them.
- Have fun with them.
- Be interested in what they're interested in.

If you do favor one child, do you know why? Does it make sense to continue to treat that child with special care? Sometimes the way to remedy this situation is not to stop treating that one special, but to find a way to treat them all special. Spend some time with your hard-to-get-along-with child, doing something he likes. Enhancing the relationship will feel good and will minimize the amount of sibling rivalry and tension in the home.

**A Parent's Cue Card**

*"Let's do something for a couple of hours on Saturday. You pick what to do and let me know. If it doesn't cost too much, we can do it."*

### Hold the Star Accountable

Because of your positive relationship with the favored child, you are apt to cut him too much slack, give him too much credit, and believe him too often when he is stretching the truth. In short, when you interact with him, you wear rose-colored glasses.

*Don't automatically believe everything the star tells you.* We all have blind spots. That's why we need each other. If you find you are the only one who believes a story your child tells, he may be fooling you. Check things out. Help keep him honest.

*Hold the favored child accountable.* Granting privileges or other benefits because he's the favored child won't work forever. If you send your star into the world with the idea that he deserves special treatment, he won't have the needed skills to work and persevere until he gets what he wants.

It's often difficult for parents to be objective about how they are treating their children. That's why it's important to listen carefully to what each child is telling you and look critically at your own behavior. When you are careful to treat each child fairly and to make clear why one child receives privileges that another doesn't, you will go a long way in forestalling anger.

## Recommended Books

Adele Faber and Elaine Mazlish. *How to Help Your Children Live Together So You Can Live Too*. New York: Avon Books, 1998.
Nancy Samalin and Catherine Whitney. *Loving Each One Best: A Caring and Practical Approach to Raising Siblings*. New York: Bantam Books, 1996.

# 5

# Parental Abandonment

## Marita: An Abandoned Child

Marita's dad, Tony, still lives in town. The divorce is final and the fighting has ceased. Custody was awarded to Marita's mother, Carol. Dad was given visitation every other weekend, sixty days in the summer, and alternating holidays. The court dictated the time but not the commitment.

Thirteen-year-old Marita just completed the seventh grade. It was a difficult year because she and her mother moved and she had to change schools, but she adjusted and still got a B average. Both parents were pleased with her effort and accomplishments. As they settled into their respective routines, Marita looked forward to spending time with both parents. She liked being with her father on the weekends. They went out to eat together and often went to concerts. Marita's life wasn't like it was before the divorce, but perhaps this would be okay after all.

Dad promised a fun weekend. They would leave Friday night to go to the Denver Zoo. One of Marita's favorite things was visiting a zoo, so naturally she was very excited. Thursday night Carol told Marita that Dad had to cancel the weekend plans. There was no explanation, other than they would go some other time. She didn't see Dad at all that weekend.

The next time Marita went for visitation, she sensed that things had changed. The apartment looked different somehow. On Friday evening they went out to dinner and had a good time, but on Saturday about noon Roberta arrived at the apartment. Dad met her while in one of the chat rooms on the Internet. Dad was excited about having Marita meet Roberta and they all went out to a movie. Marita didn't like this at all. Roberta was nice, but Marita wanted to have fun with just Dad.

Dad canceled the next visit but promised to take Marita to the zoo the next time they were together. That happened the next Saturday. Dad arrived on time and Marita anticipated a great day! But as she walked to the car, her heart sank. There in the front seat sat Roberta. As if that wasn't bad enough, there were also two kids in the backseat. Dad brought Roberta and her two children. It was a miserable day for Marita. She'd hoped for a fun day with just Dad. She and Dad fussed and fought with each other the whole time. Marita thought Dad paid more attention to Roberta's kids than to her.

Over the next few months Dad's allegiance shifted from Marita to Roberta and her children. After Dad and Roberta married, many promises were made and broken. At first Marita was hurt, then she became angry, and then finally apathetic.

Dad was still in town but he'd walked out of Marita's life. Tony made himself an absent parent (A.P.).

## Abandonment Generates Anger

The abandonment itself and the repercussions from it may be causing your child's anger. Parental abandonment generates anger because of the following:

- There is nothing the child can do about it. The child couldn't stop the A.P. from leaving and she can't make him return.
- She may feel blamed or responsible for the parent's absence but doesn't know what she did to cause the problem.
- She feels frustrated, believing a confrontation with the A.P. would push him even further away.
- She's missing out on an important and fun relationship.
- She's envious and jealous of friends who have a positive relationship with their parent.
- She's embarrassed to tell others that her parent is missing.
- She needs the relationship to help her feel good about herself.

Could abandonment be an underlying reason for your child's anger?

# Typical Responses to Abandonment

The child's anger is based on the loss of the parent, the frustration of trying to get him to return, and the implications of the absence. Depending on their age, children may respond to the abandonment in the following behavioral or relational ways:

| Behavioral Response | Relational Response |
| --- | --- |
| Regressing to younger behavior: thumb sucking, not controlling bowel or bladder, talking baby talk | Limiting their view of the absent parent to only his good points |
| Throwing temper tantrums—number and seriousness may increase | Putting one parent on a pedestal and defending every minute flaw or problem |
| Having trouble separating from a parent, e.g., at day care (they fear losing the committed parent) | Giving no credit/gratitude to committed parent |
| Being worried and fearful about how basic needs will be met | Discounting or minimizing importance of other relationships |
| Getting sick, having bodily complaints, or losing appetite—attention seekers | Testing to see if other people like them |
| Having trouble sleeping, nightmares | Setting other people up to reject them |
| Playing more aggressively | Not investing in other relationships |
| Disobeying, being less cooperative, acting up to get negative attention or punishment | Blaming others and taking no responsibility for the relationship |
| Achieving less in school, letting grades drop, cutting, or getting into trouble with the law—may be attempts to reinvolve the absent parent | Looking to peers for support and help |
| Acting sad, angry, depressed, or even suicidal because of the abandonment | |
| Escaping by using drugs or being sexually active | |
| Being sexually active to receive attention | |
| Being angry at the committed parent | |

If one parent has abandoned your child, and her behavior and relationships are consistent with these signs, it's quite likely she is struggling with issues concerning the abandonment.

In general, children who struggle with abandonment deal with their anger in the following ways:

*They are angry at the committed parent.* The committed parent is often confused by this anger, saying: "Don't be mad at me. I'm not the one who abandoned you." While this is a true statement, the issue isn't abandonment. The child believes she can't be angry at the A.P. without pushing him even further away, or

completely ruining any chances of his returning. The committed parent thus becomes the object of the child's anger.

*They are really good or really bad.* One eight-year-old child told me,
"If I'm really good, Dad will want to be with me." Obviously
this child believed her good behavior would bring the A.P. back
into the relationship. If this doesn't work, her anger and frustration make it easy to shift to the opposite pole of being very
bad. One teen ran away from home, hoping her father would be
concerned enough to talk with her. When he wasn't, she shifted to the next option—apathy.

*They dump their anger on a convenient person.* Teachers, siblings, and
peers are often handy targets of the anger of a child who feels
abandoned.

*They are apathetic.* If there is nothing the child can do to woo the
parent back into the relationship, she quits trying. Nothing
works, so she will do nothing.

## *Parental Plan*

### *Provide Pertinent Information*

This can be an extremely difficult step for you, the committed parent. After all, why should you provide a way for your child to contact
the person who has shown absolutely no interest in being a parent?
You may think, *opening this can of worms won't solve anything, and my child
may think she can go live with her father, which I will absolutely not allow.*

I understand your concern, but having information about the A.P.
allows your child to more easily move through this stage of her adjustment. The connection is for your child's benefit. You don't have to
like your child's dentist for him to help your child with an aching
tooth. If you have full custody of your child, you don't have to consider
letting your child live with the A.P. When your child is eighteen, it will
be her decision, but until then it isn't a possibility—unless you want it
to be. So when your child asks, provide relevant information, which
could include pictures, letters, newspaper clippings, and personal

items. If you have the parent's address, talk with your child about writing to the A.P. If actually given an opportunity to communicate with the parent, your child may do so, but don't force her. It may take her some time to make that decision. I recommend writing a letter instead of calling. Writing helps your child clarify her thoughts. Another advantage is that she can write the letter and then choose not to send it. Calling is often done impulsively at a time when the conversation will go poorly. If a contact is made, it should be a positive one.

### A Parent's Cue Card

"When you are ready, I have some information about your dad you might find interesting. I knew by the time you were a teenager, you'd want to know more about him. Please let me know when you are ready to look at the information."

### Don't Overcompensate

Let's follow the typical progression of a situation in which a parent feels guilty or sorry for her child and overcompensates for the absence of the other parent.

1. You feel sorry for your child.
2. You give her things.
3. She likes the things.
4. She begins to feel she deserves them.
5. She develops a sense of entitlement.
6. She's no longer appreciative.
7. She gets things because you owe her, not because she works for them.

Perhaps understanding that this isn't a healthy chain will help you deal with the links under your control. Your child needs to deal with her feelings and thoughts regarding her A.P.

> ### A Parent's Cue Card
>
> "I've tried to make up for Dad by giving you more gifts on your birthday, hoping you wouldn't focus on the fact there was no gift, card, or call from Dad. I'm sorry he doesn't contact you on your birthday, but it isn't helping either of us for me to keep overdoing it. We both need to adjust to his absence."

### Share Your Feelings

Share with your child your feelings about the situation, but don't be overly negative. Your thoughts and feelings influence your child's view of the A.P. What you want from the absent parent may be different from what your child wants, so keep in mind these two points:

*Your child needs to decide for herself how she feels and what she wants from the A.P.*

- This is her relationship and she needs to determine what she wants to do with it.
- Allowing the child and A.P. to work out their relationship keeps you out of the middle and out of a position of blame.
- Typically it's unnecessary for you to point out the negative aspects of the relationship. Especially as your child matures, she's able to see who really cares for her.

*If you cast the A.P. in a totally negative light, it may adversely affect your child.*

- Your child may have to counteract your negativity by being positive about the A.P. when in fact she would like to complain about him.
- If she is the same sex as the A.P., your negative comments may be generalized to all people of that sex, including the child her-

self. Similarly, if she is of the opposite sex, she may believe that all people of that sex aren't good people.

- If she gets to know the A.P., she may find things aren't as bad as you portrayed them, causing her to question other things you have told her.
- It doesn't allow for changes and differences in relationships. The A.P. may be a poor parent but would make a good adult friend. That relationship would likely be beneficial to your child. Don't burn a bridge that isn't yours. If it needs to be burned, your child will know when and how to do a better job.

---

### A Parent's Cue Card

"Even though you know how I feel about your dad, the most important thing is for you to decide how you feel. This is your relationship and you need to deal with it in a way that makes sense to you. Whatever you decide to do will have my support. I will not allow you to live with him now, but once you become an adult, you will have total freedom to do as you wish."

---

### Help Your Child Reach Resolution

In some situations the parent gradually shifts out of the scene. In others the parent left, or perhaps died, before your child really knew him. Curiosity and confusion concerning this situation seem to surface more strongly during the junior high years when identity issues become more prominent. Developmentally, teens are in the process of answering these two questions: Who am I? What can I do? Information about the other biological parent is crucial in this process because it helps your child answer these two related questions: What am I made of? Am I worthwhile or valuable?

The other parent's absence greatly limits your child's ability to reach positive, clear conclusions. As the parent who has tried to hold this all together, you may feel frustrated and helpless to assist your child through this time. However, there are several things you can do to help her come to a resolution.

*Encourage her to ask questions about her absent parent.* Her interest may be painful for you, but without your encouragement, she may not talk about her thoughts.

---

### A Parent's Cue Card

"We don't often talk about your dad, and I know sometimes when we do, I tend to cry a little. I really want you to feel free to ask any questions you have about him. You might be a little hesitant to ask because you don't want to make me cry. I appreciate that you care about my feelings, but the important thing at this point is for you to feel free to ask any questions you

---

might have. I'll do my best to answer them as honestly as I can. Some topics are just so important we must talk about them—whether I cry or not. So, do you have any questions you'd like to ask now?"

---

*Reassure her that she wasn't the cause of the parent leaving.* She needs to deal with the reasons for the parent's abandonment. Usually the options she considers are:

1. I did something drastically wrong, causing the parent to leave.
2. I'm defective in some way—otherwise the parent would have stayed.
3. The parent has problems or reasons for leaving that are independent from me.

You must be honest with your child. If she did something to contribute to the tension in the family, it's fine to talk with her about it. But she should not be held responsible for a parent's leaving, even if she told the parent to leave. A parent's leaving is not a decision for a child to make. It's an adult decision, and the adult needs to take responsibility for it.

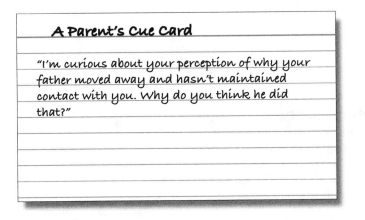

> ### A Parent's Cue Card
>
> "I'm curious about your perception of why your father moved away and hasn't maintained contact with you. Why do you think he did that?"

Usually the answer to the question falls into one of the three categories listed above. Helping your child talk and think about each one will assist her in reaching a reasonable conclusion. Generally the reason for the A.P.'s departure falls within option 3: The parent has personal problems or reasons—not related to something the child did.

*Validate her feelings about the situation.* Many children don't know how they feel. Their feelings are all wound up in a big ugly ball usually labeled "anger." Because there can be many feelings involved, you might check with your child to see if she also feels sad, confused, guilty, frustrated, embarrassed, depressed, overwhelmed, lonely, or jealous. Check chapter 17 to help her determine how she feels and what she might constructively do about it.

*Help her deal with the parent's absence and what it means to her.* Dealing with loss involves identifying her feelings and expectations regarding the relationship. What does she want from the A.P.? You can help her talk about this.

In leading teenagers in an Absent Parent Group, I usually ask them to think about areas in their lives that have been influenced by

---

### A Parent's Cue Card

"I've wondered how you feel about your dad's not being around. There are days when you seem to be angry and times you seem to be sad. How do you feel?"

---

### A Parent's Cue Card

"I was thinking about you and Dad and wondering how life would be if he hadn't left. How do you think your life would be different if he were still around?"

---

not having that parent around. The ones that usually come up as being significant include:

*Relationships:* They don't feel confident in them or understand how they work.

*Self-esteem:* They don't feel good about themselves. If they were great people, the A.P. would still be around.

*Achievement:* Why bother? Things don't work out anyway.

*Attitude:* Who cares?

*Cooperation:* There is no point. It doesn't get you what you want.

*School:* They don't care and it takes too much energy.

*Roles:* They're a victim and can't do anything about their lot in life.

*Outlook on life:* Nothing works out and they're depressed.

---

### A Parent's Cue Card

"Dad's absence has probably influenced you in several ways. You know you might not feel as good about yourself because he left. We can't bring him back. He'll have to make that decision. However, we can choose how we respond. Let's talk about the specific way it's influenced you. In what areas do you think his leaving has had an impact?"

---

You may also want to check chapter 6 to learn more about dealing specifically with the loss, and chapter 10 for dealing with mind-sets.

*Remind your child of what she does have.* Help her to feel good about these things. An A.P. can become your child's primary focus. If you spent all of your time thinking about a bad thing that happened in your life, how would you feel? That's probably the same way your child feels. It's therefore extremely helpful to remind her of other people in her life who care about her and appreciate her talents.

---

### A Parent's Cue Card

"I know you really want to have your dad's approval and to know he's proud of you. I think he is, but he just can't communicate that to you. However, there are a lot of other people who care about you and are proud of you. Who do you think really appreciates and cares about you? Give me the names of those people who are on your cheering squad."

---

*Assist your child to realistically assess her abilities and talents.* What does it mean if the A.P. doesn't recognize your child's qualities? The child may believe her abilities are of no value unless they are affirmed by the A.P. We know this isn't true, but your child may not. Accuracy is important. If your child is going to make good decisions, she needs accurate information. I usually have teens complete the following sentences. You could have your child fill out the answers and talk with you about them.

1. From the feedback I receive from others, I'm good at . . .
2. From the feedback I receive from others, a few of my good qualities are . . .
3. Things I can do really well include . . .
4. Qualities I like about myself include . . .

Encourage your child to think through her answers until she seems to have a realistic and accurate perception of her good qualities and abilities.

There may be nothing more hurtful to a child than to feel abandoned and unloved by a parent. Such a situation requires patience and sensitivity on the part of the remaining parent. Try to focus on your child's needs in light of the hurt she is experiencing and don't take to heart your child's seeming indifference to you.

## Recommended Book

Claudia Jarratt. *Helping Children Cope with Separation and Loss.* Cambridge, Mass.: Harvard Common Press, 1994.

# 6

# Losses

## Matthew: A Relocated Child

As children reach junior and senior high school, a move to another city can be very painful. They are forced to change schools and move away from their friends—who at the time are much more important than parents! They don't like the move but feel powerless. This is quite aggravating for teens who feel they can do anything and believe their parents are "stupid."

Fifteen-year-old Matthew was one of these teens. His parents were transferred to Cheyenne from Colorado Springs. He loved the Springs because he was popular in school, successful in soccer, had a girlfriend, and felt rooted in his house, school, community, and youth group. He tried everything he could to stay. Nothing worked. He moved. He's angry and depressed.

## Christopher: A Child in Grief

Christopher was eight years old when Sandra, a single mother, brought him in for counseling. She worried because the consequences of his anger were becoming serious. She received calls from the school complaining about Chris's bullying on the playground and his yelling at the teacher. He is a "good kid" but becomes very angry with little provocation. His grades had dropped from As and Bs to Ds and Fs. Sandra reported that he also misbehaves at home. He yells at his two younger brothers, Ash and Arthur, and is quite mouthy to her. He doesn't listen or obey. If Sandra wants him to do something, she must pay him. She wants to be firmer with Chris, but it's so difficult. Chris won't accept her authority and argues about everything. Sandra's tired. The burden of having to be "both the mom and the dad" weighs heavily on her shoulders.

Sandra thought Chris might still be angry about his father's death, but that was about eighteen months ago. Dad was killed at the age of twenty-nine by a drunk driver. Even though Chris and Dad were very close, Chris never cried. Sandra noticed Chris was becoming more controlling of the entire family. As a self-appointed junior parent, he "disciplined" his two younger brothers and wouldn't allow Sandra to go out. If Mom insisted on going out with friends, he demanded she "look bad so no man would want to talk with her."

Because Sandra didn't like seeing Chris so sad, she bought things for him to enjoy. A new toy was about the only thing that would bring a smile to his face. He wouldn't talk about Dad but would sit by himself and look at pictures of Dad and him together.

Certain factors hinder one's ability to cope with loss. Let's check the ones that Chris faces:

| Chris | Your Child | Variables Making Grief More Difficult |
|---|---|---|
| | | *Status of Relationship* |
| x | | Importance of relationship to survival and safety |
| x | | Perceived importance of relationship |
| | | Conflicted relationship—unresolved anger and hostility |
| | | Unfinished business, unresolved issues |
| | | Mad at deceased just before she died or at one point wished her to be dead |
| | | *Circumstances of Death* |
| x | | Out of the usual death sequence, which is grandparent first, then parent, then child |
| | | Suicide—anger and guilt are more of a problem |

**Chris**  Your Child                    **Variables Making Grief More Difficult**

*Circumstances of Death cont'd.*

|   |   |   |
|---|---|---|
|   |   | Homicide—anger is stronger |
| x |   | Unusual circumstances—long-term suffering, drunk driver |
| x |   | Length of life: Short life is more of a tragedy |
| x |   | Suddenness—no opportunity to prepare for the loss |
|   |   | Being the one to find the person—trauma of having that picture in your mind |
|   |   | Unsuccessfully trying to revive the person |

*Previous Experience*

|   |   |   |
|---|---|---|
| x |   | First major loss, unsure what to do or how to act |
|   |   | Many losses in a short time period: The child has too much to handle |

*Personality Style*

|   |   |   |
|---|---|---|
|   |   | Dependent, trouble doing things on his own |
|   |   | Rigid, trouble adapting to new situations, lacks flexibility |
| x |   | High need to be in control |
| x |   | Discomfort with emotional issues, difficulty talking about self |
|   |   | Avoids emotional issues instead of dealing with them directly |

*Family Variables*

|   |   |   |
|---|---|---|
|   |   | Poor parental modeling, no control or too controlling of emotions |
| x |   | Difficult expectations: Be the "man of the house," be strong |

*Social Variables*

|   |   |   |
|---|---|---|
|   |   | Limited support—no one available or willing to support |
|   |   | Taboo against talking about death or the deceased |

*Concurrent Stressors*

|   |   |   |
|---|---|---|
|   |   | High number of significant stressors |
|   |   | Financial concerns: Child may be aware of potential problems |

Do any of these fit your child? The more of them you check, the more support and direction your child will need to work through his grief.

## Types of Loss

There are many types of losses that can impact your child and your family. Have any of these occurred in your family?

- death of grandparent, parent, sibling, friend, pet
- divorce or separation
- custody—child loses daily contact with a parent and the dream of how things would be
- remarriage—child loses sole attention of parent
- birth of sibling—child may lose role or position
- sibling moves out of the house or gets married
- move (relocation)—child loses friends, school, familiar settings, future plans
- friend moves
- loss of a dream
- injury resulting in significant change—athletic injury may end a sports career
- abortion or miscarriage

## Losses Generate Anger

A loss of any kind may be at the root of your child's anger. Think back on any losses your family has experienced. Did the loss have a serious impact on your family? Was it a significant loss for your child? Loss and the accompanying grief can be difficult to cope with because they involve so many different issues and areas of concern.

### Physical Concerns

Your child may experience these physical responses to the loss:

- hollowness in the stomach
- tightness in the chest
- over-sensitivity to noise

- shortness of breath
- weakness in muscles
- lack of energy
- dry mouth
- sleep disturbances and nightmares
- appetite disturbances
- sense of depersonalization—watching himself as if in a dream

*Emotional Concerns*

Grief generates intense emotions. How well does your child deal with his feelings?

- *Sadness.* Is sadness okay or does your child turn it into anger? Boys may need encouragement and permission to be sad rather than mad.
- *Anger.* Does your child have a way to work through his anger? See chapters 17–21.
- *Helplessness.* Boys particularly may need help in determining what they can do.
- *Anxiety.* What will happen now? How will he cope? If it is a loss through death, he experiences anxiety and probably fears his own death.
- *Guilt.* What might your child feel guilty about? Help him realistically assess the situation.
- *Survivor guilt.* Why did the other person die and not him?
- *Confusion.* How does he make sense of all of this? How can he go on?
- *Finality of death.* Your child can't go back and change the last interaction with the deceased. Did he say or do something he regrets? Discussing what was generally true about the relationship helps your child look beyond a poor last contact.

*Spiritual Concerns*

We all have beliefs about God, life, death, and the way things ought to be. What does this loss do to those beliefs? How does your child incorporate this event into his beliefs?

- Significant losses can rock the foundation of your child's beliefs. He may have to reexamine his beliefs and whether they hold up under such loss.

- He may be mad at God. Is that okay, or must he hide his anger?
- He may be angry about comments made by the priests or clergy. Comments meant to comfort are often misinterpreted. If your child is angry about a comment, talk about it with your child.
- He may have many questions with no answers. I'm a good person, so why is this happening to me? Why did she have to die? Will I ever see him again? What's "dead" like?

### Control Issues

Death reveals how little control we have over some circumstances. Children often believe their parents can fix anything. Is this the first time your child has seen how little control you really have?

Because of the loss, you may shift into over-protecting your child. At the same time, he may push for control by demanding more privileges and freedom.

### Cognitive Issues

What we think and the meaning we attach to events are sometimes as important as the event itself. Which of these thoughts might your child be having?

- I'm very scared. My world isn't as safe as I thought.
- I never thought it could happen to me.
- It shouldn't have happened to her. She was too good to die.
- Relationships can't be trusted.
- Life is more fragile than I thought.
- I'm not a good friend or a safe friend to have. If you become my friend, you might die.
- If you are good and work hard, these things shouldn't happen to you.
- Why can't I remember anything? I've never been this forgetful.

### Parental Issues

Parents don't grieve in the same way or on the same time frame as children. This can cause great tension or loss of support for the parents.

Any kind of loss and the changes brought about by the loss may be causing your child's anger. Loss generates anger because:

- There is nothing your child can do to stop it or make the changes go away.
- He has to adjust to the changes, most of which he doesn't like.
- His life is significantly different. He doesn't get to do some of the things he used to do and he misses those activities and relationships.
- The hurt and pain "sneak up" on him and hit him at unexpected times.

Could a loss be an underlying reason for your child's anger?

## Typical Responses to Loss

Depending on their age, children may respond to a loss in the following behavioral or relational ways:

| Behavioral Responses | Relational Responses |
| --- | --- |
| Complaining of physical symptoms like those of the deceased | Avoiding contact with others, being away from home as much as possible |
| Having trouble sleeping and having nightmares about the deceased | Withdrawing emotionally |
| Taking on characteristics of the deceased, talking like she did, doing the chores she did, assuming her role in the family | "Building walls" to keep others away |
| | Giving deceased parent "sainthood status" |
| Regressing to earlier ways of acting; may revert to thumb sucking, not controlling bowel or bladder, talking baby talk | "Parenting" the emotionally distraught parent |
| Having trouble separating from a parent, e.g., at day care | Looking to peers for support and help |
| Being anxious about how basic needs will be met | Unwilling to share thoughts or feelings |
| Playing more aggressively | |
| Disobeying, being less cooperative, acting up to get negative attention or punishment | Relating to others as though the deceased would, parenting younger siblings |
| Achieving less in school, letting grades drop, cutting, or getting into trouble with the law | |
| Withdrawing emotionally or physically: shutting self off from others, spending more time in room or away from home | |
| Escaping by using drugs, being sexually active | |
| Acting sad, angry, depressed | |
| Being moody, exploding over minor issues | |
| Being more of a control freak | |

If your child has experienced a significant loss and your child's behavior and relationships are consistent with these signs, it's quite likely he's struggling with grief.

Children who struggle with losses often deal with their anger in several ways:

*They bottle it up inside and don't talk about it.* Death and other significant losses are difficult for some children and adolescents to talk about. Boys may find it especially difficult to identify and talk about their feelings. They are prone to cope by doing something rather than talking. But verbalizing their thoughts and feelings is very helpful for both males and females.

*They are apathetic.* There's nothing the child can do about the loss, so it's easy to take this mind-set into other areas of their lives. Why bother?

*They dump their anger on a convenient person.* Their anger can be contained only so long until there is bound to be an explosion. This may happen when an innocent person says something or does something that taps into the child's anger about the loss.

*They become depressed.* When the child's anger isn't dealt with directly, it often turns into depression. Depressed kids:

- Lose their zest for life.
- Become lethargic.
- Have trouble sleeping—getting to sleep and staying asleep.
- Lose their appetite and then weight.
- Lose interest in things they used to enjoy.
- Lose interest in relationships, sex.
- Withdraw from regular activities they used to enjoy.
- Are sad, tearful, and apathetic.

*They become suicidal.* Kids who can't see an end to their pain and who have lost hope of things improving may view suicide as a viable choice. They are at greater risk if they:

- Experience a devastating incident.
- Have a family history of suicide.
- Have a history of previous gestures or suicide attempts.

- Have a coping style of avoidance.
- Consume alcohol or use drugs.
- Have nothing to live for and have no hope that things will improve.
- Have a plan for committing suicide.
- Have a lethal plan.
- Have a lethal plan with access to the means (gun, rope, pills, car).
- Won't make a verbal or written promise not to hurt themselves.

Dr. Janice Wood Wetzel in her book *Clinical Handbook of Depression* cites Schneidmen and his colleagues, who list four categories of clues to suicidal behavior.[1]

1. *Verbal Clues:*
   - Direct verbal communication: "I want to die." "If that happens again, I'll kill myself."
   - Indirect verbal communication: "I can't stand it any longer." "She'd be better off without me."
   - Subtle indirect verbal communication: "You'll be sorry when I'm gone." "This is the last time I'll see you."
2. *Behavioral Clues:*
   - Direct behavioral clues: Any action that uses tools of suicide: knives, razors, guns, pills.
   - Indirect behavioral clues: Putting affairs in order, making a will, writing good-bye letters, giving away prized possessions, sudden improvement of depression.
3. *Situational Clues:*
   - Anxiety-provoking situations: breakup of a relationship.
   - Loss of hopeful options: Therapy, girlfriend, and/or accomplishing something didn't produce the desired outcome.
4. *Syndromatic Clues:*
   - Depression: Can't see that things will improve. Has no energy to keep going.

- Dependence-dissatisfaction: Feels too dependent on others and is highly dissatisfied with his lot in life.
- Defiance: Will consider suicide to make a point.

If your child exhibits these signs, contact your pastor, physician, or counselor. Remove lethal weapons, such as guns or pills, get a commitment that he won't hurt himself, don't allow him to be by himself, and deal with the issues that cause him to be suicidal.

 ## *Parental Plan*

The four steps in this plan are based on J. William Worden's four grief tasks as found in *Grief Counseling and Grief Therapy*.[2]

### *Help Him Accept Reality*

It's hard to deal with loss. Shock and denial are initially helpful because they give people time to rally their resources to begin coping with the loss. Getting stuck in denial prevents the necessary grief work. Denial often takes these forms:

- Pretending the person is gone (like on a vacation) but will be returning.
- Eliminating reminders of the person (taking down pictures, moving out of the house or city).
- Refusing to talk about the loss—the death of the person, the career-ending injury.
- Refusing to acknowledge the resulting changes.
- Minimizing the importance of the loss ("I was going to quit soccer next year anyway").
- Keeping very busy so there isn't a moment to think or feel.
- Replacing the pet or person with another to eliminate the hole left in one's life.
- Doing exciting or dangerous activities as a distraction.
- Using drugs or alcohol as an avoidance tactic.

As parents, you can assist your child to accept the reality of the loss by:

- Talking about the person and the resulting changes.
- Looking at photo albums or video tapes of the person.
- Making a scrapbook page especially of that person.
- Visiting the cemetery and putting flowers on the grave.
- If the loss is a move, remembering fun times at the old house and laughing about them.
- Drawing pictures of the old house.
- Listening to the child's preferences about a new house.
- Reassuring him he isn't going crazy.
- Expressing confidence in his ability to deal with the loss.

## What Do I Say?

| Helpful Things to Say | Things That Are Not Helpful to Say |
|---|---|
| "I was really sorry to hear about the death of your friend." (It's okay to say "death.") "I'm sorry about your injury." | "I understand how you feel." Even if you have experienced a similar loss, you don't know how he feels. |
| "I'm sad for you." The statement is personal and indicates you are comfortable talking about emotions. | "Cheer up. This too will pass." This minimizes the importance of the loss. |
| "How are you doing with all this?" The question invites your child to share if he chooses to do so. | "It was God's will." This isn't the time to become theological. The comment doesn't usually provide comfort. |
| "It's hard to know why this happened." There aren't any easy answers to difficult situations. | "It all happened for the best." You don't know that. This minimizes the tragedy of the situation. Clichés don't comfort. |
| "I'm here for you." This offers your support. | "You need to get involved in some activity." Don't encourage escape. |
| "What's the hardest part for you?" This shows your interest in the difficult aspects of adjusting. | "At least you have other friends." This minimizes the importance of the loss. |
| "Let's talk again tomorrow." This lets the child know you are available to her. | "Let me know if I can help." This places the expectation for reaching out on the grieving child. Find something you can do and do it. |
| "It's been a while since your friend died. How are you doing?" This lets the child know that you care and that the loss isn't forgotten. | "It's time to put this behind you." This isn't your call to make. |

Sometimes it's best not to say anything. You don't have to fix the problem. Actually you can't fix the problem. Sitting quietly with your child and supporting her are good things to do.

### Help Him Deal with the Pain

The more significant the loss, the greater the pain. You can support your child in dealing with the pain by:

- Helping him feel safe: Turn on a night light; check the room before he goes to bed.
- Talking about the schedule, including daily activities so he knows what to expect.
- Helping him identify specific feelings (anger, guilt, anxiety, fear) concerning the loss.
- Encouraging him to journal about how his life changed as a result of the loss.
- Providing material so he can draw a picture of his favorite time with the deceased.
- Providing a notebook to be put on his night stand so he can write down things if he's awakened in the night.
- Listening to him.
- Monitoring his behavior and activities so he isn't completely numbing his pain through alcohol or drugs.
- Expressing confidence in his ability to deal with the loss.

---

**A Parent's Cue Card**

"It's important to talk about how we feel and how we hurt. Sharing the pain makes it easier to get through it. We are a strong family. Let's talk with each other instead of trying to avoid or numb the pain."

*Help Him Adjust to the Loss*

Life will never be the same. Your child's world has been significantly altered by the loss. He doesn't like it and doesn't want to deal with the changes. Coping with those changes and adapting to them allow him to rebuild his life.

Children who struggle at this point may:

- Pretend nothing has changed.
- Cling to the way things have always been done.
- Want to cover all of the responsibilities done by the deceased as a way of pretending she is still present.
- Refuse to go places or do things he used to do with the deceased.
- Have trouble allowing new people into his life.

You can support your child to deal with the changes by reminding him of his strengths, his ability to deal with difficult issues, and his available resources.

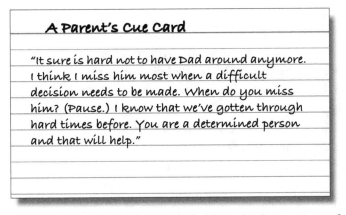

### A Parent's Cue Card

"It sure is hard not to have Dad around anymore. I think I miss him most when a difficult decision needs to be made. When do you miss him? (Pause.) I know that we've gotten through hard times before. You are a determined person and that will help."

Matthew—the relocated child at the beginning of the chapter—was able to express what he wanted in the new house. He was allowed to call a friend in the Springs once a week, and his parents let him invite a couple of his buddies up for spring break. They also encouraged Matthew to get involved in sports, which he did. This helped him meet new friends and feel more comfortable in the new school.

Sandra told Chris he didn't need to do all of Daddy's jobs, because those were adult jobs that she would do. She gave him a job he could handle. She didn't want Chris to be the "man of the house," but he could do one job that Daddy used to do. This clarification really helped Chris feel better. The task was something he could do. After this discussion he stopped bossing his two younger brothers around and began playing more with them.

*Help Him Move On*

Moving on is difficult. It's hard to suddenly stop investing time, energy, and commitment into a lost relationship or situation. What has been lost can no longer hold the same position in your child's life. If it's a loss through death, the child must understand that detaching from the deceased doesn't mean she wasn't important. Your child can still love her, miss her, and think about her, but he can't keep living as though the deceased were still alive.

People who can't let go of their grief and invest in the present or in the future often:

- Hold exclusively to past attachments.
- Make decisions based on the wishes of the deceased.
- Remain loyal to the narrowly defined wishes of the deceased.
- Resist making new attachments to other people and other relationships.
- Make decisions that interfere with their growth.
- Sabotage change and progress.
- Need permission to move on with life.

You may help your child by:

- Providing support to say good-bye or adjust to a new situation.
- Helping him work through obstacles that interfere with his moving on.
- Giving him permission to stop grieving and start living.
- Sanctioning new relationships or involvements.
- Encourage new activities.

### A Parent's Cue Card

"I know you really miss your old friends, and we're glad that you've stayed in touch with them. Avoiding new friendships here, though, doesn't help you feel better. How about inviting some people over for pizza after the game?"

Matthew's parents assisted him by encouraging his involvement with new people through sports, the youth group, and the drama club. They supported exploration into community activities.

Sandra talked more freely with Chris about Dad and explored with him new options for their lives.

Just because it has been a year or more since the loss, don't assume things are resolved and the loss no longer has an influence on your child. He may still be hurting. We need special sensitivity when our child is suffering from a loss. Talk with him about the loss and his accompanying feelings. This may be especially difficult if you too are grieving. If you or your child can't seem to get through the grief, contact your pastor or a counselor in your community.

## Recommended Books

Mary Ann Emswiler and James Emswiler. *Guiding Your Child through Grief.* New York: Bantam Doubleday Dell, 2000.

Adolph Moser. *Don't Despair on Thursdays: The Children's Grief-Management Book.* Kansas City, Mo. Landmark Editions, 1996.

# 7

# Parental Alcoholism or Drug Use

## Beth: A Child of an Alcoholic

Janet called to make a counseling appointment for her nine-year-old daughter, Beth, because of her concern about her high need to be in control and her increasing level of anger. Janet wasn't exactly sure why Beth was having a difficult time.

Beth has two older sisters, Melanie (fifteen) and Teresa (thirteen). The children get along reasonably well. They have their usual sibling fights but generally seem to appreciate and care about each other.

Janet and John, biological parents of the children, have been married for sixteen years. John is extremely busy at work but rearranged his schedule so he could attend the counseling sessions.

Janet and Beth arrived early for the first appointment. Janet appeared to be an organized woman who was used to getting things accomplished. They were both very friendly and quite articulate. They told me that the family had moved to Cheyenne about three years earlier when Dad was transferred with his company. Beth likes her school but has trouble making friends. She tends to keep her emotions bottled up inside and then explodes over little things. The family is active in church, but apparently Dad isn't too involved with the family because he's so busy at work.

I wondered if there was missing information because usually families with this picture don't feel they need counseling. I decided to meet with them separately.

As Janet and I talked, she told me, "John is very busy and very grouchy. He's a good husband and a faithful provider, but over the years he's gradually checked out of the parenting duties and the family fun."

At this point she stopped talking and tears welled up in her eyes. After a brief period of silence she said, "I'm worried about John's drinking. Since the transfer, it's become more of a problem. He stays up late watching television and drinking." She talked more about her concern and said she was sure if it became an issue when John was present, he would stop coming in for the sessions.

When I talked with Beth, she brought up Dad's drinking problem. She said she and her sisters often talk about it. Beth actively tries to get Dad to stop drinking by telling Dad to quit, putting things in his drink, hiding bottles, and pouring out open containers.

## Parental Alcohol or Drug Use Generates Anger

Parental use of alcohol or drugs and the accompanying behaviors may be causing your child's anger. In this chapter we will focus on alcoholism, but drug abuse creates the same problems and concerns for your child. Alcohol or drug use generates anger because of the user himself and because of the accompanying family concerns.

Regarding the drinking parent, your child may be angry because:

- Parental expectations may vary from day to day. The child may be punished for something one day and laughed at for doing it the next.
- Parental behavior is unpredictable, with large mood swings and erratic behavior.
- The drinker can't be counted on to attend ball games, concerts, or other activities.
- The drinker may be very hard to please.
- The drinker makes promises he doesn't keep.
- The child can't stop the parent from drinking. She may feel blamed or responsible for the parent's drinking.
- The child is frustrated with the lack of a close relationship with the parent.

Family issues also generate anger:

- The using parent doesn't make amends for his poor choices.
- The home is not a secure, stable environment. It's not a "normal" family.
- There is little family fun.
- It's not okay to talk about feelings; the only emotion expressed is anger.
- Issues aren't resolved; they're swept under the rug.

Could parental drinking be an underlying reason for your child's anger?

## Typical Responses to Parental Alcoholism

Depending on their age, children may respond to alcoholism in the following behavioral or relational ways:

| Behavioral Responses | Relational Responses |
|---|---|
| Having temper tantrums—number and seriousness may increase | Withdrawing emotionally |
| Playing more aggressively | "Parenting" the emotionally distraught parent |
| Having trouble sleeping, nightmares | Avoiding contact, being away from home as much as possible |
| Disobeying, being less cooperative, acting up to get negative attention or punishment | Looking to peers for support and help |
| Being "in your face" defiant, especially when they are physically able to hold their own | Unwilling to share thoughts or feelings about situations |
| Achieving less in school, letting grades drop, cutting classes, not turning in assignments, being disrespectful | Protecting the parent who drinks |
| Being irresponsible in areas that are important to the person who drinks | "Agreeing" not to talk about the drinking or becoming completely focused on the drinking and overlooking other positive things the parent does |
| Pushing limits at home, school, or in the community, resulting in legal difficulties | Keeping their feelings to themselves |
| Experimenting with alcohol, marijuana, or other drugs | Choosing not to trust others as they learn that people don't follow through on what they promise |
| Withdrawing emotionally/physically, spending more time in their room or away from home | Taking charge of the relationship and other parenting duties |
| Escaping by using drugs, being sexually active | |
| Being clearly angry at one or both parents | |
| Pushing themselves to work very hard and be successful | |
| Being in control all of the time | |

If a parent has a drinking problem, and your child's behavior and relationships are consistent with these signs, it's quite likely she is struggling with issues concerning the alcoholism.

In general, children who live in an alcoholic family deal with their anger in the following ways:

*They are angry at the nonalcoholic parent for not fixing the situation.* Understandably, the child turns to the other parent to remedy the situation. Because the parent can't do that, she is the focus of the child's anger. She may think, "If Mom can't fix the situation, then at the very least she should remove me from it."

*They are really good or really bad.* If the child is really good, she thinks the parent won't become angry and be pushed into drinking. As time passes and the child realizes that being perfect doesn't solve the problem, she may choose to misbehave. Misbehaving allows the child to show the parent her anger and may help the parent to stop drinking to help the child with her difficulties.

*They drink or use drugs.* As the child's anger and frustration become stronger, she seeks ways to feel better. She knows from example that drinking or using drugs are powerful ways of avoiding negative feelings. She tries alcohol and discovers it temporarily makes her feel better. Liking the results, she may begin a coping style of avoiding her feelings through drinking.

*They are angry at the parent who drinks.* Some children finally reach a point where they express their anger directly toward the drinker. This is seldom received or heard.

 ## Parental Plan

### For the Using Parent

HONESTLY AND OPENLY EXAMINE HOW
YOUR HABIT IMPACTS YOU AND YOUR FAMILY

It's easy to minimize the amount of time, energy, and resources devoted to drinking. Stop and take a look at how much time you drink, think about drinking, recover from drinking, make excuses about drinking, talk about drinking, and argue about drinking. Spending your time this way means it isn't spent in other ways, like interacting positively with your family or children. One of the chief complaints from children regarding their parent who has a drinking problem is, "He never has time to do things with me."

### CHOOSE TO STOP DRINKING

*Pick a day to stop using.* If you are going to stop, you have to find a time to do that. When will you start to stop?

*Go public with your decision.* Tell someone of your goal. This helps you be more accountable and gives you more support.

*Make effective use of countering.* "For decades, research has shown that countering—substituting healthy responses for problem behaviors—is one of the most powerful processes available to changers. . . . When you remove troubled behaviors without providing healthy substitutes, the risk of returning to old patterns remains high."[1] Instead of sitting at home and drinking, you could go out to a movie with your child. Instead of avoiding a difficult issue, talk with your spouse about it.

*Use environmental control techniques.* The environmental control technique means "restructure your environment so that the probability of a problem-causing event is reduced."[2] If you are serious about being sober, don't put yourself in positions that increase the probability of drinking. You don't go to happy hour or stop at the bar on the way home. You remove beer or drugs from your home.

*Increase your incentive to stay sober.* Give yourself positive messages and pats on the back for your progress. Focus on the positives of not drinking, and remember the negatives. Enlist the assistance of your spouse. Be clear on what you need. Join Alcoholics Anonymous (AA). Join a small group that will support you and hold you accountable.

Some parents become very angry when they realize that simply quitting drinking doesn't give them the desired results. Alcoholism is more than just drinking. It's an avoidant lifestyle of not dealing with feelings, problems, or relationships. When I ask parents to stop drinking *and* deal with their issues, anger, and relationships, many think I'm asking too much. But those who commit to these tasks find great rewards in a renewed relationship with their children and spouse. It's hard, but it's worth it.

### For the Non-using Parent

#### DON'T SOFTEN THE CONSEQUENCES

It's important that you not try to soften the consequences that your spouse experiences because of his drinking. At first glance this may seem cruel. However, consequences help us all choose to make different decisions. Removing or softening the consequences makes it easier for people to continue in behavior that isn't good for them. If you want your spouse to stop drinking, dealing with the consequences full strength will help him rethink his choices—so don't dilute them.

### Focus on Legitimate Responsibilities

Are you or your children responsible for making your spouse drink? Whose responsibility is it to stop him from using or drinking? The person who uses or drinks is responsible for starting and stopping. You can't make him drink by something you do. There are many ways he could respond, so if he drinks, it's because he chose to drink. If you or one of your children try to make him stop drinking, two things occur: 1. You've assumed responsibility for his drinking, and because you can't control that, you are doomed to fail and then feel guilty about it. 2. By taking more responsibility for the situation, you give your spouse permission to take less responsibility.

There is great relief in understanding that neither you nor your children can stop the drinker from drinking, and nothing you can do will make him drink if he doesn't want to do so. Once you grasp these responsibility principles, explain them to your children.

#### TAKE TIME FOR FAMILY FUN

It's easy to focus on the problems so much that you forget to have any fun. If there is no fun, the problems seem even larger. Find ways to increase the positives in your family.

#### TALK ABOUT FEELINGS

By watching her alcoholic parent, your child will likely reach these two conclusions: 1. Avoid feelings. 2. Drink to feel better. She thus learns to cope with situations by avoiding her emotions, beginning a

> ### A Parent's Cue Card
>
> "It's not your responsibility to stop your father from drinking. Only he can stop himself. We can't do it and we're wasting energy on trying. I love him and I know you do too, but we need to focus our energy on doing things we can control and we can make better. I don't expect you to do anything to make him stop drinking."

lifestyle of avoidance. By shutting down her emotions she's submerging pain and confusion, which creates an atmosphere where alcohol is welcomed.

Identifying emotions and using them to develop a positive plan of action is a skill that can be learned (see chapter 17 for help in determining how you feel). Janet purposely began asking Beth to identify how she felt about situations concerning her father. At first it was difficult, but with some encouragement, Beth was able to tell her. Interestingly, the better she got at that, the less angry she became.

> ### A Parent's Cue Card
>
> "Understanding how you feel helps you figure out what to do, so we're going to talk more about how we feel. Then we can figure out what we can do to make the situation better."

DEAL WITH ISSUES INSTEAD OF AVOIDING THEM

*Talk about issues and concerns; don't sweep them under the rug.* You don't have to have a solution to talk about an issue or concern. Sometimes simply talking about it helps people feel better. Don't be afraid to just talk.

*Reach some type of resolution.* You don't have to develop the perfect solution. Coming up with a tentative solution that will help things move ahead is a step in the right direction. Do something rather than avoid the issue.

---

### A Parent's Cue Card

"Sometimes you don't talk with me about your feelings and ideas because you don't think it will matter. Well, it does matter to me, and I want to hear your thoughts. You are a part of this family and you may have ideas that will make it better for all of us. Let's put our ideas together and see if we can come up with a plan that will make things better. I want us to deal with problems rather than pretend they don't exist."

---

Clarifying responsibility, identifying feelings, understanding issues, and resolving problems gives your children a sense that they have control over their lives, reduces their guilt for not fixing things out of their control, and reduces their anger. Even if your spouse continues to drink, you can still make a difference in this situation. Overcome the situation; don't let it overcome you.

## Recommended Books

John C. Friel and Linda Friel. *Adult Children: The Secrets of Dysfunctional Families.* Health Communications, 1988.

Gilda Berger. *Alcoholism and the Family (The Changing Family).* Franklin Watts, 1993.

# 8

# Parental Overindulgence

## Tiffany: An Overindulged Child

Tiffany, the older of two children, was almost ten years old when her biological parents, Tammy and Bob, brought her in for the first appointment. They were concerned about her temper tantrums at home and at school. She had great difficulty keeping friends as she always had to have her way. Mornings were the hardest because Tiffany and her mom usually fought over what she should wear to school. She would persist until Mom would angrily surrender with, "Fine, wear whatever you want! You are the one who looks silly, not me." Tiffany won.

Tammy grew up as the oldest daughter of four children in a single-parent household. Her mom's job didn't provide for much above the bare necessities, so clothes were passed down from child to child. Bob, a sergeant in the Army, felt guilty about being away from home so much, but that was just "part of military life." While away, he faithfully e-mailed and called when he could. He always sent interesting and expensive gifts from his remote assignments. Tammy was the primary caregiver in the family and seemed very committed to her children, Tiffany and Travis, who is eight years old.

Bob and Tammy were told early in their marriage they could not have children. When the news came of Tammy's pregnancy, they were ecstatic. Although the pregnancy was normal, the birth was premature, and Tiffany was airlifted to a larger hospital to receive more intensive care. You don't have to be a counselor to see how these factors made it easy for the parents to give Tiffany everything she wanted. In many ways, Tiffany's parents communicate to her that she is a very special child and deserves to have whatever she wants.

The parents have created a "princess," and now they want to turn her back into a "regular" child. When the family came in for counseling, the parents had already started to implement some changes but they weren't sure they were doing the right thing. Their plan was to hold Tiffany more accountable for her actions and have her work for some of the things they had previously freely supplied. They stopped doing her homework. They actually expected her to take out the trash. Tiffany, of course, wasn't thrilled with this new parental plan and was doing all she could to force them to return to the way things were. When they tried to hold her accountable she became extremely angry. Once she took an Exacto knife and cut a cushion on Mom's new couch and cut all the stripes and buttons off Dad's dress uniform. She did not like being demoted to a mere child in the family.

## Stopping the Overindulgence Generates Anger

If you give your children everything they want, expecting nothing from them, they probably won't complain. But when you want something in return or hold them accountable, look out! You will see some anger. There are several reasons for the anger:

*The child doesn't have any input into the change of rules and doesn't like them.*

*The child believes he deserves special treatment (mind-set).*

*The child no longer gets everything she wants.* This is compounded by the fact that she has never been denied before.

*The child discovers the "earn-what-you-get system" is harder than the "entitlement system."*

*The child doesn't perform well and therefore doesn't earn much of what she's used to receiving.* She hasn't had the practice of working hard and persevering at a task. She feels awkward and isn't happy about the rewards of her labors.

# Typical Responses to Overindulgence

Children who have been overindulged may respond in a number of ways:

| Behavioral Responses | Relational Responses |
| --- | --- |
| Expecting to receive special privileges and gifts because of who they are not because of what they've done | Having relationships based on what others can give to them |
| Showing little appreciation for what they have and not taking care of it | Expecting others to save them and meet their demands |
| Expecting rewards for every little thing they're asked to do | Getting what they want by making others feel guilt or sympathy for them |
| Demanding their own way | Using other people |
| Whining or throwing huge temper tantrums when things don't go their way | Having little empathy for others—their needs aren't important |
| Exerting very little effort on assigned tasks | Having trouble cooperating for the good of the family or group |
| Having little persistence—if something is hard, they just give up | Having trouble keeping friends of their own age |
| Minimizing their contribution to a bad situation or problem | Having negatively focused relationships: Parents focus on what the child is not doing—homework, chores, cleaning room |
| Avoiding responsibility by shifting focus to what the other person did or didn't do | Creating tension in parental or caregiver relationships |
| Blaming others | |

If your child's behavior and relationships are consistent with these signs, it's quite likely she will become very angry if you begin to limit your indulgence.

In general, overindulged children, who aren't getting what they want, deal with their anger in several ways:

*They may throw temper tantrums.* They may not know what else to do, or they may throw the tantrums because they work!

*They may stage stubborn sit-down strikes.* You can't make them do anything, and they aren't going to do anything until you give them what they want!

*They may blame you for their problems.* Because they are so special, it can't be their fault. It therefore must be your fault!

*They may wait you out.* They may choose to do nothing, causing a drastic decline in their achievement. They believe you will step in and help them out.

*They may express directly their anger toward you.* Because they aren't particularly concerned about your feelings, they may say and do some very hurtful things.

*They may seek assistance from others who historically have given them what they want.* Typically there are several people who will give them what they want and make you feel terrible in the process.

## *Parental Plan*

### *Admit to Your Overindulgence and Stop It*

Parents usually give too much because of difficult birth circumstances, the child's physical problems, parental guilt about their child care, parental hardships in the parent's childhood, or because they simply feel sorry for their child. No doubt these are all significant issues that encourage parents to give what immediately makes their child happy. If you believe your child deserves to be overindulged, you will continue to give her everything she wants. But you must ask yourself if you are happy with the kind of person she is becoming. And can you continue to provide her with what she wants for the rest of her life?

If you conclude you must change the way you interact with your child, the time to start the change is NOW. The longer you wait, the harder it becomes to make the changes. Now is the time to act. It will be difficult, but you can do it and it will be worth it.

What would happen if you stopped overindulging your child? The authors of *Changing for Good*[1] recommend completing a Decisional Balance Scale when considering change. The scale is provided below and some possible responses are filled in. Complete the scale relative to your specific situation to weigh the pros and cons of stopping your overindulgence. For change to occur and be maintained, the pros must outweigh the cons in number and importance. Trying to implement a plan while the pros are few and unimportant will result in a failed plan.

By stopping the overindulgence of my child, I would expect the following pros and cons. (Cross out the ones that don't apply to you. Fill in your own responses.)

### 1. Consequences to Self (What would happen to you?)

| Pros | Cons |
| --- | --- |
| • I'd feel better about my parenting.<br>• My spouse would support me and we would be working better as a team. | • My child wouldn't like me.<br>• She'd yell at me.<br>• I'd experience more tension and stress.<br>• I might receive criticism from others who think I'm being mean. |

### 2. Consequences to Others (What would happen to others?)

| Pros | Cons |
| --- | --- |
| • If my child worked, she would realize some of her strengths.<br>• My spouse would feel better because he/she would no longer be the only one who says no. | • My child wouldn't get what she's used to getting.<br>• She would fail at school. |

### 3. Reactions of Self (How would you feel about yourself?)

| Pros | Cons |
| --- | --- |
| • I would see myself as a more courageous parent.<br>• I would feel confident I'm doing the right thing. | • I'd probably feel mean and guilty, thinking I'm treating her too harshly. |

### 4. Reactions of Others (How would others feel about you?)

| Pros | Cons |
| --- | --- |
| • Other children in the family would probably support holding their sibling more accountable.<br>• My spouse would feel very positive about my change. | • My child would likely think I'm mean.<br>• Others may not understand or think I'm too mean. |

After you and your spouse have thought about the situation and you have identified numerous and strong pros for limiting your over-indulgence and you have decided that the cons don't seem as important, you are ready to make changes. When is a good time to stop the overindulgence? No matter when you stop, your child won't like it. If you can't stop now, talk with your spouse and agree on a date when you will change the way you reward your child. Go public with your decision! Advise the grandparents, baby-sitter, aunts, uncles, and your little princess. Doing so will help hold you accountable and may enlist the assistance of others.

### Develop Reasonable Expectations, Rewards, and Consequences

Making the change will be difficult. Your little princess may beg, whine, threaten (suicide, runaway, pregnancy), manipulate, cry, and plead to get you to change your mind. The expectations, rewards, and consequences must be thought out, thoroughly discussed, and agreed on by both parents. If you aren't committed to them, you will crumble when your child pressures you to return to the old way of dealing with her. Reasonable expectations include:

- doing her chores
- making a C average or better in school (adjust for ability and special circumstances)
- earning and budgeting her allowance
- playing nicely with her siblings
- doing without or waiting for some things she wants
- helping out with family needs, not just meeting her own needs

You will need to specify your expectations, the rewards for meeting them, and the consequences for not doing them. (See chapter 26 for more specific information on developing expectations and consequences.) For example, your expectation may be that your child turn in all her homework and have no missing assignments. The reward for this could be one night (either Friday or Saturday) to go out and be with friends. However, if she does not meet the expectation, the consequence would be no weekend time out of the house with friends.

Make sure both parents are committed to the expectations, rewards, and consequences and be prepared to follow through on them. Otherwise, your child has no real reason to change. She may be the princess, but you must establish yourselves as the king and queen.

## Advise Your Child of the Change

Even though your child probably won't believe you're changing the way she gets things, tell her anyway. When she protests and doesn't want the change to occur, you can simply refer her back to the new plan.

---

### A Parent's Cue Card

"Sweetie, because of the special circumstances concerning your birth and then almost losing you when you were born, your father and I have given you too much. This was fine at first, but now it has gone too far. We are frustrated, and you aren't learning responsibility. You must learn in life that most of the time you get what you earn. When you get a gift you didn't earn, it should be greatly appreciated. We are therefore making some changes. We expect you to work

---

and earn things, and we won't be doing as much for you. It's time you did some of these things for yourself. This will take some time to adjust to, but we know it will make things better for all of us. We believe this change is necessary for you to become more responsible and for us to feel better about how we are raising you. Here's a list of the things we expect you to begin doing and what we will do to help this transition." (Have an extra copy of the list already made as this first one may end up in the trash!)

---

## Give Her What She Earns

This step begins the hard work of stopping yourself from overindulging your child and expecting her to work. If she does nothing, she gets nothing. If she works hard, she should be rewarded accordingly.

---

### A Parent's Cue Card

"This is the way the world works, and I'm not doing my job if I don't prepare you for the world."

OR . . .

"If I don't work diligently at my job, I get fired. We want you to be able to keep a job."

---

Talking isn't likely to work. This step in the process is characterized by doing and acting rather than talking and explaining. You must act differently so your child can see what she gets is based on what she gives. If you don't do this, things won't change. You must start and lead the way if she is going to follow.

*Be prepared to be tested.* She won't like your changes and will push you to return to the "entitlement system" where she received without putting forth any effort. She won't comply with your expectations until she sees it's the only way to get what she wants. Hang tough and don't give in. Parents must support each other to stay firm!

*Contact the people your child may turn to when she wishes to avoid responsibility. They need to be firm and not rescue her from her deserved consequences.* If everyone begins to hold your child accountable, she will see that she must change. This will help her make the adjustment quicker and with less difficulty.

### Teach Empathy for Others

Princesses (and all children in general) focus on what they want and how they feel, often missing how others feel. Part of moving past the self-centeredness is realizing that other people have feelings as well and their feelings matter as much to them as the child's do to her. Awareness of others is the beginning of shifting from the totally self-absorbed focus. This can be started by simply asking your princess how she thinks other people might feel given their circumstances. You can ask this question about someone in the store, an actor in a television show, yourself, one of her siblings, or anyone you encounter. Once she's thought about how the other person feels, she's already shifted her focus. Knowing how the person feels usually provides some direction for an appropriate way to respond.

*Consideration* is an important part of empathy. To help your child be more considerate of others you may:

- Talk with her about how you are considerate of others.
- Point out ways other people are considerate of her.
- Allow her to see how you consider others when you make decisions.
- Analyze television fights; talk about what each person might do to make things better.
- Point out the impact of consideration in friendships.

It will not be easy to change the way you have interacted with your child if you have overindulged her for several years, but for the future health of your child, you must try. Be prepared for a difficult time ahead when your child will strongly resist your commitment to be less indulgent and to treat her fairly. When you are tempted to go back to your old ways to have some peace, remember the goal before you and keep believing that with persistence you can reach it.

## Recommended Book

H. Stephen Glenn and Jane Nelson. *Raising Self-Reliant Children in a Self-Indulgent World: Seven Building Blocks for Developing Capable Young People.* Rocklin, Calif.: Prima Publishing, 1989.

# Part 2

# Improving Problem-Solving Skills

When a child doesn't know how to solve her problems, it compounds the difficulties in her life. Helping your child acquire the skills that will help her solve problems will reduce her frustration and anger.

# 9

# The Tool Box

## Jasmine: Angry Responses

Jasmine is a short, slightly overweight eighth grader with a temper problem. She used to be rather quiet and passive, enduring quite a bit of teasing and harassment from her two older sisters. About the time she went through puberty, she decided she was no longer putting up with any more garbage from them. Holding her anger in had come to an end! Now when anything happens she doesn't like, she comes unglued. She goes after not only her sisters but anyone at school or church who gives her a hard time. She went from the extreme of doing nothing to the other of hurting people. I hoped to get her to choose some middle-ground responses. First, she had to recognize the tools she was using to express her anger.

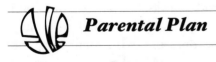 *Parental Plan*

*Identify Anger Tools*
Help your child identify her anger tools.

---

### A Parent's Cue Card

"In his tool box, the carpenter has a variety of tools to use for specific jobs. Having the right tools and choosing the right one for a specific job makes him a skilled and successful carpenter. Because each tool has a unique function, one tool typically can't be used to start and complete every job. The carpenter's tools are a lot like the anger tools we use. What tools do you have in your anger tool box?"

---

Jasmine identified the following:

1. Hitting: "If my sisters do something I don't like, I hit them. I hit them first and really hard so they won't think about hitting me back."
2. Yelling: "Sometimes I just yell at the other person. This works well in Sunday school. They don't want me to yell, so they do what I want to get me to be quiet."
3. Swearing: "Sometimes I use bad words because they bother people and then they leave me alone."

After your child has identified all the tools she can, feel free to add to the list a few that you have observed.

Talk about each of the tools your child identifies. Discuss that some situations may need those responses, but certainly not all situations. Even though hitting, yelling, and swearing are inappropriate, refrain from judging them at this point. If you judge them, she will defend them instead of moving to the next step of evaluating them.

### Help Her Evaluate Her Tools

How well do your child's anger tools work? Encourage your child to evaluate her anger responses by identifying the tool, determining which tools she typically uses first, second, and so on, identifying the positive and negative results of using the tool, and rating how happy she is with the tool, with 1 being very unhappy and 10 being very happy. In the table below I've given two examples:

**Anger Tool Evaluation**

| Tool | Order of Use | Positive Results of Using This Tool | Negative Results of Using This Tool | Tool Rating (1–10) |
|------|--------------|-------------------------------------|-------------------------------------|--------------------|
| 1. Yelling | second | People pay attention to me. My opinion is voiced. I feel strong. | People pay attention to my volume, not my message. I get into trouble. | 5 |
| 2. Hitting | first | People give me what I want. Nobody messes with me. | I get suspended and grounded. Some people don't want to be with me. | 7 |

Identify four tools your child uses and fill out the information asked for in the chart. Have your child fill out one for herself as well. Once you've both finished, compare the results. (You may also want to evaluate your own tools.)

> ### A Parent's Cue Card
>
> "Here is a table you can use to evaluate your anger tools. You take this one and fill it out for you, and I'll take one and fill it out too. When we have them filled out, let's compare them and see how they look."

*Encourage your child to evaluate the timing and circumstances when she uses her anger tools.*

When eleven-year-old Brent became angry at school, he stubbornly refused to do what anyone asked him to do. With this attitude, he could change a simple adult request into a three-day suspension with very little effort.

To address this issue, I said, "Brent, your mom tells me you can be really stubborn. Sometimes people call this quality you have 'stubbornness,' and sometimes they call it 'determination.' Did you know that stubbornness is a great quality because it helps you keep going when it would be easier to quit? So one of the anger tools you have is the ability to keep going when it's not easy. That's a great tool, Brent. The key, then, is knowing when to use it. Not doing what the teacher wants you to do will get you into trouble, but not giving up when you have a big project will get you an excellent grade. It's all in knowing when to use the tool and when to leave it in the tool box. Will you think about situations and make a decision about when to use your stubborn/determined tool this week?"

Brent's response was, "Sure. Nobody ever told me that being stubborn could be good."

Using the list of tools you've compiled on the Anger Tool Evaluation form, talk with your child about the timing and use of her tools.

### Identify New Tools

Wanting Jasmine to have a few more choices in her responses, I asked her to tell me her favorite ice cream. She looked at me strangely and asked, "What does that have to do with anything?"

I responded, "Well, Jasmine, having lots of options is a good thing. Let me give you an example. When you are hungry for ice cream, are you excited about going to Baskin-Robbins Vanilla Ice Cream Store? No, you want to go to Baskin-Robbins 31 Flavors Ice Cream Store. We prefer going to the store with thirty-one options rather than the store with only one option. With more choices you can pick the flavor that currently sounds appealing. Similarly, with anger, it's good to have many choices of how to deal with a situation. So besides the responses you've listed, what else might you do when you are angry?"

She thought for a while and added a few more tools to her list:

compromising
asking for what I want
using my sense of humor
trading something for what I want

Be sure to praise your child for any appropriate tools she's added to the list. If there are only inappropriate tools on the list, you certainly may point that out.

> ### A Parent's Cue Card
>
> "It looks like you have only tools on the list that would get you into trouble."
>
> OR . . .
>
> "Wow! I'm really pleased not only with the number of tools you've added, but also with their quality. These are really good tools, and I've seen you use a couple of them! Nice job."

Talk with your child about other positive tools you've seen her use. Suggest a couple that she already possesses but doesn't use very often. Encourage her to practice those for the upcoming week. When you see her try to use them, reinforce the effort. Check with her to see how she thought they worked. Share with her some of the tools you use. Practice using some different ones and let her know how they worked.

## Recommended Books

Amette Geffert and Diane Brown. *A Toolbox for our Daughters: Building Strength, Confidence, and Integrity.* Novato, Calif.: New World Library, 2000.

Bradley Barris. *When Chicken Soup Isn't Enough: Managing Your Anger in an Increasingly Angry World.* Mountain View, Calif.: Mind Matters Seminars Home Study Programs, 1999.

# 10

# Mind-sets

Mind-sets are beliefs that determine how your child views a situation and dictates possible solutions. Negative mind-sets prevent progress, greatly increasing the child's anger. Identifying and changing your child's unproductive mind-sets allows him to see more options in solving his problems, thereby reducing his frustration and anger.

## Eric: Stuck

Let's meet Eric, a thirteen-year-old junior high student who has good grades and hasn't been in any major trouble. He has one older brother who is very athletic. Eric's parents divorced when Eric was ten years old, with Mom receiving custody of both children. During a large portion of Eric's life (ages four to eight), his parents' conflict was quite intense. When they argued, Eric retreated to his room and put a pillow over his head so he couldn't hear them.

Loretta, Eric's mother, referred him for counseling because he seemed depressed. During the first meeting we talked about what bothered him.

"Eric, tell me about the things that really bug you."

"Dad and I aren't getting along and I wish he'd just leave me alone. He doesn't listen to what I say to him and I'm tired of it. I just want to get away from all of my family. My brother doesn't do his share of the chores, and she [Mom] still gives him all of his privileges. I'm sick of it all and I need to get away."

"I guess you've had it with all of them. You particularly want Dad to leave you alone. Does he try to spend time with you?"

"Yes, but I'm through with him. He doesn't listen, and he favors my brother too. They both like throwing the football around."

"You really dislike the favoritism. Eric, what do you think you could do to make things better with Dad?"

"Nothing. I don't want to get along with him. I've been talking with Mom about getting an unlisted telephone number so he can't call me."

 ## *Parental Plan*

*Understand Mind-sets*

Mind-sets are tricky because you can be caught in one and not know it. Here is an exercise (which I think came from a very old *Weekly Reader*) you can do with your school-age child to help him understand a mind-set. Say to him: "I'm going to spell some words and I want you to tell me what they are."

| *You spell:* | *He says:* |
| --- | --- |
| McDonalds | McDonalds |
| McCoy | McCoy |
| Macbeth | Macbeth |
| MacArthur | MacArthur |
| machinery | MacHinery |

People generally recognize the "mc" or "mac" word pattern and assume it applies to all of the words on the list. In only four examples they develop a mind-set, making it easy for them to say "MacHinery" instead of machinery. Point out to your child how he adopted a mind-set that allowed him to treat all the words identically, when in fact they are different. Similarly, a child may believe he can do nothing about a current situation, because he learned earlier in his life that he had no control over circumstances. So even when he *can* do something (mostly because he has changed and matured), he views the previous and present situations as identical and continues to do nothing. The mind-set limits his willingness to try, keeping him caught and feeling hopeless.

### Identify Your Child's Mind-sets

It's not difficult to identify mind-sets. Observe your child and think about the beliefs underlying his actions. Let's return to Eric and identify his mind-set. Review the observations I made from talking with Eric:

- Eric couldn't stop his parents from arguing, so he withdrew to his room.
- He believed there was nothing he could do about his situation.
- Because he couldn't be athletic like his older brother, he didn't find Dad's favor.
- He deals with problems by trying to avoid them.
- He seeks environmental solutions from others (changing the phone number).

Do you see any themes? Eric's mind-set could be encapsulated in this statement:

"Eric, you believe there is nothing you can personally do about your problems except to hope other people will make changes in the situation."

"I suppose so. I hadn't thought about it like that."

"The problem with this mind-set, Eric, is that it allows and even pushes you to be completely passive. The only thing you can do is wait until someone else fixes the situation for you. This must be extremely frustrating for you, which is probably why every once in a while you explode in anger."

"You're right, I don't think there is anything I can do—which really bugs me."

We identified several things that bugged him and talked about what he could do about them. I then had him talk with his mom about them and they negotiated some changes. He felt much better.

What mind-sets operate in your child's beliefs? Here are a few common ones:

| Mind-set | Resulting Action | Remedy | Parental Action |
|---|---|---|---|
| My parents are mean, so I'll never get more privileges. | He does nothing to show parents he is responsible, resulting in great limitations on what he can do. | By being more responsible, he reassures parents he can make good decisions and earns more privileges. | Parents notice when he is responsible and encourage it. |
| Parents favor my brother because he is a boy. | She can't become a boy so she does nothing to improve her relationship with her parents. | By doing her chores and interacting respectfully, she discovers they like her after all. They just choose not to reward bad behavior. | Be positive with your daughter. Prioritize battles. Hold all children accountable to the same family standards. |
| I'm not a likeable person otherwise Dad (or Mom) wouldn't have abandoned me. | He's negative and angry when he interacts with others, pushing them away. Because of this behavior, he has few relationships. | Be pleasant and take the risk that people might like him if he allowed them to get to know him. | Reassure him that the parent left for personal reasons, not because of who he is or what he did. |
| I can't do anything about my current situation. | Believing she can do nothing to improve the circumstances, she does nothing. | She does something, even a small thing, under her control that could make a difference. | Emphasize times when her actions resulted in change. Reinforce cause-effect connection. |

Do any of these fit for your child? A negative mind-set may be present if you:

- Observe that your child consistently exerts no effort when a little effort would make a huge difference in the outcome.
- See that your child has a defeated attitude.

- Hear your child say, "It doesn't make any difference what I do, it won't work" or "There's nothing I can do about that, so there is no use in trying."

### Evaluate the Child's Flexibility

Dr. Ross Green, in his book *The Explosive Child,* describes children who explode, not because they think it will get them what they want, but because they can't think of anything better to do. These children get caught in a mind-set with their frustration building, and because they lack the flexibility to do anything different, they blow up.

> These children do not choose to be explosive and noncompliant—any more than a child would choose to have a reading disability—but are delayed in the process of developing the skills that are critical to being flexible and tolerating frustration or have great difficulty applying these skills when they most need to.[1]

### Help Your Child Reevaluate and Shift His Mind-set

Encourage your child to think about the time and circumstances when the mind-set was established. Then help him to see how things have changed since then. Remind him of how he has grown both physically and cognitively since the mind-set was established. This will help him reevaluate the present situation and change his mind-set.

---

**A Parent's Cue Card**

"I know you think things won't change and there is nothing you can do about it. But don't forget that you were only five years old when the incident occurred. You are now _____ years old and you've certainly matured a lot since then. If the same thing occurred today, I know you would respond differently. That was all you could do then, but it isn't all you could do now. If it did happen today, what would you do?"

---

*Encourage New Behaviors*

Breaking out of a mind-set simply requires that your child recognize it and stop acting as though it were true. ("I'm not good in math so there's no point in studying," thus proving that he's not good in math.) As long as he acts consistently with the mind-set, nothing changes. Eric believed he couldn't do anything about his problems, and when he did nothing, things didn't get better. I gave him this direction:

"Because of your mind-set, you are either too passive or too aggressive. Neither of these extremes works. This week I want you to consciously choose to do something—even if it is very small—about the things on your list of problems. When you come in next week, let's talk about what you did—what seemed to work and what didn't. Pay close attention to how you feel during the time you do something and later as well."

Eric came in the following week, looking much brighter. On several occasions he chose to speak up instead of keeping quiet. He was surprised at how many people actually listened to what he said and how much better he felt.

To help your child try new actions that are incompatible with the old mind-sets, you may:

- Encourage him to try a new behavior.
- Recognize and reinforce his actions when he does act differently.
- Have him examine whether his new behavior felt better to him.
- Reinforce the positive cause-effect connection so he sees that the more he acts in a certain way, the better he feels.

It will take time, effort, and patience to help your child discover detrimental mind-sets and do something about them. Don't get discouraged if progress seems slow. Sit down with your child at regular intervals to discover and evaluate mind-sets. Give him feedback on your observations of how well he's doing at changing.

## Recommended Book

Ross Green. *The Explosive Child.* New York: HarperCollins, 1998.

# 11

# Avoidance and Procrastination Problems

Successfully completing tasks on time increases your child's confidence and self-esteem and decreases her frustration and anger. Assist your child to deal with issues and complete projects in a timely manner.

## Ashley: Procrastinator

Ashley, a popular and very social seventh grader, lives with her mom and younger sister. Her father died of cancer when she was in fourth grade. Even though she's brighter than the average student, Ashley has no interest in doing any academic work. She goes to school "to be with her friends and eat lunch." Ashley usually does quite well on tests but is failing four classes because she doesn't turn in any of her homework. She starts to work on major projects the night before they are due. Her mom, Emily, recently began an evening routine of sitting with her and checking each assignment to make sure it was finished. This plan doesn't appear to be working because Ashley still doesn't turn in her completed work. Emily is extremely frustrated and fears Ashley will flunk the seventh grade. The more Emily talks about the importance of doing homework and passing, the more Ashley seems to avoid doing her work.

Ashley has often succeeded in getting her mother's last-minute help on projects and then getting a pretty good grade. She appears to be happy with this plan, so she probably isn't motivated to change. Emily has decided, however, that she doesn't want to enable Ashley's procrastination and reinforce her poor planning, so she has been thinking about what she might do differently.

 ## *Parental Plan*

### *Explore Reasons for Procrastination*

There are a multitude of reasons why your child may procrastinate. Here are a few for your consideration:

| Your child procrastinates because: | Possible direction to pursue: |
| --- | --- |
| She thinks she's still doing fine. | Emphasize points of reality: a teacher conference, feedback from others regarding her progress, time left before the project is due. Ask her to tell you about the signs she believes would be indicative of difficulties. If these signs appear, point them out to her, suggesting that she may now need to be concerned. |
| She simply doesn't want to do the task. | Listen carefully to find out why she doesn't want to do it. Check out alternatives to the task, showing choices available and their consequences. |
| She's lazy. | Work with her to help get her started. Reinforce cause-effect link. Give her only what she earns. Don't save her from consequences. |
| She's fearful and isn't willing to try. | Help her identify specific fears. Develop a plan to address those fears. Reinforce *any* effort. |
| She lacks confidence. | Identify specific strengths. Remind her of past successes. Help her risk. Break tasks down into smaller doable pieces to reinforce effort and success. |

| Your child procrastinates because: | Possible direction to pursue: |
|---|---|
| She is angry and uncooperative. | Understand why being angry and uncooperative is a reasonable response for her. Deal with the anger, limiting its negative influence. Help her see how her anger and uncooperativeness are causing her more problems. |
| She likes the deadline adrenaline rush. | Find other ways to get the rush without harming her grades and future. Build in a reward she would view as a rush (going to a concert, staying up all night). "Good, safe, exciting rushes" are better than bad rushes. |
| She doesn't understand the importance of the task. | Make sure you've explained the importance of the task. Have her tell you how she will deal with the repercussions of not doing the task. |
| She has different priorities. | Listen to her talk about her priorities and their consequences. Affirm your priorities by attaching rewards and consequences to them. |
| She's focused on other important issues. | Identify these issues and help her cope with them. Other concerns interfere with her concentration and sap needed energy. |
| She ignores long-term consequences. | Tie the present into future goals and identify doors she may be shutting. If she can't see the long-term consequences, make sure short-term rewards and consequences are clear and meaningful. |
| She doesn't want to succumb to your wishes or threats. | Remove yourself from the power struggle. Sometimes the only way to win is not to play. Let her know that the choice is up to her, and the consequences will be hers alone as well. |
| She's committed to doing it her way. | Imagine with her that she did do it her way and evaluate how it worked. Allow her to do it that way and see how it works. Is it more important that the job be *done,* or that it is done *your* way? |
| She doesn't like the person (teacher, boss) so she won't perform for him. | Remove the teacher from the focal point. The issue is passing or failing, not the popularity of the teacher. Make it a challenge to get along with the teacher. Encourage your child to find something positive about the teacher. Schedule a meeting with the person to discuss concerns and the relationship. |
| She sees no value in working on or completing the project. | Fill out a balance sheet (see chapter 8), discovering the positive benefits of doing the task. Assist her to find a reason that is meaningful to her. |

| Your child procrastinates because: | Possible direction to pursue: |
|---|---|
| She has no energy or may be depressed. | Check for depression and consider counseling or medication. Being depressed makes it hard to care or have the energy to do the work. |
| She can't concentrate and has trouble staying focused on task. | Clarify your expectations and increase rewards. She may have attention difficulties: counseling or medication may be helpful (see chapter 15). |
| She knows the material and doesn't think she should have to do the busy work. | Arguing this point usually doesn't work. However, you can let her know it's unfortunate she isn't receiving credit for what she knows. She will have to decide what to do about the system. You can let her know how the poor grades will affect her. |

Even though we've covered eighteen reasons why your child may procrastinate, the main reason probably is because it works. If you ask her to take out the garbage—or do some other task—she will likely put it off. It may turn out that someone else does it or you forget about it altogether. So her procrastination is reinforced. She learns, If I put things off, I don't have to do them at all.

---

### A Parent's Cue Card

*"I'm worried about your tendency to put things off. It looks like you've chosen to put the big history project off until the last minute. So I can quit worrying, would you please tell me about your plan for completing the project?"*

---

### Help Her See the Cost of Avoidance

Talking to your child about her avoidance usually doesn't have much impact, so parents must increase the negative cost of the procrastination before their child will consider changing her actions. Isn't this what the policeman does by giving us a ticket? How can Emily increase the cost of avoidance for Ashley? This can be done by:

*Setting firm limits on what she will do and when she will help with Ashley's projects.* By limiting her assistance, Emily understands that Ashley may do poorly. In fact she may need to fail a couple of projects before she believes Emily won't help her. By helping your child continue in a poor habit, you may avoid the immediate negative consequences, but you also reinforce poor coping habits and generate long-term problems. Preventing your child from receiving a poor grade also prevents her from learning to take more responsibility for her choices.

*Rewarding Ashley according to how much timely effort she exerted.* As a parent, you have the ability to reward any type of behavior you wish. If you want your child to work and not procrastinate you can heap huge rewards on projects that receive an A or on projects that are turned in on time. Emily could offer shopping trips for Ashley and her friends at the mall if the projects receive an A.

*Having a "fine" associated with late work.* Emily can check with the teacher to see if the work is turned in late. For each day the work is late, Emily loses a weekend day's privileges.

*Having Ashley evaluate her own performance.* If you've talked and talked about the negative aspects of putting things off, stop talking! Instead of your talking about procrastination, have your child assess her project and how much time it will take. She may decide that to get a good grade, she must start working sooner. It will be tempting to record her statement and play it back to her the next time she procrastinates, but don't. She'll get it figured out. She needs only one reason that makes sense to her to deal with the problem in a timely manner.

*By not saving her.* In the story of the prodigal son in the Bible, the young man came "to his senses" when he had no food and remembered that his dad's servants had plenty to eat. The outcome of his wrong decisions motivated him to change his actions. The same will happen with your child if you allow the consequences of her decisions to influence her choices. If you can't watch your child deal with the pain caused by her choices, close your eyes or leave the situation. Don't save her from being "hungry" because that's what will help her make better choices.

*Help Her Improve Organizational Skills*

Some teens procrastinate by choice, others by default. Organizational difficulties can cause the same problems as purposeful procrastination. If your child doesn't know when an assignment is due, she may be reminded of it the day before when other students talk about it. She will then come home and start the flurry of activity like Ashley. Does your child have difficulty organizing herself? Talk with her about how much organizational problems interfere with her meeting assignment deadlines.

---

### A Parent's Cue Card

*"I've noticed there are times when you wanted to have a project turned in on time, but you were uncertain of the due date. Sometimes you don't have the material you need to complete the project on time. How much of the problem is related to getting yourself organized?"*

---

Here are a few things you could offer your child to help get her better organized:

- A day timer. Many schools provide one, so check to see if her school does. There are also good electronic ones, and computer software planners.
- A specific notebook or file folder that "clicks" with your child.
- Homework sheets listing each class, the assignment, and the due date.
- Daily note to and from the teacher outlining assignments.
- Weekly progress reports so your child knows relatively soon when problems are developing.
- A file cabinet with folders for each class.
- An organized locker. She may need your help in organizing it. The counselor may be willing to help, or you may recruit an upperclassman to provide some assistance.

*Reinforce Strengths*

Your child may avoid doing certain tasks because she hasn't experienced success in those areas. Unfortunately, avoiding them and not dealing with them in a timely manner ensures a poor performance. A reminder of her specific strengths and past success in similar endeavors may help her tackle the problem while she has adequate time to do a good job.

---

### A Parent's Cue Card

"You are a very creative individual, which is the main skill this project requires. Do you remember the assignment last year that Mrs. McDonald gave you? It was very similar to this one. What grade did you get on it? I bet if you worked as hard on this one as you did that one, you'd also get an excellent grade."

---

Because of all the dynamics in your child's life, it may take a while to determine the causes for her procrastination and an appropriate remedy. What you can begin doing right away, though, is letting her take responsibility for her own actions. It may be painful for you to watch, but in the long run it will be best for your child.

## Recommended Books

Linda Sapadin. *Beat Procrastination and Make the Grade: The Six Styles of Procrastination and How Students Can Overcome Them.* New York: Penguin USA, 1999.

Jerry and Kristi Newcomb. *I'll Do It Tomorrow: How to Stop Putting It Off and Get It Done Today.* Nashville: Broadman & Holman, 1999.

# 12

# Speed Problems

Moving too quickly causes your child to miss important cues and to do poor-quality work. Having to do the work over increases his frustration. Additionally he's angry with you or a teacher for making him do it again. Doing a reasonable job the first time would reduce his anger and frustration.

## Robbie: Mr. Speed

Robbie is ten years old and is in the fourth grade. He's known as "Mr. Speed." He does everything in high gear. He thinks fast, talks fast, and walks fast. He always has his homework done before his mother arrives home from her work. He always finishes his math quiz before the allotted time is up, even if the last several problems just have random numbers written for answers. He can do his weekly household chores in less than five minutes.

Of course there are some negative trade-offs for this speed: He usually has to redo his homework after supper because it's so sloppy he can't even read it. He's making a D in math because of his careless mistakes, and his mom, Grace, sends him back to redo his chores at least twice before they are acceptable.

Robbie is the fourth of five children. He has two older brothers, one older sister, and one younger sister. He lives with his biological parents. Kerry is a stockbroker and Grace is a real estate agent. The parents believe that competition brings out the best in people. Kerry and Grace are very proud of their children because they are generally high achievers who have a zest for life.

Kerry called for the counseling appointment because he and his wife were concerned and a little confused about what to do with Robbie. All of their other children are quite successful. They do well in school, complete their chores in a very responsible manner, and require little parenting attention. Kerry and Grace spend a great deal of time following after Robbie, picking up after him, and making him slow down and do things right. They never had these problems with the other kids.

What's going on with Robbie and his family? When I thought about this, I came up with some questions:

- Because the family values competition, is there room for cooperation?
- Have the parents overemphasized competition?
- Can Robbie compete with his siblings in other areas besides speed?
- How do his siblings establish themselves as unique and special individuals (athlete, artist, musician, scholar, beautiful . . .)?
- Are there legitimate areas available in which Robbie can excel?
- Can Robbie compete academically with his siblings and peers?
- How confident is Robbie in his abilities?
- Does he get to go to lunch early after he finishes his test? Does he get to watch television only after he's completed his homework?
- Is Robbie bothered by his situation, or are only the parents bothered?
- Is an ADD/ADHD evaluation warranted?

 **_Parental Plan_**

*Structure*

Why is Robbie so speedy? Is it his nature? Is it the attention? Is it the reinforcement? Why is he always in high gear?

When I talked with Robbie, I discovered that he hurries through jobs so that he can play Sega. I asked him what the rules were about homework.

"My parents said I couldn't play video games until my homework was done. At first they said I could play after school for a little while but then they changed their minds. I can't play until my homework is done."

"What do you think about that rule?"

"Well I think it's a dumb rule, so I just rush through my homework and then I can play the games."

Robbie's speed with his homework and other jobs seems to be caused by his desire to have time to play. That's not a big surprise. In fact it's quite typical of most kids. They want to minimize the amount of time working and maximize the time playing. Kerry and Grace were obviously aware of that as well when they set the rule—No video games until chores and homework are done.

The parents did a good job monitoring the situation, knowing their child and providing direction. Normally this would work. Robbie dealt with this rule by "doing what was required" very quickly so he didn't have to waste much time before getting to play. He knew he'd have to do more homework later, but at least he got to play some after school and before supper. Once this was clear, the parents chose to modify the rule. There are a lot of ways to do that, but the important piece was to provide structure that addressed the quality of the job—not the speed. Of course, both parents needed to be in agreement with the new rule. They thought and modified the original rule to No Sega until chores and homework are done and they've been checked as being satisfactory by a parent.

This means that he can't play Sega until his chores and homework are satisfactorily completed and checked. What is the impact of the rule change? The hour he has at home before Grace arrives is now not available for Sega use. (Sometimes I don't support the enforcement of a rule when parents aren't home, but because there are so many children in the house, somebody would tell the parents if the Sega was turned on.) Robbie can still rush through his responsibilities, but what would he do then? He wants to play video games, which he can't do. So if he rushes through and his parents assess his work as unsatisfactory, he has to then take after-supper time to make things acceptable, further delaying his Sega time. Modifying the structure by changing the rule made it easier for Robbie to do a better job on his tasks the first time. Obviously, there's no guarantee, but the parents have increased the probability of Robbie slowing down and doing a good job the first time.

We checked with Robbie's teacher to see what occurred after major tests. Once the children finish the test, they're allowed to play on the computer. We asked the teacher that Robbie not be allowed to work on the computer. He could draw or read quietly at his desk, but no computer. She was willing to support the request. Because Robbie could no longer be first on the computer, he spent more time working on the test because he didn't like to read or draw. Modifying the rules and rewards helped Robbie slow down and do a better job, greatly reducing his frustration.

### Reinforce Accuracy, Not Speed

When possible, it's always good to work on a problem on several different levels. By changing the rule, Kerry and Grace helped Robbie slow down. We learned that when Robbie slows down, he does better work. But the parents can also work at a different level by reinforcing quality work with increased rewards. They made a deal with Robbie.

"Robbie, your father and I know that you really like to play video games. When I work hard and do a good job, I'm rewarded with a bigger check. We want to provide you with a similar deal. When Dad and I check your homework and see that it's neat and complete, we'll throw a quarter in the pot toward a new video game. If you get a quarter every night—Monday through Thursday—we'll throw in an extra dollar as a bonus. So if you do a good job on your homework, you could earn two dollars per week toward a new game. How does that sound to you?"

Kerry and Grace used their parental reinforcer ($) to motivate Robbie. Some parents don't like doing this because they don't think children should be paid for what they are supposed to do. Kerry and Grace decided to do the bonus for the homework and not for the chores. In many of these situations there isn't a clear-cut right or wrong. Money can be a good motivator. If it works and both parents are supportive of the plan, go for it.

### Emphasize Cooperation, Not Competition

There are a lot of people in this family, and they are very competitive. The parents make an excellent living through very competitive professions. Competition is highly valued. Robbie picked up on this value and incorporated it into his life by being fast and first. Robbie may not be the best at some things, but he is always done first. This was a slot or role in the family that was available and he could fill. Robbie's claim to fame is his speed. Even though this role provides quite a bit of attention for Robbie, it also creates a great deal of frustration.

I talked with the parents about two concerns:

*Toning down the competition within the family.* There always has and there always will be competition among siblings. But when it becomes too competitive and cooperation is lost, it's time to rebalance the scale.

To help tone down the competition, I encouraged the parents to:

- Stop using the name "Mr. Speed" when referring to Robbie.
- Not compare children in the family with each other.
- Not set up competition among the children for their parental attention.
- Focus on cooperation among family members.
- Make sure they rewarded cooperation.

*Finding strengths Robbie has that would allow him to compete successfully.* Switching the focus of the competition can be a successful way of keeping its value and having it serve Robbie in a positive way. I encouraged the parents to identify Robbie's strengths and focus on those rather than his speed.

### Consider an Evaluation for ADD or ADHD

If your child has trouble focusing and can't seem to slow himself down, make sure you read chapter 15: Focus Problems. Children who can't slow down may benefit from an ADD or ADHD evaluation and a trial period of medication.

But what about Robbie? Sending Robbie in for an evaluation at this point isn't warranted. He does not show many of the characteristics associated with ADD or ADHD. His speed doesn't have much to do with a focusing difficulty but is more of a competitive problem. We have a plan in place to see if it will help him slow down and be more accurate in his work. If the plan is successful, there's no need to pursue additional services.

Many children are in the habit of rushing through tasks that they dislike so they can get to more enjoyable pursuits. If this commitment to speed is causing frustration or otherwise interfering with your child's success, an effort should be made to determine what is behind the preoccupation with speed and how to encourage more productive behavior.

## Recommended Books

Edward Hallowell and John Ratey. *Driven to Distraction.* New York: Pantheon, 1994.
Cames Cristi. *ADHD: A Teenager's Guide.* Plainview, N.Y.: Childs Work/Childs Play, LLC, 1996.

# 13

# Information Problems

Identifying and using available information improves the quality of your child's decisions. This will increase her ability to resolve problems and reduce her frustration and anger.

## Annie: Needing Information

John and Marie referred their seven-year-old daughter, Annie, for counseling because she wouldn't do the simple things they requested. Their frustration was high because they thought Annie was deliberately being defiant. Marie was very critical of Annie, even though she tried to be positive. This whole situation embarrassed Marie and caused her to doubt her parenting skills.

Annie was extremely quiet when I talked to the family together. Even after I excused the parents to the waiting room, Annie remained silent. Sometimes it's easier for children to talk if they are slightly distracted, so I found my thirty-five-piece puzzle and laid it out on the floor. I discovered a great deal more about her problem than I'd anticipated. She didn't say much, but what she did spoke volumes.

Annie took two puzzle pieces and put them together to see if they fit. When they didn't, she laid them down, picked up two more pieces, and tried to put them together. She worked, using this trial and error method, for about five minutes, finding only two pieces that fit together. She grew tired of the puzzle and moved on to other toys in the office.

Being curious, I called her back to the puzzle and said, "Annie, have you noticed that some of the pieces have straight edges?"

"So," was her only response.

"If you put all the straight-edged pieces together, you've made the out-side of the puzzle, the border. Let me show you." I then put together a couple of edge pieces.

This rekindled her interest and she put together several of the edge pieces. Having completed the border, she then finished the rest of the puzzle. She was delighted with her success and exclaimed, "I did it!"

John and Marie are college-educated parents who treat Annie as though she were a miniature adult. They expect her to know what to do and they become upset when she doesn't make the "obviously" right choice. It seemed that Annie was quite capable of making good decisions, but she was just missing important information—at least with the puzzle. Once she had the information she needed, she made good choices.

I talked with John and Marie about providing more information and direction for Annie.

"It may be that Annie's resistance to your requests is not defiance but uncertainty about what she's supposed to do. If that's the case, providing more direction and helping her identify pertinent cues will help her respond appropriately. Will you try doing that to see if it works?"

The parents did a good job of increasing the amount of information available to Annie, and she responded! Annie became more talkative and the parents' frustration greatly declined.

 *Parental Plan*

*Gather Information*

Help your child observe how she gathers information to make de-cisions. I encourage children to become curious about how and why they do what they do. As humans we have the ability to observe ourselves—to step back and assess what we do while we are doing it. You, your spouse, and your child gather information in a consistent manner. Knowing your pattern allows you to make adjustments.

After observing, I asked the following children questions about their style of gathering data: "Anthony, have you noticed that your girlfriend is the only person you talk to when you seek information? You find out what she thinks and that becomes your decision."

"Tina, have you observed that you make your decisions based on whether you like the person, instead of on information about the situation? If you don't like the person, you don't obtain enough information to make an informed decision."

"Will, you seem to need exhaustive information about the circumstances before you are able to make a decision. Do you know why you have to have so much information?"

"Sue, it appears that you find out what your mother thinks about a decision, and then you do the opposite. Why do you suppose you do that?"

Watch and you will be able to identify your child's style of obtaining information. You could then ask your child questions to help her become aware of her pattern. Help her evaluate her style to see if she needs to change it.

### Gather Adequate Information

Does your child take time to gather adequate information before making a decision? Children rush through the process and make quick decisions for some of the following reasons:

*They are anxious about the subject.* Increase your support and talk with your child about the information.

*The topic is too threatening.* Help your child identify why this topic bothers her, and remind her of strengths she has.

*The child is in a hurry to go on to other things.* Remind her of the cost of rushing through the task.

*The decision isn't important to the child.* Help her see the importance of making a good decision. Structure her schedule so she will take time to obtain the needed information and think about what to do.

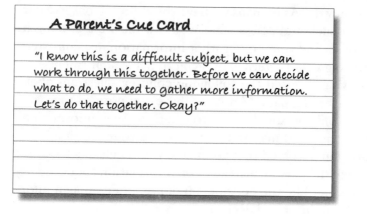

### A Parent's Cue Card

"I know this is a difficult subject, but we can work through this together. Before we can decide what to do, we need to gather more information. Let's do that together. Okay?"

### A Parent's Cue Card

"I know you are bothered by this, so let's understand why. If we deal with the fears, we will be in a better position to make a good decision."

### A Parent's Cue Card

"Deal with it properly now and you won't have to mess with it later."

---

### A Parent's Cue Card

"I know this decision isn't important to you right now, but it will have a big impact on your future. I want you to think some more about this. Let's talk about these issues before you go to the mall."

---

## Respond to Pertinent Cues

Annie missed the meaning and importance of the straight-edged pieces in the puzzle. Your child may also be missing cues that would help her make better decisions.

I often tell adolescents about the cues I missed when I got my last ticket. I was driving down the street and decided to check my "To Do" list. When I looked up, the traffic light turned to red. Unfortunately I was going 30 mph and was already in the intersection, so there was no way I could stop. As I went through the intersection, I noticed the police car sitting at the light. I missed two very important cues: the traffic light and the police car. Because I missed both of them, I received a fifty-dollar fine.

What cues are important to notice in your child's situation? After your child has identified a problematic situation, you may:

1. Ask her to identify the meaningful cues that would help her know how to act.
2. Help her understand why the cues are important.
3. Determine with her ways to respond to those cues.
4. Talk with her about the consequences of ignoring the cues.

As an example, we'll use eight-year-old Samuel, who has trouble making and keeping friends.

## Problematic Situation: Trouble Making and Keeping Friends

| Meaningful Cue | Importance of the Cue | Ways of Responding to the Cue | Consequences of Missing the Cue |
|---|---|---|---|
| Facial expressions of his classmates. | The expressions let him know if his peers are happy or upset with him. | Ask if he's doing something that bothers others. Make adjustments in how he acts. If people are frowning, he could stop what he's doing. If people are smiling, he could continue doing what he's doing. | He may continue behaving in ways that push his peers away from him. |
| Body language. | It gives him an idea of how they are feeling if they aren't talking to him. | Ask for feedback. Change what he's doing. | He keeps doing what he's doing that irritates his peers. |
| Tone and volume of voice. | It helps him determine if peers are upset with him. | Stop doing what he's doing that's irritating others. | Peers stop talking to him and ignore him. |
| Verbal messages: "You always talk about yourself." "You stink." "You're a cry baby." | Peers are giving very direct cues as to what bothers them. | Listen even though it may hurt. Determine what's true and what isn't. Deal with the true ones and make improvements. | Peers stop talking to him because he doesn't listen. He then misses out on information that would help things improve. |

Once Samuel was aware of these cues and began using them, he experienced fewer conflicts with his peers. He knew he was making real progress when he was invited to a peer's birthday party.

### Make Choices Based on Adequate Information

Using the information about the straight-edge pieces, Annie was able to put the puzzle together. Because she was successful, she felt very proud of herself.

Typically, decisions are only as good as the information on which they are based. If your child has limited or faulty information, how can she expect to make a good decision? Identify areas where you believe your child makes decisions without having adequate information. Would she agree with your assessment? Encourage her to make her decisions based on adequate information.

---

### A Parent's Cue Card

*"Most of my worst decisions were made because I made a snap decision without enough information. Make sure you have adequate information about your problem before you make a decision."*

---

Learning to make good decisions is often a lifelong process. The lessons need to begin in childhood so that children learn how to gather adequate information and how to respond to pertinent cues before making choices. When we learn to make good choices, we avoid much frustration and anger.

## Recommended Books

Ruth Peters. *Overcoming Underachieving.* New York: Broadway Books, 2000.
Adele Faber and Elaine Mazlish. *How to Talk So Kids Will Listen and Listen So Kids Will Talk.* New York: Avon Books, 1980.

# 14

## Solution Problems

A child becomes frustrated and angry when he is unable to come up with workable solutions to his problems.

### John: His Faulty Solution

John (fifteen years old) wasn't popular in elementary school or seventh grade. In eighth grade when he gained popularity, his first priority was to spend as much time as he could with his friends. His parents didn't agree with his priorities, believing that grades and family should be at the top of his list. To help John prioritize, his parents limited the amount of time spent with his friends. Both sides had a solution to the problem: The parents' solutions were that John bring up his grades so that he could have more free time on the weekends and that he invite his friends over to the house and spend time with them there. John's solutions were to sneak out and try not to get caught and if he got caught and grounded, to sneak out anyway.

When the family came to the office, they were stuck in the negative cycle of John sneaking out and the parents increasing the amount of time he was grounded. No one was happy, and John was grounded until he was at least seventeen years old.

Like John, children often encounter solution problems. Your child may have locked onto a faulty solution.

*It hasn't worked.* He's tried the solution for a long time, but it just isn't a workable solution to the problem. He may think: *The solution is good. I just need to stick with it a while longer.*

> ### A Parent's Cue Card
>
> *"You've tried that solution for a long time now. I don't think it's going to work. Are you ready to try a new one?"*

*It is a variation of a solution that hasn't worked.* Your child is trying to do something differently, but the new solution is just a modification of the old one that doesn't work. Hence it won't work either.

> ### A Parent's Cue Card
>
> *"This solution looks like a variation of the last one you tried that didn't work. What do you think?"*

*It can't work.* He's committed to a solution that cannot solve the problem.

*The solution distracts him but won't solve the problem.* He's given up on solving the problem and now just wants to avoid it. This solution lets him feel like he's doing something about it.

**A Parent's Cue Card**

"Logically I don't see how this solution could ever work. Maybe you should try another option."

**A Parent's Cue Card**

"This solution keeps you from thinking about other solutions that could work. Don't you want to get rid of this problem?"

*The solution is easy but doesn't work.* He doesn't want to do the hard work involved in actually resolving the problem.

**A Parent's Cue Card**

"While this solution is easy, it doesn't move you along the road toward solving your dilemma. It's like looking for something you lost under a street lamp because the light is better, even though you lost the item down the block."

*The solution is a quick fix but doesn't deal with the long-term problem.* He's doing something that helps in the short run but doesn't deal with the underlying issues, so the problem will continue to be a long-term concern for him.

---

### A Parent's Cue Card

"This fixes the short-term problem, which is good, but it doesn't do anything toward fixing your long-term problem."

---

*The solution avoids the necessary changes to solve the problem.* He doesn't want to deal with the real underlying issues, which would demand that he change his actions. He isn't ready to do that.

---

### A Parent's Cue Card

"You can't expect to come up with a solution that solves the problem unless you change the way you are acting. This solution doesn't address any of the needed changes. You won't make progress until you are ready to change."

 ## *Parental Plan*

### *Evaluate Current Solutions*

Identifying and evaluating the specific solution being used is sometimes enough to bring about change. John had locked onto a solution that accomplished his main goal, but at a great cost to other areas of his life. When a goal becomes extremely important, it usually limits a person's flexibility because he doesn't want to risk not achieving the goal. John wanted to be with his friends because he finally was receiving the affirmation he desperately needed. At this point in his life, being popular was crucial. He focused only on what he wanted to do and what his parents needed to do to help him, refusing to look at what he could do to help himself. Helping adolescents shift their focus usually requires: 1. having parents give a clear message about the proposed solution, and 2. finding ways to empower the child to take charge of what he wants (in a positive way).

John's parents were hesitant to tell John they would never give him free rein with his friends because they didn't want to risk his becoming angry and sneaking out even more. But with my encouragement they told John clearly and firmly they would not give him complete control of his free time. He responded quite angrily! But with this option gone he is more likely to move to exploring other options, because he still wants to be with his friends.

Most adolescents want to be in charge of their life because they "know everything" and are invincible. They usually respond if I can find a way to empower them. I often point out they could get more of what they want if they: 1. put themselves in the best possible position to negotiate, and 2. present a workable plan. Doing so gives them power over their situation and moves it beyond the impasse.

While this conversation didn't immediately lead to a shift in the solution John used, it did cause him to think more specifically about the solution he'd adopted. Having to own an imperfect solution by identifying it and saying it out loud creates mental friction. This motivated John to come up with another solution that encompassed more of his goals.

Interestingly, the parents were also locked onto a specific solution because of the importance of their goal of keeping John safe and getting him into college. Clearly, both sides were trying to meet important, understandable needs. The problem lies in the solutions, not in the needs.

Use the following questionnaire to help your child evaluate his solution:

### Solution Evaluation

*Problem.* Specifically state the problem:

*Solution.* Specifically state what you do to resolve the problem:

1. On a scale of 1 to 10, with 1 being the solution doesn't work at all and 10 being the solution works perfectly, how would you rate the effectiveness of your current solution?

2. What important goals does this solution accomplish?

3. What important goals does this solution ignore?

4. What does it cost you to adopt this solution?

### *Focus on Solutions under the Child's Control*

Trying to make a solution work that is out of the child's control leads only to anger and frustration. The only behavior your child can control is his. This is where the solution must lie.

Stephen Covey in his book *The Seven Habits of Highly Effective People* contrasts proactive people and reactive people. To illustrate, he describes all the concerns an individual may have as being contained in a Circle of Concern. Within that circle there is another circle, the Circle of Influence. An individual can do something directly about those concerns located within the Circle of Influence but can do nothing about those concerns outside of this circle. The Circle of Influence may expand or shrink.

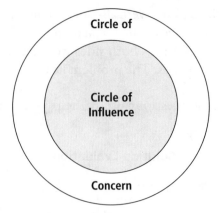

Proactive people focus their efforts in the Circle of Influence. They work on things they can do something about. The nature of their energy is positive, enlarging and magnifying, causing their Circle of Influence to increase.

Reactive people, on the other hand, focus their efforts in the Circle of Concern. They focus on the weakness of other people, the problems in the environment, and circumstances over which they have no control. Their focus results in blaming and accusing attitudes, reactive language, and increased feelings of victimization. The negative energy generated by that focus, combined with neglect in areas they could do something about, cause their Circle of Influence to shrink.[1]

Using Covey's concepts, I said, "John, you have only so much energy available to use. You may invest your energy in the Circle of Concern over which you have no control. Focusing in this circle means you blame your parents for being too restrictive and compare your situation to those of your friends who have more freedom. Or you may invest your energy in the Circle of Influence. Focusing in that circle means you work on bringing up your grades and building trust with your parents. Let's talk about each of those energy investments."

Together, we then developed this cause-and-effect illustration. You may want to do the same with your child.

## Circle of Concern

| Investment | Outcome |
|---|---|
| Focus and work on things outside of your control. Try to coerce your parents to increase your freedom. | • Frustration, anger, discouragement<br>• Nothing accomplished, no progress<br>• Increased tension with your parents<br>• Poor grades, ruining scholarship opportunities |

## Circle of Influence

| Investment | Outcome |
|---|---|
| Focus and work on things you can control. Study, turn in your homework, do well on tests, and don't sneak out. | • Encouragement, hope, optimism<br>• Progress is made<br>• Improved relationship with parents<br>• Your grades improve and you receive more time with your friends |

### A Parent's Cue Card

"The choice is really yours. Where are you going to invest your energy?"

### *Brainstorm Other Possible Solutions*

This step seems to work best when parents first acknowledge the importance of the child's needs. Then they assist the child in coming up with possible solutions that would meet the need and also be acceptable to them.

John's parents acknowledged that it was important for him to enjoy his friends, to be liked by them, and to have time with them. By recognizing the needs first, the parents shift their focus from Are these needs important enough to be met? to How can these needs best be met?

Once John knew his parents were working with him to meet an important need, his attitude brightened and he participated in brainstorming other ways to be with his friends.

Brainstorming requires generating a large number of solutions that haven't been filtered through the practical screen. See if you can generate with your child twenty-five solutions to his problem. Several of them will actually be workable solutions. Some will be impossible.

Once John understood his favorite solution—sneaking out to be with his friends—wouldn't work, he began working in the Circle of Influence by doing his homework, turning it in, bringing home a weekly progress report, and not sneaking out. His grades immediately improved, and his parents rewarded his effort with increased time with his friends on weekends. They also arranged to have several of his friends over for a twenty-four-hour Jim Carrey movie marathon.

It is relatively easy to generate a number of solutions to a problem, but they will be helpful only if the child uses them. Whether he does or not is under his control. If he chooses to disregard them and stick with a solution that doesn't work, he will continue to be frustrated and angry. Parents can help their child by following through on consequences that they have explained will result from inappropriate solutions. Consistency here will help the child control his behavior. Very few solutions (maybe none) work all of the time, so it's good to have some different choices. Don't let your child become discouraged with one solution that may work only part of the time. There are plenty of solutions out there! But he will only find them if he keeps looking!

## Recommended Books

John Rosemond. *Teen-Proofing: Fostering Responsible Decision Making in Your Teenager*. Kansas City: Andrews McMeel, 2000.
Cynthia Ulrich Tobias. *The Way They Learn: How to Discover and Teach to Your Child's Strengths*. Colorado Springs: Focus on the Family, 1994.

# 15

# Focus Problems

The ability to focus is the ability to concentrate on a specific task and ignore other stimuli. When a child is able to do this, he will make progress toward reaching his goals. If he is unable to focus, he will be plagued by frustration, anxiety, and anger.

If your child has trouble focusing, parent and school interventions may greatly reduce his frustration and help him be more successful. If he's diagnosed with ADD (attention deficit disorder) or ADHD (attention deficit hyperactivity disorder), you may also need to seek medical assistance. We'll concentrate on the parent interventions but also provide summary information concerning school and medical help.

## Kyle: Easily Distracted

Seven-year-old Kyle was referred for counseling by his biological parents, Al and Jill, and his second-grade teacher. Parents reported that Kyle:

- Has always been hyperactive.
- Won't listen to what they tell him.
- Makes impulsive decisions.

- Doesn't seem to learn from his past mistakes.
- Has trouble remembering things he is supposed to do.
- Fidgets all the time.
- Has great difficulty focusing on school assignments, chores, or any task except playing Nintendo—which he plays for hours.
- Is in trouble at school for constantly talking and disrupting the class.
- Has problems getting along with other students, particularly on the playground.
- Has few friends and isn't invited to birthday parties or after-school gatherings.
- Is angry with his teacher for embarrassing him in front of the class.
- May not pass second grade because his grades have dropped so much.

Al and Jill have been married for ten years and enjoy a stable, healthy relationship. While both parents work outside of the home, they have the flexibility to be involved in many family activities. Most of the time they discuss important parental decisions and reach a compromise they both can support. They have one other child, David, who is five years old.

When we met, Kyle was pleasant and polite, but easily distracted. If I talked very long or made my sentences too complex, Kyle would stop listening. He would then interrupt me and ask about objects in my office. To help him focus on what I said, I:

- Said his name.
- Asked him to look at me.
- Kept my sentences short, containing only one major thought.
- Used very simple words.
- Asked only one question at a time.
- Asked for immediate feedback on what he heard.
- Thanked him for paying attention.

Don't get the wrong idea; Kyle is a very bright child. He just has trouble staying focused. Understanding his history, his constant fidgeting, and his high level of distractability, I was relatively sure he met the criteria for an ADHD diagnosis.

What about your child? Does he have some of the same difficulties as Kyle? If so, consider the following parental interventions.

# Parental Intervention

### Build Parent-Child Relationship

How do you think Kyle feels about himself? If you were fired from your job, routinely embarrassed in front of others, couldn't get along with peers, couldn't manage your thinking or emotions, and felt like you'd greatly disappointed your family, how do you think you would feel? After Kyle felt comfortable talking, he confided in me that he wanted to run away because he didn't like school. Kyle, and other kids with difficulties, need someone to balance out the negative thoughts and comments they hear and feel about themselves. As a parent, you can help that balance by:

- Being warm and responsive to your child.
- Having fun with him.
- Affirming him and letting him know how important he is to you.
- Identifying and praising his strengths.

Children can make it through a lot providing they feel they have someone on their side. If you don't support your child and cheer for him, who will? (Be aware, though, that long-term struggles with hyperactivity and lack of progress can really take a toll on a parent's ability to continue to hope and cheer. If this describes you, pursue school and medical assistance and find a support group.)

Accept the fact that your child has a problem but don't make that his identity. This is how one parent introduced his child to me: "This is Johnny, my ADD child." Having a difficulty should not be his identity!

### Provide Structure

If your child currently doesn't have the ability to organize himself, the schedule and structure you provide will give him a sense of security and provide cues to help him make good decisions.

If a situation doesn't provide clear expectations and cues prompting specific behaviors, your child will make poor decisions and experience more difficulties. Imagine what driving would be like if all of the driving cues—the signs, lights, lane markings—were removed! That is why a child with focusing problems typically doesn't do well with free-time situations, like recess, school parties, lunch, field trips, and weekends, where the cues aren't evident and clear. Kyle received many of his discipline slips for his aggressive actions on the playground. Here are some guidelines for determining a daily structure for your child:

*With your spouse, determine a schedule you both can support.* Important specifics to include are bedtime, study time, chore time, and wake-up time. These don't have to be the same for every child, but they do need to be reasonably fair.

*Talk with your child about the schedule, getting his input.* You don't have to accept his ideas, but listen to them and incorporate them into the schedule when possible.

*Post the schedule on the refrigerator so everyone has access to it.* Family members can then refer to it when they have questions or need reminders of what to do.

*Follow the schedule religiously.* If your child's bedtime is sometimes 8:30 P.M., sometimes 9:15 P.M., and sometimes 10:00 P.M., guess what time he will push for each night? Does that nightly argument help you feel good about each other? By following the schedule, your family adjusts to the routine. The other positive benefit is that once a routine is established, our bodies also adapt to that schedule. If you stick with a 9:00 P.M. bedtime, your child's body shifts to settling down at that time. Establishing a specific bedtime routine, like getting into pajamas, putting clothes in the hamper, brushing teeth, reading a story, praying, and then turning out the lights, will also help reduce the amount of bedtime conflict.

*Let your child know well in advance, with several warnings, if you change the routine.* Stick with the schedule as closely as you can. Giving advance notice of changes will help family members adjust.

### Use Specific Discipline Strategies

Proper discipline will reduce everyone's frustration and make it easier for your child to control himself. It won't guarantee that he always makes the decision you'd like him to make. Here are some specifics that will help:

*Be clear in your limits and expectations.* If the external cues are as confusing as his internal cues, your child won't know what to do.

What he will then do is determined by what impulsively looks the most fun at the moment. This certainly is not a good way to make decisions!

*Focus on and tell him what you want him to do, not what he didn't do or did wrong.* Say, "Please chew with your mouth closed," instead of, "Don't chew with your mouth open." Scolding him for what he did wrong doesn't correct the problem, creates problems in the relationship, and usually isn't remembered anyway. Asking him to do specifically what you want assists him to do it correctly and gives you an opportunity to praise him. This builds the relationship and helps him feel successful. Success is a good thing for all of us, but it's especially good for someone who hasn't had much of it.

*Redirect his inappropriate actions to appropriate ones.* This is more effective and requires less energy than getting him to stop doing something. You could say: "Please take the hose you have and water the flowers there in the flower bed." This works better than telling him to stop wasting the water by making designs on the concrete driveway.

*Use mild consequences you can consistently enforce.* Consequences do have some impact, but don't expect them to be the magic bullet. The sureness of the consequence is more important than its severity. If you use time out, a good rule of thumb is a minute for every year old (four years old equals four minutes; nine years old equals nine minutes in time out). Using shorter consequences can also be very effective for a teenager. If he doesn't do his daily chore, he loses his privileges for only the next day. Taking away his privileges for a week may greatly reduce his motivation to do the chore for the rest of the week!

*Use the child's desire to earn privileges.* Your child can be pulled easier than he can be pushed. If your child wants a specific privilege or toy, you may use that as a reward for certain behavior. He then is motivated to do what he can to manage his actions.

*Gauge how much your child can manage.* Avoid too much stimulation, keep good supervision, and don't set him up to handle more than he's capable of. If he does become overwhelmed, you may have him look at you, take a few deep breaths, and think specifically about what you want him to do next. Direct him to focus on the next step you want him to do, and begin to do it.

*Use the "one step and praise" approach.* Give one request at a time and reward completion of that one task. If your child has significant focusing problems, giving a three-stage request is completely unreasonable. You can reduce your own frustration and increase his sense of success by asking him to do one task and then letting him know he did a good job. Then go on to the next one. This method will require some time on your part, but it would take even more time to scold, tell him again, get upset, and then do it yourself.

### Teach Positive Coping Skills

When a child has problems with focusing, it interferes with many areas of his life, including socialization. Kyle has few friends and usually isn't invited to birthday parties or after-school activities. He's a nice enough kid but he just misses several crucial cues, causing him to act socially inappropriately. His parents have taught him to behave according to social norms, but he needs reminders to slow down and think about how he should act.

Your child needs to develop social skill cues concerning gratefulness, empathy, listening, sharing, waiting his turn, and being interested in others. Reminders, cues, gestures, prompts, signs, and signals help your child remember how to act appropriately in social settings. Kyle's impulsiveness interferes with his being thankful, understanding how others feel, and sharing. If he sees what he wants, he impulsively takes it—even if it belongs to someone else or it is currently being used. When reminded, he knows what to do; he just needs the cue.

To help Kyle listen more, we developed a signal to cue him to stop talking and listen. Because Kyle knew that "listen" begins with the letter L, we used sign language to make the letter L. The parents would say his name and then sign the letter L. With a little practice in the counseling session the parents became quite good at getting Kyle's attention and showing him the L. Kyle stopped talking when he saw the letter. They then tried it in a variety of settings with good success. Because Kyle was talking less and listening more, his peer relationships improved.

*Assist with Homework*

Because Kyle experiences school as a negative place, do you think he's excited about doing schoolwork at home? Al and Jill knew his grades were bad so they tried to help him learn at home. This usually caused a fight and often ruined the entire evening. We talked about ways they could help Kyle learn while minimizing the negative interactions.

*Set up a specific place to work on homework.* Find a comfortable place where there will be minimal interruptions. Near the television, phone, or central pathway through the house would not be good places.

*Set a time limit.* Depending on your child's age, start with a schedule of two five- to thirty-minute study times per evening. You may even set a timer so he can see how much time is left.

*Allow breaks.* This allows him to refresh himself and relax a bit.

*Remove distractions.* Remove toys and other things that would distract him.

*Provide significant and immediate rewards for effort.* If your child has reached a goal, give out the rewards immediately after the study time.

*Reinforce connection between reward and effort.* Help him see the connection between his effort and the positive feelings that accompany success.

---

### A Parent's Cue Card

"Your father and I have been thinking about your frustration with school. You are a smart kid and very capable of learning. We want you to feel better about school. To do that we're going to start a brief study time in the evening. It will be for only fifteen minutes, so you won't have to feel like you will be stuck at the kitchen table forever. After you are done, we will read a story

> together. Getting some of your work done at
> home will help you feel better the next day at
> school."

## School Intervention

If your child has problems with focus, he is probably experiencing difficulties in school. Dr. Larry Fisher in his workshop "New Directions in ADHD"[1] indicated that the child's school performance improved when the teacher:

- Assigned a seat near the teacher (so she is the most likely focus) and away from distractions.
- Got eye contact from the student when presenting verbal instruction.
- Wrote instructions on the board.
- Provided simple, clear, consistent instructions on what to do and repeated them, checking to see if the student understood.
- Encouraged the child to ask for help.
- Helped a lot at first and then reduced assistance.
- Gave extra time to complete assignments; helped with organization.
- Didn't put time pressure on or set up competition.
- Enforced the rules consistently, not harshly.
- Avoided ridicule, used praise and rewards.
- Caught him being quiet, on task, working.
- Gave quiet reminders, cues to get back on task.
- Encouraged positive self-talk.

Dr. Edward M. Hallowell and Dr. John J. Ratey, in their "50 Tips on the Classroom Management of Attention Deficit Disorder," offer the following additional classroom suggestions for assisting a child with focusing problems.[2]

- Ask the child what will help.
- Remember that ADD kids need structure. Make lists.
- Post rules.
- Repeat directions. Write down directions. Speak directions. Repeat directions.
- Make frequent eye contact.
- Have as predictable a schedule as possible.
- Go for quality work rather than quantity of work.
- Monitor progress often. Children with ADD benefit greatly from frequent feedback.
- Break large tasks into small tasks.
- Seek out and underscore success as much as possible.
- Try a home-to-school-to-home notebook.

In addition to your child's teacher, the school may also have a counselor, social worker, nurse, psychologist, and other supportive staff. They are there to help your child succeed. If you have questions or concerns, contact one or all of them. You may find you work better with one of them. If your child needs help, ask! Keep on asking until you get the help you need. Work together!

## Medical Intervention

Here are a few facts about the current research conclusions regarding ADD:

- Boys are four times more likely to have this illness than girls.
- The disorder is found in all cultures, although prevalences differ.
- The fact that ADHD runs in families suggests that inheritance is an important risk factor.
- Hyperactivity and inattention are more common in children who were exposed to high quantities of lead, who had a lack of

oxygen in the neonatal period, and whose mothers smoked during pregnancy.

- The most effective treatment includes the support and education of parents, appropriate school placement and intervention, and medication.

- "Some investigators have noted that the parents of hyperactive children are often over-intrusive and over-controlling (Carlson et al., 1995). It has therefore been suggested that such parental behavior is another possible risk factor for ADHD. However, others have noted that, when children are treated with methylphenidate, there is a reduction in parental negativity and intrusiveness. This suggests that the observed over-intrusiveness and over-controlling behavior of the parent is a response to the child's behavior rather than the cause (Barkley et al., 1985)."[3]

- "Inattention or attention deficit may not become apparent until a child enters the challenging environment of elementary school. Such children then have difficulty paying attention to details and are easily distracted by other events that are occurring at the same time; they find it difficult and unpleasant to finish their schoolwork; they put off anything that requires a sustained mental effort; they are prone to make careless mistakes, and are disorganized, losing their school books and assignments; they appear not to listen when spoken to and often fail to follow through on tasks (DSM-IV; Waslick & Greenhill, 1997)."[4]

Understanding why your child acts the way he does may help you relax and focus on what you can do to help. If your child meets Criteria A–E, as outlined in the *Diagnostic and Statistical Manual of Mental Disorders,*[5] he would be diagnosed with ADD.

### Criteria A

Either 1. or 2.
  1. Six (or more) of the following symptoms of inattention have persisted for at least 6 months to a degree that is maladaptive and inconsistent with developmental level:
     a. Often fails to give close attention to details or makes careless mistakes in schoolwork, work, or other activities
     b. Often has difficulty sustaining attention in tasks or play activities
     c. Often does not seem to listen when spoken to directly

    d. Often does not follow through on instructions and fails to finish schoolwork, chores, or duties in the workplace (not due to oppositional behavior or failure to understand instructions)

    e. Often has difficulty organizing tasks and activities

    f. Often avoids, dislikes, or is reluctant to engage in tasks that require sustained mental effort (such as schoolwork or homework)

    g. Often loses things necessary for tasks or activities (e.g., toys, school assignments, pencils, books, or tools)

    h. Is often easily distracted by extraneous stimuli

    i. Is often forgetful in daily activities

2. Six (or more) of the following symptoms of hyperactivity-impulsivity have persisted for at least 6 months to a degree that is maladaptive and inconsistent with developmental level:

*Hyperactivity*

    a. Often fidgets with hands or feet or squirms in seat

    b. Often leaves seat in classroom or in other situations in which remaining seated is expected

    c. Often runs about or climbs excessively in situations in which it is inappropriate (in adolescents or adults, may be limited to subjective feelings of restlessness)

    d. Often has difficulty playing or engaging in leisure activities quietly

    e. Is often "on the go" or often acts as if "driven by a motor"

    f. Often talks excessively

*Impulsivity*

    g. Often blurts out answers before questions have been completed

    h. Often has difficulty awaiting turn

    i. Often interrupts or intrudes on others (e.g., butts into conversations or games)

## Criteria B

Some hyperactive-impulsive or inattentive symptoms that caused impairment were present before age 7 years.

## Criteria C

Some impairment from the symptoms is present in two or more settings (e.g., at school [or work] and at home).

## Criteria D

There must be clear evidence of clinically significant impairment in social, academic, or occupational functioning.

*Criteria E*

The symptoms do not occur exclusively during the course of a Pervasive Developmental Disorder, Schizophrenia, or other Psychotic Disorder and are not better accounted for by another mental disorder (e.g., Mood Disorder, Anxiety Disorder, Dissociative Disorder, or a Personality Disorder).

If your child meets the diagnostic criteria of A–E, she may benefit from a medical evaluation and a trial dosage of a stimulant medication like Ritalin. Dr. Fisher likened the medication to brake fluid. Research indicates that children with focusing problems have a shortage of a chemical substance in their brain known as dopamine. Increasing the amount of dopamine increases their ability to control themselves and stop themselves from being distracted. A car that has good brakes but no brake fluid would be very difficult to stop. Pushing harder and harder on the brake pedal won't make the car stop any more than yelling, screaming, or demanding will make your child control himself.

Medication may be considered because of its positive influence: "The short-term benefits of medication include a decrease in impulsive behavior, in hyperactivity, aggressive behavior, and in inappropriate social interaction; and an increase in concentration, in academic productivity, and in effort directed toward a goal."[6]

Some parents oppose medicating their child. This is certainly understandable, and you should approach the option with caution. It's been my experience, though, that parents who oppose medication have weighed the evidence against using it but have often overlooked the costs of *not* using the medication. These costs may include:

- poor peer relationships
- low self-esteem
- school failure
- family conflict
- involvement in illegal activities, like shoplifting, burglary, and joy riding
- loss of the excitement of learning

If you've tried the parental and school interventions and still find your child struggling, it's time to explore a medical intervention. If your child truly needs the medication (just like the car needs the brake fluid), you will see a remarkable improvement in his behavior. The medications methylphenidate (Ritalin), dextroamphetamine (Dexadrine, Adderall), and clonidine (Catapress) are initially taken seven days a week so parents can monitor the effectiveness of the medication and the side effects.

Look at both sides and count the cost of taking and not taking the medication.

It is comforting to parents to know that something can be done for their child's focusing problems. Often, as we have seen, the parents are able to undertake the needed intervention. But school intervention and medical intervention may be needed as well. Parents are richly rewarded for their efforts when they see the positive changes in their child.

## Recommended Books

Russell A. Barkley. *Taking Charge of ADHD: The Complete Authoritative Guide for Parents*. New York: The Guilford Press, 2000.

Grad Flick. *Power Parenting for Children with ADD/ADHD: A Practical Parent's Guide for Managing Difficult Behaviors*. New York: The Center for Applied Research in Education, 1996.

# 16

# Problems with Giving Up Too Easily

Children often experience failure because they quit too soon. When they learn to persevere, they have a greater chance of success, reducing the causes of frustration and anger.

## Carl: Wanting to Quit

Carl (fifteen years old) shuffled into the office and slumped onto the couch. His blond spiked hair had wilted into a strange wet porcupine look. I don't think it was the way he wanted it, but from his demeanor, he didn't appear to care. He looked very tired and quite discouraged. From the previous session, I knew he hadn't been very successful in his wrestling season, so I wondered if he'd lost another match.

"Carl, you look tired and discouraged. Are you okay?"

"I guess. It's been a tough day. I lost another match and so I told the coach I wouldn't be at practice on Monday. I just can't win a match. I quit the team."

"It's been a tough day and you're feeling really defeated. May I tell you a little story?"

"I suppose you will, so go ahead."

I told him about a basketball player who was struggling in a big game. As I told him the story, I held up my fingers to help keep track of the shots. "This basketball player shot his first shot and missed. So he was 0 for 1. How do you suppose he feels?" I asked.

"Not too good," Carl answered. "He's probably disappointed."

"His teammate got the ball," I continued, "and passed it to him. He shot, and missed again. So he's now 0 for 2. How do you think he feels now?"

"Not any better," Carl said. "He's probably wondering if the whole game is going to go bad."

I went on. "He got another pass, shot, and missed again. So he's now 0 for 3. How is he feeling now?"

Carl sighed. "He's getting discouraged. He isn't shooting well and his teammates are probably starting to bug him."

"He shot, and missed again. He's now 0 for 4. How is he feeling? What do you think he might do at this point?"

"He's really feeling bad. He might be thinking about quitting, about coming out of the game."

"Carl, what happens if he quits right now?"

"He doesn't score any points, he feels awful, and he had a bad game."

"That's true. If he quits right now, he's stuck with those terrible feelings, and the opportunity to change them would be gone. But if he keeps playing, he has a chance of improving his numbers. Let's say he does persevere. He shot again, and made it! He's now 1 for 5. Now how do you think he's feeling?"

Carl brightened slightly. "He's probably feeling a little better."

"He shot again," I said, "and made it! He's now 2 for 6. Now how do you think he's feeling?"

"He's probably feeling even a little better. The team is probably happier with him too."

"Carl, you have a good understanding of how the basketball player would feel if he pulled himself out of the game when he wasn't doing as well as he expected. How do you think he kept going?"

"I'm not sure. Maybe he remembered some of the days when he made more baskets."

"You know, that's a really good thought. We know from research that when people feel lousy, they tend to recall lousy memories. When people feel better, they tend to recall more encouraging memories. So having him consciously remember some good times would be helpful. Good thought!"

"Thanks."

"So why did we talk about all this?"

"Because you think I need to be reminded of the good things that come from not quitting. You want me to keep going so I'm not left with the feelings I have right now. I'm right, aren't I?"

"Yes, Carl, as usual, you are right on. So what are you going to do? Do you want to keep the feelings you have right now or do you want to trade them in for some better ones?"

"I don't know. Sometimes it's just really hard to keep going."

 *Parental Plan*

### Remind Him of His Strengths and Resources

"Sometimes it's just really hard to keep going." When your child hits that point, what does he do? It's easy to quit. But quitting at a bad point removes the possibility of changing those nasty feelings. Being reminded of his strengths and resources may provide him just enough encouragement to persist a little longer—just long enough to be successful!

When your child is overwhelmed, you can:

- Share from your experience, focusing on helping your child identify his emotions and dealing with them, and letting him know about other resources.
- Invite him to look at his resources and not the opposition, because where he focuses to a large degree determines how he feels.
- Reassure him that God is actively at work in his situation.

- Pray for him.
- Help him see and be able to use his resources to deal with the situation.

I usually tell discouraged kids my "moving the office furniture" story to help them shift from focusing on the problem to remembering the resources they have to successfully cope.

In my office we frequently move furniture to accommodate the needs of specific counselors. We have one couch that has two recliners built into it. Let me tell you, it's heavy! I hate it when it has to be moved. However, if Ronn and Jay (two of the bigger and stronger men in the office) move or help move the couch, it doesn't seem to be nearly as heavy. Why is that so?

I'm sure you have a story as well to point out the fact that with proper strength and resources problems shrink in difficulty. Does your child know and use his resources? Help him see them by reminding him of his abilities and his past successes with similar situations.

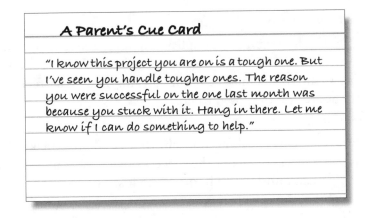

### A Parent's Cue Card

"I know this project you are on is a tough one. But I've seen you handle tougher ones. The reason you were successful on the one last month was because you stuck with it. Hang in there. Let me know if I can do something to help."

*Watch for a Mind-set of Failure*

This was Carl's first attempt at athletics. He actually was doing quite well but didn't feel that way. He constantly compared himself to his older brother who was a gifted athlete. The mind-set Carl struggled with came from a comment his dad made: "You won't ever be a successful athlete, like your brother." He really wanted to prove Dad wrong but he also had doubts about his ability. He went out for wrestling because he wanted to participate in a team sport that would give him a taste of athletic competition. Whether he won a match or not, he was reaching his goal. But that's hard to keep in mind, especially when the negative mind-set is strong.

The mind-set of some children is that no matter what they do, they will fail. Has your child learned to fail? If he has, you may see him:

- Quit before he gets involved.
- Quit before he makes progress.
- Quit just as he is about to succeed.

If he thinks failure will always be the final outcome, why try?

We saw in chapter 10 that a mind-set is learned from specific circumstances and/or experiences. Reviewing those and determining how things have changed allows your child to act differently. Doing this will help him change his mind-set.

### Reinforce Any of His Effort

Your child won't accomplish anything unless he exerts some effort. But he may be so discouraged, he can't muster any effort to tackle the problem. Yet doing nothing is why he feels so terrible. What are you supposed to do?

PARENTAL POINTERS

- To feel good about himself, your child must make the effort.
- To feel good about the success or victory, it must be *his* victory. It can only be his victory when it's his effort.
- Sometimes victory must take the road through defeat.
- Your child may prefer "my failure" over "our victory" because there's little joy for him in sharing the victory.
- You can search for and reinforce any minuscule bit of effort your child makes, but you can't make it for him.

PARENTAL DIRECTION

- Find and reinforce even the tiniest amount of effort.
- Be pleased with any effort. (You don't have to be satisfied, but you do need to be pleased.)

- Point out and reinforce the connection between his effort and his progress.
- Point out and reinforce the connection between his effort and his feelings.
- Be pleased with his progress before exhorting him to continue.
- Don't correct everything. If nothing is ever good enough, he'll quit trying.

*Break Down the Problem*

How do you eat an elephant? The only way you can eat an elephant is one bite at a time. Now, it may take a little while, but if you keep eating, you can eat an entire elephant. If you think about eating one in a single bite, you won't try. The way you define a problem and approach it determines solutions and results.

Carl hasn't won a match, feels lousy, and sees quitting as the way to end his pain and humiliation. Quitting would give him distance from the pain but it wouldn't resolve the issue nor change his feelings.

Help your child think only about the next step that will lead to accomplishing his goal. Encourage him to focus on that step for now and to try not to think beyond it.

---

### A Parent's Cue Card

"I want you to think about what you need to do to get ready for and get through your wrestling practice on Monday, and only Monday—not the rest of the week, just Monday."

---

PARENTAL ASSISTANCE

- Help your child break the big insurmountable problem down into smaller doable problems.

- Encourage him to focus on the smaller immediate goals because they will not seem overwhelming.
- Direct him to work first on the smaller goals that are easy to accomplish. This creates an atmosphere of success and builds confidence.
- Help him set up timelines for completing the smaller goals. This keeps your child moving, which is crucial to his success.
- Monitor his progress.
- Record the completion of his goals in some visual way so he can see and celebrate his progress.
- Encourage your child to tell a friend about his goals. Public goals are more likely to be accomplished, and the emotional support from a friend is invaluable.

I talked with Carl after school on Monday. He'd gone to wrestling practice and was feeling much more optimistic. He thought he would have enough energy to get through the next meet. Who knows, he might even win his match!

### Increase His Motivation

"We've tried everything to motivate our bright, underachieving eighth-grade son. He tested really high, but he's flunking. Tell me what to do and I will do it."

It's difficult when you reach this point. Usually when parents say this, it means they've tried both option 1 and 2:

*Option 1.* Be very firm, structured, and punitive. This can go all the way to "We've taken everything out of his room except his mattress and blankets. Everything else he had to earn back. He didn't care. It didn't work."

*Option 2.* Tell him he's responsible for his choices. "We've tried telling him it's his life, his grades, and he will be the one who has to take the eighth grade over again. He didn't care. It didn't work."

In many cases, options 1 and 2 are simply slight modifications of the same solution. This solution won't work, thus neither of the options will work. You might ask, How are they the same solution when they are so different? Good question. They are the same solution because you as a parent are trying to make your child do something he doesn't want to do. The real solution is to transfer ownership of the problem to your child. It's your child's responsibility to take care of his grades and chores. He has the most power to fix his situation. You can't do it for him, and you can't make him do it, but you can encourage him and hold him accountable when he doesn't do his part. Here's what you *can* do:

- Express confidence to your child that he will figure out what to do to handle his problem.
- Supply encouragement and consequences for his actions. Parents are responsible for supplying consequences. Children are responsible for utilizing them in making their decisions. You can only do your part, expecting your child will do his.
- Minimize the amount of attention paid to his negative choices and behavior.
- Accept the fact that any consequences you might impose won't guarantee the right changes in your child's conduct.
- Respect his decisions and allow him to deal with the results of those choices.
- Tell your child that the consequences may help him think, but real change will occur only when he decides he's ready.

Before leaving this section, let's talk about internal and external motivation. Internal motivation is found within a person: his conviction to do quality work, his drive for success, his desire to overcome and accomplish, his wish to succeed. Internally driven motivation is usually the stronger of the two types of motivation. External motivation is money, prestige, being noticed by others, and recognition—things others can give for a job well done. External motivators usually have limits on their use. If you've been given and have eaten five big candy bars, another candy bar probably isn't a big motivator.

Some children give up because they are discouraged and don't think they can be successful. Others give up, not because they're discouraged, but because they simply don't want to do the work. In both cases motivation can be a problem. The following table provides some ideas to increase your child's motivation.

| | To Prompt His Internal Motivation | To Increase His External Motivation |
|---|---|---|
| **Your Child Is Discouraged** | Remind him of his strengths Remind him of past successes in similar situations Talk with him about the kind of person he is: "You are a survivor, not a quitter." Show him your confidence in him and his abilities | Increase rewards, perhaps temporarily, in order to get him moving Increase support Be pleased and supportive of any effort If your child is depressed, an antidepressant medication may be needed—contact your family physician |
| **Your Child Doesn't Care** | Remind him of your expectations Let him know his choices are up to him Ask if he's happy with the way things are going for him Affirm your belief that when he chooses to deal with issues he will be successful | Clarify consequences and rewards Be firm and consistent in using consequences Don't interfere with natural consequences Make desirable rewards available, but don't push them and don't nag him Minimize the amount of time spent trying to fix the problem Be matter of fact—non-emotional—about the problems and in enforcing the consequences |

You may be frustrated with a child who gives up too easily because you know that with a little more effort, he would be successful. The responsibility for completing the project belongs to him and you must let him carry it. He needs your support and encouragement but he must accomplish the goal himself. Your part is to show your interest and to remind him that his effort produced the desired result.

## Recommended Books

James Prochaska, John Norcross, and Carlo Diclemente. *Changing for Good: A Revolutionary Six-Stage Program for Overcoming Bad Habits and Moving Your Life Positively Forward.* New York: Avon Books, 1994.

Cynthia Ulrich Tobias. *Every Child Can Succeed: Making the Most of Your Child's Learning Style.* Colorado Springs: Focus on the Family, 1995.

# Part 3

# Managing Anger

Often children are unable to control their angry outbursts. Teaching them how to manage their temper will reduce their frustration and anger. I advocate a five-step method that I explain in the following chapters. It's called A.N.G.E.R.: A—assess feelings; N—neutralize emotions; G—gauge anger; E—engage the correct person; and R—resolve the situation.

# 17

# Assess Feelings

*When Your Child Responds Only in Anger*

An important step in dealing with anger is identifying the feelings behind it. Correctly identifying your child's underlying feelings and responding to them generates more choices for resolving the situation. Let's consider Derrick, who had trouble feeling anything but anger.

## Derrick: Stuck in Anger

Derrick, a husky ninth grader, was very angry. He hadn't talked much in the previous groups, but today he looked like he was about to explode.

"Derrick, you don't look so good today. How are you doing?"

"I'm really mad at this dude named Frank. He's trying to make the moves on my girlfriend. As soon as this group is over, I'm going to punch him out."

"You're really mad at him. What did he do?"

"He tried to sit with Annie at lunch yesterday and then called her last night. He's talking trash about me, so I'm going to smack him."

"What does Annie think about Frank?"

"I'm not going to have that jerk moving in on Annie. I'm going to mess him up good."

"Derrick, how are you and Annie getting along?"

"We'd be doing fine if this jerk wasn't fouling things up. He will learn not to mess with me."

"Derrick, listen to me for a moment. Tell me about your relationship with Annie."

"We're fine. Frank is screwing things up and I'm going to set him straight. That's all there is to it."

Derrick chose to focus on his anger toward Frank, instead of dealing with his fear that Annie was losing interest in him. Identifying the fear would allow him to talk with Annie and address concerns in their relationship. Avoiding his feelings beneath the anger greatly concerned me because Derrick had only a few things he could do if he remained focused on the anger.

## *Parental Plan*

### *Stop*

*When we stop doing what we normally do, it's easier to identify our feelings.* We are all "feeling" creatures. While some children and adolescents are very aware of their emotions, others have no idea how they feel. Many young people have trouble identifying any emotions other than irritated, mad, and really mad! Psychologist Neil Clark Warren wrote, "Anger is not a primary emotion, but it is typically experienced as an almost automatic inner response to hurt, frustration, or fear."[1] "When you find yourself angry, you can often gain considerable information about what is going on in you by asking yourself what you are hurt or frustrated about or what is frightening you."[2] Dr. Warren's point: Identifying the primary emotions, instead of focusing on the anger, provides needed information. Your child can then use this knowledge to develop an appropriate action plan.

Identifying the underlying feelings can be difficult, especially if emotions are stirred, confusion is rampant, and a poor situation escalates. To most accurately identify his underlying feelings, your child must STOP what he's currently doing (arguing, yelling, throwing things, whining, blaming) and ask himself, *How do I feel?* The answer to this question must be a feeling word not a thought word. Feelings and thoughts are very different.

Please note that the question is not "How do I want to feel?" or "How should I feel?" We feel how we feel, and trying to change that distorts the information we need. Disliking his weight, your child could adjust the scale in the desired direction. But changing the scale, like censoring his feelings, makes the information of little use because it's inaccurate. Acting on the anger, instead of on the correctly identified underlying feelings, usually causes problems.

### Determine Feelings

*A child needs to know how he feels.* To help a child learn to identify his feelings beneath his anger, I often use the following poster and ask him to point to a face that looks the way he feels. Your child is not likely to be able to identify his feelings without your help and practice. You may want to keep this poster handy to assist your child in identifying his underlying emotions.

Use these five "feeling questions" to help your child identify his feelings as you look at the poster together.

1. What situation, person, or thing triggered your anger?
2. Why did the situation, person, or thing prompt your anger?
3. What feelings were beneath your anger? Derrick felt insecure and scared that Annie was losing interest in him.
4. What may have caused you to shift from the underlying feeling(s) to the anger? Derrick shifted to the anger to avoid feeling insecure and vulnerable. He's tough when he's angry.
5. How would your actions be different if you responded to the underlying feeling(s) rather than the anger?

Answering these five feeling questions will provide the necessary emotional input needed to cope more effectively with the situation.

### Take Charge of the Feeling

Knowing his real feelings and responding to them instead of reacting in anger allows your child to deal more appropriately with the situation. When feelings are identified and understood, the child gains

**Feelings Poster**

needed information for dealing with difficulties. Once your child understands his feelings, he's in a position to develop a rational plan. Otherwise, the anger will control your child—like Derrick—by limiting the choices he can use.

Consider the following example of identifying the feelings beneath the anger and then responding to those feelings.

| If Your Child Feels . . . | Then He Could . . . |
| --- | --- |
| frustrated | get help, develop a new plan, let go of situation |
| guilty | apologize, make amends, confess |
| confused | ask appropriate questions for clarification |
| exhausted | get some rest, support, or direction |
| frightened | take action to ensure safety |
| sad | feel the sadness, cry, decide to be sad rather than mad |
| jealous | identify why he's jealous, look at his strengths, determine an effective way to respond using his strengths |

In Derrick's case, Frank is only a symptom of the problems in his relationship with Annie. Had Derrick identified his fear that she was losing interest in him, he might have talked with Annie and worked out the problems. As it turned out, Derrick found Frank later that day and punched him (one of the limited options available if he focuses on the anger), resulting in a three-day suspension. While Derrick was gone, Annie broke up with him and started to go out with Frank. Derrick's anger helped produce his greatest fear.

Pursuing the anger often confuses the issues and makes the situation worse. When children remain focused on the anger, avoiding their underlying feelings, they are likely to experience negative results. Dealing directly with the underlying feelings clarifies the situation, provides more choices, and allows them to work toward a positive resolution.

Even though your child has successfully assessed his feelings, he may still be too emotional to begin to deal with them. Calming himself down before responding to those emotions prevents an impulsive blowup. Let's move to the next chapter to learn how to neutralize the strong emotional feelings.

## Recommended Books

Don Kindlon and Michael Thompson. *Raising Cain: Protecting the Emotional Life of Boys*. New York: 2000.

William Lee Carter. *The Angry Teenager: Why Teens Get So Angry and How Parents Can Help Them Grow Through It*. Nashville: Thomas Nelson, 1995.

# 18

# Neutralize Emotions

*When Your Child Acts without Thinking*

It is our tendency as human beings to act on our anger as soon as we feel it, but delaying our anger response can have an amazing impact on how we feel. Immediately acting on angry feelings generally produces negative results. "Most of the time we conclude, expressing anger makes people angrier, solidifies an angry attitude, and establishes a hostile habit."[1] Does your child sometimes have so much steam in her you think she is going to blow? Can you see it coming out of her ears? Simply letting it fly can have many negative effects on others and on the angry child.

## Carla: A Quick Temper

Carla was a very pleasant twelve-year-old when she was in my office. According to school reports, she wasn't always that way. She had been in several fights, suspended four times, and was on the verge of being expelled when the school referred her for counseling. Her mother was in prison for bad checks, and her dad had a severe drinking problem. When Dad was home, he was often physically abusive to Carla. Many abuse reports had been made to family services, resulting in Carla's placement with her maternal grandmother.

The school referred Carla for counseling because of her quick temper and her inability to control herself. She would "go off" on people if they did anything to annoy her. Her grades were bad even though she was bright. She didn't work well with others and wouldn't work at all for a teacher she disliked. Even though she was in a lot of trouble at school, she didn't want to be kicked out.

I have a traffic light in my office that I use for a variety of conversation starters. Carla was playing with the switches, turning on the different lights. When she lit the yellow light, I said, "Carla, what does the yellow light mean?"

"It means caution. You're supposed to slow down."

"So it's a warning that the light is about to turn red. What do you think would happen if there wasn't a warning light?"

"People wouldn't have a chance to stop before the light turned red. They would just crash into the other cars. There would be a lot more crashes."

"Yes, I suppose there would be a lot more crashes with more people being hurt. That would be too bad. You know, Carla, I've been thinking about how you go off on people without much warning. It would be helpful if there were a yellow light to caution you to slow down. Then you could stop your anger before you crash."

"That would be good."

"Carla, do you know what a trigger is?"

"Sure, it is what you pull to shoot a gun."

"Right. The trigger is what starts the explosion. Carla, if we could identify the triggers that start your anger explosions, we could use them as a 'yellow light warning' that you are about to crash. You could then prepare yourself to handle the anger so you wouldn't get into trouble. Do you know what tends to make you mad?"

"No."

"Hmm, let's think a minute and see if we can come up with a list of things that usually make you mad." With the help of my probing questions, Carla identified the following list of triggers that are quite certain to upset her. We also determined the people usually involved.

| Trigger | Person |
|---|---|
| being teased | peers at school |
| being hit | Dad |
| being ignored | teacher, peers at school |
| being criticized | Dad, Mom, teacher |
| being cussed at | Dad |
| being promised something and it not happening | Dad |
| being told no | Dad, Mom, Grandma, teacher |
| having her plans changed | Dad |
| not being included in play | peers at school |

In the week that followed, Carla watched for these triggers and she worked on controlling her anger when she saw them. She kept herself out of trouble for the week, earning praise for her efforts. Carla liked being out of trouble and reported it really wasn't too hard to control herself.

 ***Parental Plan***

### *Identify Anger Triggers*

Identifying your child's anger triggers alerts her to restrain her anger before it builds. What prompts your child's anger? What prompts yours? Neither of you may know, but together you certainly could come up with a list of the things that usually evoke anger in both of you. After explaining how triggers work, ask your child to give you some ideas about your triggers. Assist her in figuring out hers.

Being aware of her triggers warns your daughter about upcoming danger, just as the yellow light warns you that the light will soon be red. Once you and your child have identified her triggers, you may alert her in certain situations by stating: "Yellow light ahead."

C.J. is a bright fourth grader who definitely has an anger problem. He lost his recesses for the rest of the school year in March because he couldn't control his anger. We did all the things I did with Carla, but it didn't work. C.J. knew all the right answers to my questions and could tell me everything he would do to prevent an angry outburst. Unfortunately every time he had an opportunity to show me he could control himself, he didn't. I was quite frustrated and so was C.J.

One morning, a student named Tommy teased C.J. and called him a "chicken." C.J. got in his face, called him a bad name, and then cussed at the teacher who tried to prevent a fight.

As I sat with him, trying to figure out what to do next, I suddenly realized the problem. I had been focusing on the last few minutes right before the blowup. If C.J. could change the way he acted at that point, he could avoid trouble. But at that late stage, it was very difficult for him to control himself.

"C.J., if we went out west of town, we could find some railroad tracks. What do you think would happen if you stood on the tracks, put up your hand, and motioned for the train to stop?"

"The train would run over me because it can't stop very well once it gets going."

"You're right, and the same thing happens with your anger. Once you get really angry, you have difficulty stopping. When you try to control yourself, your anger just runs over you and you do things that get you into trouble. Let's think about your anger as a chain with many links. The last link is the TROUBLE (consequences) you receive for making a poor choice. The next to the last link is what you do when you blow up—cuss and name call."

I drew a chain on the board and labeled the last two links.

"C.J., we've been trying to change what you do in the next to the last link, but by then it's sometimes too late. Let's back up, look at earlier links, and change what you do there so you don't get to the last two links. If we do that, you won't build up so much frustration. Let's review what happened this morning, starting with the last link and working backward."

Using Linehan's framework,[2] I followed up on each of the links in the chain that hooked the vulnerability to the problem behavior (name calling and cussing).

### Consequence (Last Link)

"What consequences did you get?"

"I got suspended for three days, and I was grounded at home for a week."

### Problem Behavior (Next to the Last Link)

"What did you do that got you into trouble?"

"I called Tommy a bad name and cussed at the teacher."

Intervention: "When you're upset, you could choose to keep your mouth closed until you've calmed down. If you controlled your mouth, you wouldn't be in as much trouble."

### Action Link

"What actions did you take that moved you closer to name calling and cussing?"

"I got right up in his face and gave him a dirty look."

Intervention: "Moving away from him would keep you from doing something you will be punished for."

### Body Sensations Link

"Where in your body do you feel your anger?"

"I feel my anger in my face, and it gets all hot."

Intervention: "When your face gets hot, you could recognize it as a cue that you are starting to get out of control. Moving away at that point will keep you out of trouble."

### Cognition Link

"What were you thinking that made it easier to call him names?"

"I thought, He has called me names in the past and nobody did any-thing about it, so I'm going to call him a name to get even."

Intervention: "Instead of thinking about what he called you, think about the trouble you got into the last time you called someone a bad name. You can choose what you think about."

### Event Link

"What did Tommy or others do that made it easier to move toward name calling?"

"Tommy laughed and said I was too chicken to do anything to him."

Intervention: "How else could you have responded to being laughed at and dared? There are many ways to respond. Let's come up with some other choices."

### Feeling/Emotion Link

"What feelings or emotions did you experience?"

"Well, I was embarrassed because a lot of kids were watching, and I wasn't sure how I was going to get out of the situation."

Intervention: "Think about your best response when you've been embarrassed. What did you do then?"

### Prompting Event (Trigger)

"What triggered you to act this way?"

"He teased me and laughed at me."

Intervention: "What would happen if you laughed with him? How else can you respond to teasing?"

### Vulnerability

"Why does teasing bother you so much?"

"I've been teased all of my life and I'm not going to take it anymore."

Intervention: "Teasing is a 'yellow light' for you. What can you do to keep it from bothering you so much?"

When we finished talking, the board looked like this:

Developing the specifics in the chain produces more points of intervention, increasing the probability of a positive outcome. With more places to break the chain, C.J. had more opportunity to avoid the final link where he received negative consequences. If any one of the links is broken, it doesn't connect to the next link, effectively breaking the chain. C.J. began noticing the different links and found that the cognitive link was the easiest for him to change. He started telling himself that he could get through the situation without blowing up, instead of focusing on what the other person did. This resulted in fewer negative consequences!

### Delay the Angry Response

Delaying your child's angry response diminishes its intensity. This is extremely beneficial because a less intense response is less likely to get her into trouble. Sometimes the delay doesn't have to be a very long period to yield benefits. What are some practical ways of helping your child delay her response? She could do any of the following:

*Call a time-out.* Taking a time-out stops the usual pattern, preventing an escalation of tension and anger. Getting out of the situation, even briefly, allows the child to cool down.

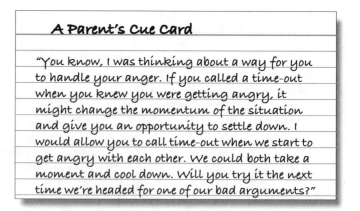

**A Parent's Cue Card**

"You know, I was thinking about a way for you to handle your anger. If you called a time-out when you knew you were getting angry, it might change the momentum of the situation and give you an opportunity to settle down. I would allow you to call time-out when we start to get angry with each other. We could both take a moment and cool down. Will you try it the next time we're headed for one of our bad arguments?"

*Take a walk to a specific destination.* Note that this is different from walking away. Most children tell me that walking away is a good idea, but because it's usually viewed as wimpy, they won't do it. So instead have your child choose a place to walk to when she needs time to cool down before responding.

*Do something to cool down.* Most people have a favorite activity that helps them calm down—listening to music, going for a drive, talking with a friend, reading a book, working on the computer, playing racquet ball, going for a walk. What works for your child? She needs to have something in mind, so when she encounters a "hot situation" she will know what to do to cool herself off.

*Decide she will respond after she has talked with you, a friend, pastor, or counselor.* This helps her wait and gives her a positive direction. Talking with a friend her age provides a different perspective on how to deal with the situation.

*Do something physical in a positive way to reduce the adrenaline.* This may include taking a brisk walk, swimming, running, or lifting weights. Counselors have often encouraged the beating of a pillow or a punching bag, but be careful of these approaches as they may actually build your child's anger rather than reduce it. The pairing of violence or punching with anger isn't usually productive.

*Act in a way that limits her undesirable responses.* This is the psychological principle of incompatible responses: Certain responses (when performed) automatically prevent your child from responding in other ways. She can't sit and stand at the same time. Listening prevents her from calling someone a name. Leaving a situation prevents her from engaging in an argument. Talking to a friend on the phone in the kitchen stops her from punching a hole in her bedroom wall. Help her identify the responses that usually get her into trouble and then brainstorm ideas of incompatible responses. Using those new responses would limit the negative ones and keep her out of difficulties.

*Set a date and time to respond and don't respond before then.* Setting a date and time gives your child the opportunity to settle down and think about what she really wants and determine the best way to get it. When a specific time to revisit the situation is established, the angry feelings are not suppressed and "forgotten."

*Count—really high if she's really angry!* "When angry, count to ten before you speak. If very angry, a hundred" (Thomas Jefferson).

*Write her thoughts and feelings down before responding to the situation or person.* Writing is a great way to delay a response and it also

helps to clarify thoughts and feelings. These notes can be reviewed later to see how things have changed. Some children
prefer drawing pictures of the situation and how they would
like to handle it.

*Fill out the anger log like the one below.* This gives your child something to do. Have her put the log in her notebook, keeping
track of the situations when she becomes angry and how she
handles them. This information will also help her identify her
triggers.

| Date | Time | Location | Trigger | Intensity (Low) 1–10 (High) | Duration | What did you do? | How did it work? |
|------|------|----------|---------|------------------------------|----------|------------------|------------------|
| 9/10 | 8:00 a.m. | Car | Sister kept changing radio sta- tions | 5 | 3 minutes | Plugged in my head- phones on por- table cd player | Great! There was no fight, and I liked listening to my music |
|  |  |  |  |  |  |  |  |
|  |  |  |  |  |  |  |  |
|  |  |  |  |  |  |  |  |

Talk with your child about the ways you restrain your anger and
share a situation when you didn't. Discuss specific ways you have
seen her delay her response. Ask if she is satisfied with the number
of choices she has in not "letting it fly." If not, help her identify other
possibilities from the preceding list.

*Use Anger-Restraining Techniques*

Actively using restraining techniques keeps your child's anger
from building.

For as churning the milk produces butter, and as twisting the nose produces blood, so stirring up anger produces strife.

Proverbs 30:33

A gentle answer turns away wrath, but a harsh word stirs up anger.

Proverbs 15:1

When your child is angry, she may not think much about what she can do to either make herself angrier or to cool herself down. She may in fact wish to avoid this responsibility, choosing instead to blame others for making her angry. But whether or not she admits it, when she is angry, she chooses to either stir up or restrain her anger. Discuss with her the following questions and anger restraining responses.

- Whom do you usually talk to when you're angry? Does this person help you to calm down or to get more stirred up?
    *Anger restraining response:* Identify someone to talk with who will help you calm down.
- When you're angry, do you blame others?
    *Anger restraining response:* Use "I" statements to ask for what you need.
- When you are angry, does it feel like your world is falling apart?
    *Anger restraining response:* Try to gain perspective by asking yourself, *How important is this situation?* and telling yourself, *This may be difficult, but I can handle it.*
- When something is not going the way you wanted or expected it to, do you assume it's going to get worse?
    *Anger restraining response:* Look for something good to come out of it (read Romans 8:28). Focus on solutions and positive problem solving. Brainstorm new solutions.
- Do you assume that the other person involved had negative motives?
    *Anger restraining response:* Try not to make assumptions. Wait to find out the truth.
- Do you go over and over in your mind the thing that upset you?
    *Anger restraining response:* Think about something positive to help settle yourself down. Ask for what you want.

It may take a little practice, but by choosing anger restraining responses, your child will be better able to manage her anger. She will begin to make better choices, resulting in less trouble!

### Minimize the Impact of Old Anger

If your child has a reservoir of old anger, it contributes to her tendency to over-respond. Anticipating situations that could trigger an outburst is beneficial for avoiding those scenes. Identify and deal with old unresolved issues, thereby draining the reservoir of old anger. Doing this will reduce the magnitude of your child's response to the current issues. Some ways that may help to resolve old issues are talking with you about the incident that still bothers her, writing a letter requesting that certain action be taken, or forgiving the person who offended her. Help your child do what she can to resolve the old issue.

If you and your child reached this chapter's goal of neutralizing your strong emotions, you reached a positive outcome. If not, you must deal with a negative one. Don't despair if you are on the negative side. It takes practice to change, and, at least, you tried. Keep working at it.

Once your child has cooled down and is in control of herself, she's in a position to begin to problem solve. When she has learned to accurately assess her feelings and neutralize her strong emotions, she's ready for the next step. Does she need to use some of the energy generated by the anger to change the situation? Relative to her goal, how much anger would be appropriate to use? In the next chapter, let's see what happens when she uses too much or too little anger.

## Recommended Books

Redford and Virginia Williams. *Anger Kills: Seventeen Strategies for Controlling the Hostility That Can Harm Your Health*. New York: HarperCollins, 1993.
Audrey Ricker and Carolyn Crowder. *Whining: Three Steps to Stopping It Before the Tears and the Tantrums Start*. New York: Simon & Schuster, 2000.

# 19

# Gauge Anger

*When Your Child Blows Up*

An angry response in some situations is warranted, but to be productive the angry person must be in control of his anger. Gauging the correct amount of anger needed for the situation promotes the best possible outcome.

## Josh: Underreacting

Josh is a thirteen-year-old junior high school student who lives with his mother. Shortly after his parents' divorce, Josh and his mother moved in with another man, Cliff, who has two children. Josh tries to obey his mom and help out, while Cliff's children do very little work and expect to be paid for everything they do. Josh's frustration is building. He's been trying to hold it in, but one afternoon he became very angry and punched a hole in the hallway to his bedroom.

When Josh and I talked about this incident, he was very remorseful and had already apologized to his mother and Cliff. He didn't want to do that again but he wasn't sure how to keep his frustration from building.

"Josh, just because you're angry and you've chosen to react, doesn't mean you have to explode," I said. "Venting all of your anger at once is almost never productive. It's just too much emotion with too little thought directing the process."

I often hear parents say, "My son would be okay if he could just get his anger out."

But unleashing anger seldom produces the desired outcome and usually creates more problems to solve. Getting it out, unloading it, or venting it according to Tavris doesn't really do what we hope it will do. Many people believe that there are benefits to ventilating your anger (see left column below), but anger actually produces the opposite effects (see right column below).[1] Simply getting it out isn't the answer.

## Getting Out His Anger

| Supposed Benefits | Actual Results |
| --- | --- |
| Improved communication with target of anger | Worsened communication with target of anger |
| Increased feelings of closeness with target | Feelings of distance from target |
| Physiological relief/catharsis | Physiological arousal, higher blood pressure |
| Raising self-esteem | Feeling terrible, lowered self-esteem |
| Solving problems instead of brooding about them | Making the problem worse |
| Getting rid of anger | "Rehearsing" the anger |
| Becoming a happy person | Becoming a hostile person |
| Getting results from the target of one's anger | Making target angry at you |

Josh knew blowing up wasn't the answer, which is why he chose to keep his anger inside. Ironically, keeping his anger stuffed inside is what actually led to the blowups.

Because many adolescents are into bodily functions, I asked Josh: "What would happen if you tried not to pee for a week?"

He laughed and said, "I don't think that would work. At some point I'd probably have an accident."

"You're right, and perhaps at a time when you wouldn't want it to happen."

"But wait a minute. Earlier you told me not to unload my anger because 'getting it out' doesn't work, and now you're telling me not to keep it inside. Which is the right way?"

"Good question, Josh. Unloading it all doesn't work, and keeping it all inside doesn't work either. These two responses are on the opposite ends of the continuum. Let's see if we can find a response that uses some anger to help you reach your goal."

To help Josh understand, we reviewed the three steps in the parental plan for gauging his anger.

## *Parental Plan*

### *Think about Consequences the Last Time He Overreacted*

Remembering previous consequences to angry outbursts can help restrain your child's current response. Josh was grounded for a week and had to pay to have the hole patched and then had to paint. Cliff was extremely angry with him, and his mother was disappointed and disgusted. Cliff's children laughed at him and teased him about being in big trouble. Josh was disappointed and embarrassed that he allowed himself to get so far out of control. He promised himself he would never again put himself in a position where Cliff's children would laugh at him. When he thought about the previous consequences and how he felt, he had a reason to not just "let it fly" again. Being specific and thorough as you remember the consequences builds a mental picture that can effectively limit outbursts.

Josh didn't like the consequences of his explosion and didn't want to repeat it. Knowing what he didn't want was helpful, but Josh also needed to figure out what he *did* want. Knowing the desired outcome provides needed direction for dealing with anger.

### *Determine the Desired Outcome in the Current Situation*

When a child is focused on the goal, this directs his behavior and limits angry outbursts. What's your child's goal? How flexible is he in the way this goal is reached?

Let's consider Tonya and her sister:

Tonya is fourteen years old and her sister, Desiree, is sixteen years old. They live with their mother, a single parent, who works until 6:00 P.M. Typically the girls interact with little conflict. But one day Desiree, who was very grouchy, had her stereo blaring. Tonya had had a tough day at school and wanted some peace and quiet.

Tonya went to Desiree's room and in her sisterly fashion "requested" that she turn down the music. Because of her bad mood, Desiree refused to turn it down.

The situation is primed to explode. If the only way Tonya can reach her goal is to get Desiree to turn down the stereo, the two are set for a big fight. This approach sets up a "win-lose" confrontation. If Tonya can "make" Desiree turn down the stereo, she wins and her sister loses. If she can't make that happen, then she loses and Desiree wins. Tonya may be able to turn this into a "win-win" situation and increase the probability of getting what she wants if she has the flexibility to modify the way she reaches her goal.

Tonya's goal is to have some "peace and quiet." Clearly one way of getting that is to have Desiree turn down her stereo. Is that the only way? In this situation, Tonya decided she could accomplish her goal by going to the nearby park and enjoying the afternoon sun. She received permission from Mom and had an enjoyable, relaxing time at the park. Each sister "won" by getting what she wanted. Tonya didn't need her sister's cooperation or assistance to reach her goal at the park.

When Tonya came in for her next session, she was very proud of herself. She reported: "I kept my goal in mind! In the past I would have shifted goals midstream. You know, from the quiet time to getting my dumb sister to shut off her stereo. But this time I didn't. Mom said she was really proud of me."

"Tonya, you did a great job of keeping your goal in mind and being flexible in how you met it. Isn't it also wonderful that you don't have any bad side effects like grounding or hard feelings with your sister?"

When your child becomes angry, is he able to clearly state his goal? How flexible is he in reaching his objective? Locking prematurely on one goal and one way of reaching it greatly limits his available choices and increases the probability of frustration and anger. If you can help him be more flexible, it may allow him to shift out of the "win-lose" scenario.

Returning to Josh, what was his goal? At first, he wasn't sure. He thought for a while and came up with these three possibilities:

- Have Mom recognize the work he had been doing.
- Have Cliff demand more work from his children.
- Have the workload more equitably distributed among the children.

As we discussed each one, Josh finally settled on the last one as the most important to him. He was really tired of having to do all of the work. To reach his goal Josh had locked onto the solution of making Cliff's children do more work. When he couldn't make them work, he became even more frustrated. Trying to accomplish something that was out of his control finally caused Josh to blow. How could he be more flexible and come up with a different solution to reach his goal? I encouraged him to talk with his mother about what she wanted him to do. If Josh was doing some—but not all—of the work, and she was happy, then he could feel comfortable quitting. He and Mom worked out an agreement on "work days." Because Josh did his part and didn't blow up, the focus shifted to how little work Cliff's children did.

What situations generally create anger in you? In your child? Does the anger keep you locked onto one goal, thereby limiting the options available to you? Identify those situations and the way you and your child have defined the goal.

*Parent*
Situation:
I defined the goal as:
I could modify the goal to be:
By changing the goal I would be able to:
I could change the way the goal is met by:

*Child*
Situation:

I defined the goal as:

I could modify the goal to be:

By changing the goal I would be able to:

I could change the way the goal is met by:

Think back on a situation and review it with your child. How else could you two have handled the situation that would have produced a different outcome?

### Gauge the Amount of Anger Needed to Meet the Goal

Overreacting or underreacting to a situation decreases the chances of your child getting what he wants. The strength of your child's angry reaction may lessen the chances of him reaching his goal. Typically most parents are concerned about the overreaction (yelling, cussing, throwing things), but the underreaction (not speaking up, pretending he's in agreement, showing no emotions) can also be a serious problem. Review the following chart and talk with your child about the outcome of his response.

**Did he reach his goal and get what he wanted?**

| Underreacted | Reasonable Reaction | Overreacted |
| --- | --- | --- |
| He's less likely to get what he wanted because he didn't state his opinion or show any emotion. | He's more likely to get what he wanted because his input was the focus of attention. | If he "successfully" intimidated others, he may get what he wanted immediately. But in doing so, he may have created negative side effects or long-term damage to the relationship. |

**What did people notice?**

| Underreacted | Reasonable Reaction | Overreacted |
| --- | --- | --- |
| They may not have noticed his response or his view on the issue. | They probably noticed his response and his view on the issue. | They noticed his angry response and dismissed his view on the issue. |

**Where was the focus?**

| Underreacted | Reasonable Reaction | Overreacted |
| --- | --- | --- |
| The focus was on what others thought about the issue. They didn't know what he was thinking or if he cared. | The focus was on what he thought about the issue. They knew he cared. | The focus was on his angry response. They thought he had "lost it," and overlooked his view on the issue. |

## How safe and effective was the response?

| Underreacted | Reasonable Reaction | Overreacted |
|---|---|---|
| Safe but ineffective response—he probably didn't get into trouble for underreacting. But this response often leads to feelings of inadequacy and depression. | Safe and effective response—he probably got what he wanted and didn't create any trouble for himself. | Unsafe and ineffective response in the long-term. He probably didn't get what he wanted and caused trouble for himself (was fired, grounded, suspended). |

## What are the implications?

| Underreacted | Reasonable Reaction | Overreacted |
|---|---|---|
| Could be indicative of fear, or an unwillingness to take a firm stand. | Could be indicative of well-planned risk taking and practice. | Could be indicative of old unresolved issues, lack of control or anger-management tools. |

What is your child's tendency? Is he more likely to overreact, underreact, or pick a reasonable response?

Initially Josh underreacted. He was angry about having to do all the work while Cliff's children played video games, but he didn't speak up. Neither Cliff nor Mom noticed there was a problem or that Josh was upset. With his frustration increasing, Josh finally overreacted, punching a hole in the wall. At this point the adults focused on the "inappropriate anger" and the property damage, totally missing Josh's concerns about the fair division of work. It was only when Josh allowed his anger to push him to a reasonable response of talking with his mother that the situation improved.

Sit down with your child and discuss how you react in difficult situations.

*Parent*
A situation I usually overreact to is:
When I overreact, people respond to me by:
My more balanced response could be to:
If I did that, people would likely respond to me by:

*Child*

A situation I usually overreact to is:

When I overreact, people respond to me by:

My more balanced response could be to:

If I did that, people would likely respond to me by:

Now that your child has learned to assess his feelings, neutralize the strong emotion so he doesn't immediately act on it, and gauge the amount of anger needed for his goal, he is now ready to engage the correct person and issue. Engaging can be difficult, so let's proceed to the next chapter for some direction.

## Recommended Books

Adolph Moser. *Don't Rant and Rave on Wednesdays: The Child's Anger-Control Book*. Kansas City, Mo.: Landmark Editions, 1994.

John Rosemond. *Raising a Nonviolent Child*. Kansas City, Mo.: McMeel Publishing, 2000.

# 20

# Engage the Correct Person

*When Your Child Expresses Anger*
*toward the Wrong Person*

Successfully resolving issues with others will greatly reduce your child's frustration and anger.

## Sydney: Angry with Mom

Sydney, a fifth grader, was referred for counseling by the school social worker because of her high number of behavioral referrals for playground fights. If things didn't go her way, she punched whoever was bothering her. Sydney hit big kids and little kids, girls and boys, her friends, and people she didn't like. The school suspended her when she kicked one of the teachers who was trying to break up the second fight in a week.

From talking with her mom, Sally, I gathered the following information: Sydney lives with her mom, who reported she's essentially been a single parent for several years as Dad never has much time for Sydney. She has one younger brother. Sally tries to do the best she can to provide for Sydney, but finances are tight. Mom worries about overcompensating for Dad's uninvolvement by giving in too much and getting Sydney more stuff than she needs. Her guilt makes it easy to feel sorry for her child when she sees how sad she looks.

Sally talked about the school referrals and described the fights. The only common theme to the fights appeared to be that Sydney wasn't getting what she wanted from the other people, so she hit them.

Dad drinks too much, limiting his finances and available time to be with Sydney. Dad tends to promise things to Sydney but usually doesn't follow through. At times Sydney is mean to Mom and calls her bad names but seems always to be pleasant to Dad.

 ## *Parental Plan*

### *Be Angry with the Correct Person*

Identifying the right person with whom to be angry allows problem solving to begin. Was Sydney really angry with all the people she hit? Some children know whom they're mad at, while others are really clueless about the object of their anger. Putting yourself in their shoes may help you determine the target of their anger. What people, given the current circumstances, might evoke anger from you? If you would be angry at that person, your child probably would be too.

How well the anger will be received and responded to often dictates where the child directs her anger. Your child may be mad at person A but focuses her anger on person B. This second person thus becomes a scapegoat, bearing the blame for person A's behavior.

Sydney knew her mother was committed to her, no matter what. She understood there was nothing she could do to push her away. Dad, on the other hand, was a completely different story. My guess was that Sydney was angry with her dad but was taking it out on her mother and anyone else who didn't give her what she wanted.

Two problems must be resolved to improve the situation:

- Sydney needs to determine whom she's angry with and what she's going to do about it.

- If Sydney does work up the courage to talk about the situation, Dad must be in a place to listen and help her reach a reasonable resolution.

Getting Sydney and Dad ready to deal with these concerns at the same time can certainly be a challenge. To begin, I start talking with Sydney. Sydney confirmed what I had guessed: She believed Dad wouldn't receive the anger well and would ignore her even more. So instead of making that mistake, she focused her anger on her mother and others at school.

### Separate Issues from Irritants

Dealing with the issues promotes resolution. Irritants are like a fever. Issues are like an infection. Managing the fever doesn't take care of the infection. The infected area must be cleaned and bandaged so it can heal.

Irritants often become the focus of arguments and family tension. Trying to fix them usually doesn't work because irritants:

are generally the symptoms of problems in the relationships
are needed as a way of expressing the emotions related to the underlying family issues
help avoid the issues that are painful and difficult to remedy
reduce anxiety by focusing people away from the real issues
change into a different form when examined (child finally does dishes when pushed but then stops taking out the trash)

Unresolved issues exert a negative influence on life, causing things that probably aren't big deals to grow into irritants. It's easy to focus on the irritants, particularly when you think you can fix them but aren't hopeful about solving the issues.

When I talked with Sydney's parents, they focused on several irritants: Sydney's bed not being neatly made and her messy closet, Dad's television watching, and Mom's need to have everything perfect. They argued about these concerns, going back to them when I tried to talk about other topics. It was difficult to talk about the underlying issues.

When I talked with Sydney alone, however, it became apparent that she really wanted Dad to stop drinking and to spend more time with her.

*Engage the Correct Person*

Being a good negotiator helps a child get what she wants. Even though engaging is a simple process, this is where kids, parents, and families most often get stuck. The first three steps in anger management (assess, neutralize, gauge) don't require cooperation from others. Engaging sharpens the focus on a particular issue and, because we don't know how the other person will respond, our anxiety increases. Engaging thus involves a certain amount of RISK. If your child is going to take the risk, she might just as well do it in a manner that minimizes the risk and maximizes the possibility of getting what she wants. How does a child engage productively?

## Productive Engaging Checklist

| Productive Engaging | Nonproductive Engaging |
|---|---|
| ☐ Talk to the person she's mad at about what's bothering her. | ☐ Talk with or dump her anger on the wrong person. Talk with the right person but not about the issue. |
| ☐ Deal with one issue at a time. | ☐ Try to fix too many problems at once. |
| ☐ Determine what she needs and what she wants to say ahead of time. | ☐ Talk only when upset and then impulsively include many other issues and concerns. |
| ☐ Don't let things build up too much before she decides to talk to the person. | ☐ Become more and more angry until she explodes, saying hurtful things that lessen her chances of getting what she wants. |
| ☐ Make sure she's cooled down and in control when she talks to the person. | ☐ Never talks with the person or does it too quickly while she's still too angry or waits so long that the issue is forgotten. |
| ☐ Meet at a good time for both of you. Make an appointment. | ☐ Force a meeting at a poor time. |
| ☐ Meet privately. | ☐ Talk to the person when others can hear. |
| ☐ Make eye contact. | ☐ Avoid eye contact. |
| ☐ Speak respectfully, watching volume and tone. | ☐ Yell, threaten, be sarcastic. |
| ☐ Make "I" statements: "I felt bad when . . ." | ☐ Make "you" statements: "You really messed up." |
| ☐ Ask clearly for what she wants. | ☐ Hint, demand, or threaten to get what she wants. |
| ☐ State what she's willing to do to help the situation. | ☐ Offer nothing to help the situation, demanding the other person do all the changing. |

"Sydney, we've figured out 'who' and 'what,' but we need now to determine 'how.' What I mean by that is: The 'who' is your dad, he's the one you are mad at. The 'what' is that you want more time with him. The 'how' is how are you going to communicate it to him so it works?

"Because what you're doing doesn't seem to work, I think it's time to try something new. In the past when you've talked with Dad about spending time with you, it sounds like you have also talked about his drinking. What do you think would happen if you stayed focused on getting more time with him and didn't mention the drinking?"

"I don't know what would happen. All I know is I don't have any better idea."

"I've found some things that help these conversations go more smoothly and have included them in this checklist. Tell me what you think about each point, and ask questions if you're not sure. When you're clear on what to do with each point, you can check it off."

I gave Sydney the productive engaging checklist, and we talked about what each section meant.

Reviewing the checklist showed me that Sydney had a good grasp of what each point meant. She was ready to engage her father in a conversation. If she successfully engages her father and they resolve their differences, Sydney's anger will drop sharply. Let's move to the next chapter to resolve some issues!

## Recommended Books

Harriet Goldhor Lerner. *The Dance of Anger: A Woman's Guide to Changing the Patterns of Intimate Relationships.* New York: Harper & Row, 1985.
Carol Tavris. *Anger: The Misunderstood Emotion.* New York: Simon & Schuster, 1989.

# 21

## Resolve the Situation

*When Your Child Perpetuates the Problem*

### Dave: Avoiding Accountability

When I first met Dave, he was a seventh grader. He was a nice-looking boy with an impish grin and a knack for pushing people's buttons. In no time at all he could find a way to evoke an angry response from almost any adult. Nothing was ever his fault. He may have been on the scene but he was always an innocent bystander. He had learned quite well from two of Mom's husbands how to avoid accountability for his actions. If he was responsible for the problem, he was beaten (not disciplined, beaten).

Even though he's now a ninth grader and Mom is married to a kinder man, Dave still clings tightly to his finely honed skill of avoiding responsibility. But his anger toward those two men for their abuse clings even tighter to him. In counseling, Dave came close to talking about and dealing with these situations, but each time he hit the same roadblock. Coming to grips with his feelings toward the stepdads meant he also had to wrestle with his mom's lack of protection. Clearly he was upset with her but their relationship couldn't tolerate that, so he swallowed his feelings. The feelings, however, didn't go away. He just acted them out on others. He engaged the wrong people. Instead of talking with Mom, he irritated others. They would then come down on him, reinforcing his belief that people weren't to be trusted. His anger toward his mom and those two men remains unresolved and continues to cause him problems.

Resolved situations look very different from those that remain a source of difficulty and aggravation. Resolved issues can be left behind; they don't require an investment of energy or worry. They no longer evoke strong emotional responses and exert little negative influence on behavior.

An unresolved issue, however, remains a focus of concern. This is true for Dave. He is stuck. His anger prevents him from letting go. A great deal of his energy is invested in trying not to think about the abuse and the lack of protection he experienced. Many environmental cues still trigger his thoughts and emotions regarding the issue, and Dave still expects to be beaten if he makes slight errors in judgment. He often thinks about how he can get even with his stepdads. He is still quite emotional about the issue and becomes very angry, with tears streaming down his cheeks, when I ask him about either of his stepdads.

Because Dave hasn't resolved his situation, he continues to respond negatively to anyone questioning his behavior. He doesn't learn from his mistakes because he's too busy trying to hide them.

Does your child, like Dave, struggle with unresolved issues? Even though people want to have issues settled, they often act in a manner that ensures the issues will remain unresolved. Let's look at six ways of responding that prevent issues from being resolved.

## Six Ways to Prevent Resolution

### 1. Seeking Revenge

Revenge is commonly thought to be a manly way of dealing with issues, as indicated by the bumper sticker: "I don't get mad. I get even." Consider the Bible's instructions:

> Do not seek revenge or bear a grudge against one of your people, but love your neighbor as yourself. I am the LORD.
>
> Leviticus 19:18

> Do not repay evil with evil or insult with insult, but with blessings, because to this you were called so that you may inherit a blessing.
>
> 1 Peter 3:9

Do not say, "I'll pay you back for this wrong!" Wait for the LORD, and he will deliver you.

Proverbs 20:22

Revenge does not have God's blessing. It isn't a good choice. Teach your child not to go there.

Revenge limits the amount of energy and thought focused on re-solving the problem. It strengthens the negative pattern, causing it to continue, and increases the seriousness of the situation because the other person usually responds to revenge with a bigger action or threat. Also revenge develops an intense negative bond with the other person. The more energy invested, the stronger that negative bond will be. This poisons perceptions, creativity, and communion with God.

Instead of seeking revenge, focus on solving the problem. Teach your child to stop his part of the "get even" cycle, because that's the place he can make a difference.

### 2. Provoking or Irritating

Justin taught me about provoking and irritating. He did it to his father. He always had a comment and had to have the last word. Because Dad seldom gave Justin what he wanted, Justin was determined to make his dad's life a "living hell." The anger rule Justin clearly stated was: "If I'm mad and upset, Dad should be too. When he feels as crappy as I, I win."

When we continue to provoke, we cause more negative energy to be invested in the relationship, eventually killing any positives there may have been. This limits the amount of energy we have to get what we want and keeps us locked into a negative response, limiting our search for more effective responses and increasing the probability of the situation escalating into a revengeful situation.

*To stop provoking and irritating others,* your child must identify and deal with specific troublesome issues and work for and ask for what he wants. Being appreciative of what he receives would also have a positive influence on others and himself.

### 3. Trying to Control Everything

I saw a T-shirt that had the following message:

**Two Things to Remember:**
1. There is a God.
2. You are not him.

I chuckled at the thought, but as I pondered the message I found myself wanting to add a few words on point number 2:

**Two Things to Remember:**
1. There is a God.
2. You are not him,
therefore you can't
control everything.

Of course that doesn't fit as nicely on a T-shirt, so it will never sell.

### DO WHAT HE CAN DO

Your child can't control everything and trying to do so drastically increases his level of frustration and anger. Discourage him from wasting energy on things he can't control. Instead, encourage him to focus on what he CAN DO about the situation.

The apostle Paul used this principle when he urged the Roman Christians to do what they could do to live in peace. He didn't expect them to be 100 percent accountable for generating peace; they were only to do what they could actually do. "If it is possible, as far as it depends on you, live at peace with everyone" (Rom. 12:18).

### LET GO OF WHAT HE CAN'T CONTROL

Our refusal to let go seals our negative involvement in a destructive interaction.

When your child tries to control everything, he must apply increasing pressure to the situation. This negative and sometimes extreme pressure creates anger in those who are controlled.

Letting go of what he can't control will lessen the child's frustration. Focusing on what he *can* control, and investing his energy in that, will encourage him and give him hope.

### 4. Rehearsing

The constant rehearsal—going over the problem again and again—stirs up bad feelings with no positive outcome. It's like practicing your lines for a play. The more you practice, the more automatic the lines become. How long do you want this play to run? The longer people stay in a bad habit, the harder it usually is to change.

Going over a problem again and again focuses on blaming others and makes things worse. Rehearsing interferes with finding solutions and builds a negative mind-set, strengthening the negative response and solidifying the situation so that it won't change.

The answer is to look for solutions rather than looking for the person to blame. Forgiveness is needed. The problem situation can improve if the focus is on individual ways to change.

### 5. Resenting

Jarred (fifteen years old) resented his younger brother Jason, who always seemed to do things right. Jason was good in athletics, made good grades, and was popular with the girls. He was never in trouble at school or at home. Jarred was most irritated by the fact that his curfew was earlier than his younger brother's.

Jarred's resentment prevented resolution of the problem because he spent his energy on building a case to be resentful. He focused on his brother and this stopped him from doing what he could do to improve his situation. His negative mind-set told him that Jason gets the privileges because of who he is, not because of what he does. This mind-set interfered with change occurring and solidified the situation.

Jarred needs to change his focus to what he can do to improve his situation. This could include complying with parental expectations so he gets more privileges, looking for solutions rather than evidence to justify resentment, and acting responsibly instead of complaining.

Jarred believed his parents "like Jason better." Because of this mind-set, Jarred refused to change his actions, which ensured a continuing earlier curfew. Never seeing how his own actions caused him to miss out on privileges, Jarred continued to resent his brother.

### 6. "Forgetting" the Problem

Anne (seventeen years old) seemed to be angry all of the time. Her parents couldn't understand the dramatic change in her demeanor. What they didn't know was that she had been raped when she was a sophomore. She believed that if they knew, they would be very disappointed, and she already felt guilty enough. Because she believed she couldn't do anything about it now, she thought trying to forget it was the best solution.

Many teens tell me they cope with a problem by "forgetting it." I tell them if they really have forgotten it, the problem is resolved. We then review the differences between resolved issues and unresolved issues. Most of them then reluctantly admit the issue isn't resolved, but they just try not to think about it. I asked Anne: "Does ignoring the rock in your shoe make it go away?" I wanted Anne to decide whether she would continue to "forget" or choose a different course to pursue.

When we choose to "forget" a problem, we minimize the importance of our feelings and their impact on our behavior. Forgetting also denies us the opportunity to do something about the problem situation. It allows the negative impact to grow and promotes inappropriate expression on other issues that may trigger anger, leaving a person stuck with negative feelings and guilt.

If we choose to deal with a difficult problem, we have to recognize our feelings and accept them as important, while realizing the cost of avoiding the issue. Develop a plan for dealing with the emotions and then identify and deal with obstacles that interfere with the plan.

Fortunately, Anne chose to face the problem and deal with some hard questions. She eventually realized the rape was truly unfortunate but not her fault. She was a victim not a bad person. Avoiding the topic had prevented her from reaching this conclusion. Once she worked this through, she felt much better and regained her energy for other positive things in her life.

## Six Ways to Promote Resolution

So Abram said to Lot, "Let's not have any quarreling between you and me, or between your herdsmen and mine, for we are brothers. Is not the whole land before you? Let's part company. If you go to the left, I'll go to the right; if you go to the right, I'll go to the left." . . .

The LORD said to Abram after Lot had parted from him, "Lift up your eyes from where you are and look north and south, east and west. All the land that you see I will give to you and your offspring forever. I will make your offspring like the dust of the earth, so that if anyone could count the dust, then your offspring could be counted. Go, walk through the length and breadth of the land, for I am giving it to you."

Genesis 13:8–9, 14–17

These verses illustrate two factors that promote resolution:

1. Find a reason to break the tie that keeps you locked together, and break it.
2. Move on with your own life in a positive direction with faith that God will honor your decision.

Unlike Abram, Ben (a seventeen-year-old senior) couldn't find a reason to stop fighting with his parents, who expect him to help out around the house. But he "does absolutely nothing except what he wants to do." Getting information about where he's going and when he'll return always resulted in a fight. When approaching the age of majority some young people, angry about their treatment as children, purposely defy parental authority. In response, parents assert the philosophy of "if you're living in my house you will follow my rules." Both sides feel justified in their anger and unwilling to compromise.

With the family tension building, I tried to help both sides find a reason to do something different with their anger. When a good reason couldn't be found, I knew it was only a matter of time before a crisis occurred. It didn't take long. One Friday afternoon, Dad asked Ben for a little bit of help with a garden project. Ben refused to help, told Dad he was going out, and wouldn't tell Dad where he was going. Dad told him it was fine to leave but not to worry about coming back.

Ben took his stuff and left. For a while he stayed at his friends' homes, changing locations every two weeks so as not to wear out his welcome. Periodically he needed money or a ride, so he asked his parents for some help. Deciding what to do about these requests can be difficult. If the parents truly don't want the child back in the house, providing the extra assistance makes sense until he reaches the legal adult age. On the other hand, not supporting him gives him a more accurate picture of what's required to make it on his own. He will then either make it or decide he needs to return home, which is eventually what happened with Ben. He ran out of friends and money. After sleeping in the park a couple of nights, he found a reason to do something different with his anger. He contacted his parents and they worked out a compromise—without counseling.

Is your child ready to seek resolution of a problem situation? If so, the following six tools will help him.

### *1. Asking for What He Wants*

Many children are hesitant to ask for what they want. Instead they often:

- Take care of the concern themselves but become resentful that other family members didn't take care of them.
- Expect others to know what they want without asking (mind reading) and become very angry when their needs aren't met.
- Hint about what they want.
- Manipulate circumstances in a negative way to get what they want.
- Take what they want by force from someone else.

To ask for what he wants, a child must know:

- *What* he wants to ask for.
- *Whom* to ask. Ask the person who can grant the request.
- The *risk* involved.

Asking directly and clearly doesn't always result in a positive response, but it certainly increases the chances of getting what he wants.

### *2. Negotiating an Acceptable Compromise*

Thad (thirteen years old) was extremely angry with his mother because she had actually thrown away two pairs of his favorite pants. Because of that, he wasn't cooperating with her. He began coming home late and not doing his chores. Mom, of course, responded to this with grounding him and telling him he would wear the clothes she bought for him. They were both angry and upset when they showed up at the office.

We started talking about the problem that sparked the conflict: the pants. In guiding the discussion, I kept the following negotiation tips in my mind:

- Talk at a good time for both of you. Most issues can be put off until both parties are ready to talk. Trying to talk at a bad time often ensures a bad outcome.
- Identify and agree on a specific issue to be discussed.
- Deal with only one issue at a time. Issues and problems are frequently intertwined. Tease them apart so they can be dealt with individually. Two issues are harder to solve than one, especially when they are stuck together. For example, "You don't like me so you never take me to the movies." Two issues need to be addressed: 1. Do you like me? 2. Why don't you take me to the movies? Dealing with them individually makes it easier to resolve them.
- Start softly and stay focused on that issue. Dr. John Gottman defines a soft start-up as one that identifies a specific behavior that needs to be changed, rather than attacking the other person's character. "Softening the start-up is crucial to resolving conflicts because, my research finds, discussions invariably end on the same note they begin."[1]
- Ask clearly for what you want. Be specific and then be willing to compromise.
- Don't let things get out of control. Only one person at a time should speak. Take a time-out from the discussion if things start to get tense.
- To start, focus on understanding each other, not on finding solutions. Once you truly understand each other, the problem may resolve itself.
- Develop a plan and try it for a specific period. You don't have to develop the perfect plan or solution. Decide on one and try it. Set a specific date to reevaluate and modify the plan.

### 3. Focusing on His Actions

Children often become so focused on what others are doing, they lose track of what they can actually do to help the situation.

Andrea, a bright eight-year-old from an intact family, was brought to the office because she and Dad frequently have nasty fights. She becomes quite angry and calls him names. Dad, whose feelings are then hurt, withdraws and avoids her for several days. We had the following conversation:

"Andrea, help me understand why the two of you get into these conflicts with each other. Your mom said that when you become very angry you say some very mean things to your dad. Why do you think these things happen?"

"Well, Dad always plays with my younger brother and hugs him a lot. I want a hug but he won't give one to me."

"So if he won't give you a hug, what do you do?"

"I get so mad that I call him bad names."

"Dad, when you get called the bad names, does it make you want to grab Andrea, give her a big hug, and tell her how much you love her?"

"No, it makes me want to avoid her."

"Okay, let me see if I get this. Andrea, you want Dad to hug you, but when he doesn't, you call him names, which pushes him further away from you. Is that right?"

Andrea responded, "If he would just hug me a little bit, I probably wouldn't call him names. Why can't he do that? He's the adult!"

If Andrea or her dad work on their parts of the problem, they will make progress. However, it's easy for them to get caught up in: If you will, I will. But if you don't, I won't. This results in an impasse. Jesus commented on these situations:

> Why do you look at the speck of sawdust in your brother's eye and pay no attention to the plank in your own eye? How can you say to your brother, "Let me take the speck out of your eye," when all the time there is a plank in your own eye? You hypocrite, first take the plank out of your own eye, and then you will see clearly to remove the speck from your brother's eye.
>
> Matthew 7:3–5

*Jesus provides the needed shift in focus:* Take your eyes off the speck in your brother's eye and examine the plank in your eye.

*He gives the proper sequence:* First take care of your responsibilities and the problems you have. Then you can help the other person.

When each party pays attention to and works on his part in the difficulty, things improve.

Andrea did her part by not calling Dad names. Dad did his part by being more affectionate. They got along much better and decided they liked that. Neither of them thought it was that hard to continue doing what each had done to make the improvements.

### 4. Shifting His Perspective

Look at the situation through another person's eyes!

I often hear from boys ages twelve to fourteen that they never get much time or attention from their fathers. That was the case with thirteen-year-old Danny.

"Dad never spends any time with me. He cares more about the dog than he does me. I've done things to get him to do stuff with me, but it never works. I don't have a dad and I don't care any more." Danny clearly cared because he was fighting back the tears. He was truly hurt and angry that Dad didn't love or care about him.

I said to him, "Danny, let's look at this from a different perspective. Let's think about how Dad views this situation. Tell me about how Dad got along with his dad."

"They didn't get along at all. They never did anything together, and then his dad died when he wasn't very old."

"Tell me, Danny, how do guys learn how to be a dad?"

"From what they saw their dad do."

"Danny, perhaps your dad is doing what he's doing, not because he doesn't care about you, but because he doesn't know what else to do. He may even think he's doing okay, because he's doing more than his dad did with him. Think about it and let me know."

Understanding the situation from his dad's point of view helped take the edge off Danny's anger. This in turn had a positive influence on how Dad interacted with Danny. Seeing the situation from another's perspective helps your child be less angry and judgmental, allowing a shift to occur in the usual interactions.

### 5. Forgiving

Forgiveness gives your child a way to resolve a situation. How do you encourage your child to forgive? Let's look at a situation where the father encouraged his son to forgive.

You may be familiar with the prodigal son story (Luke 15:11–32). We usually look at it from the prodigal's perspective. This time let's look at it through the eyes of the older, *angry* brother. How did the older brother respond to the "good news" regarding his younger wayward brother? He became angry and refused to go in to the party (Luke 15:28).

From my perspective, the older brother (let's call him Bill) had at least five good reasons to be angry.

> *Reason 1:* Verse 25: "Meanwhile, the older son was in the field. When he came near the house, he heard music and dancing." Bill was working and doing what he should have been doing, tending to the crops. He might have said, "I've been working all day. I'm hot, tired, and dirty. How could you have a party for my lazy brother without including me?" I'd be mad too. How about you?
>
> *Reason 2:* Verse 29: "But he answered his father, 'Look! All these years I've been slaving for you . . .'" In contrast to his brother, he'd been a faithful worker for many years. Doesn't that count? Yes, it does. That would irritate me!
>
> *Reason 3:* Verse 29: "and never disobeyed your orders." Bill obeyed when his brother didn't. That's supposed to be important—isn't it?
>
> *Reason 4:* Verse 29: "Yet you never gave me even a young goat so I could celebrate with my friends." Aren't rewards supposed to be connected with good work? That's not the case here. Bill didn't get a goat, much less a fattened calf. This just doesn't seem fair. Does it?
>
> *Reason 5:* Verse 30: "But when this son of yours who has squandered your property with prostitutes comes home, you kill the fattened calf for him!" Bill didn't say it, but he probably thought: *How can you reward his immoral behavior?*

Bill was angry, and in his own mind the anger was very justified. Once your child feels justified in being angry, is it difficult for him to move on? Let's see how this parent dealt with his angry son. Perhaps it will provide some assistance in dealing with your angry child. This is what he said: "My son," the father said, "you are always with me, and everything I have is yours" (v. 31). Dad thus dealt with the two major questions underlying Bill's anger:

Dad, am I still important to you?—Yes, my son. He reaffirmed
   their relationship.
Does it matter that I've worked hard?—Everything I have is yours.

After dealing first with Bill, he then moved to the prodigal son and
the issues of forgiveness and celebration: "But we had to celebrate
and be glad, because this brother of yours was dead and is alive again;
he was lost and is found" (v. 32).

My guess is that when Dad's words sank in, Bill realized he was still
important and that his efforts weren't in vain. Because Bill's concerns
and feelings were dealt with, it was easier for him to listen to Dad's
words about his younger brother. The sequence of these two comments is critical. Reversing the order with talking about forgiveness
first would likely have been unsuccessful. Bill won't listen to talk
about forgiveness until he is sure of his position. With Dad's reassur-
ance, Bill could then focus on forgiving his brother. I hope he forgave
him and joined the party.

Read the story with your child and discuss the older brother's legitimate reasons for anger, the father's affirmation of his son, and the
need for forgiveness.

"Bear with each other and forgive whatever grievances you may
have against one another. Forgive as the Lord forgave you" (Col. 3:13).
Sometimes a basis for forgiveness can be found in the situation or in
the person. When one can't be found, your child can still consider
forgiving even when the person doesn't deserve it. After all, God's
forgiveness of him was freely given—not because he did something
to earn it.

Forgiving allows your child to release the offender and himself
from the negative power of the act.

### 6. Finding Something Good in the Situation

When you and your child are driving around town or walking in
the mall, what do you see? What does your child notice? Depending
on our mind-set, the "glasses" (rose or other colors) we wear, and our
current needs, we pay attention to certain things and unconsciously
ignore other things. Our mind is like a camera as it catches a particular section of a scene. The camera can't capture the whole scene,
just a part of it. For example, let's look at this picture:

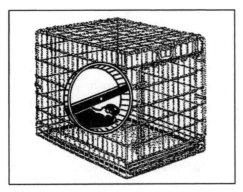

Ask your child, "How does the hamster view the cage?" He'll probably say something like:

- It's confining; it limits his freedom.
- It's restricting; the hamster can do things only within the cage and there isn't much to do.
- He doesn't like it and would be much happier outside where he could roam and explore.

Now, let's change our perspective. Step back ten feet and take another look.

This picture of the snake waiting to eat the hamster certainly gives us a different perspective. Ask your child to describe how the hamster now views the cage. He'll probably say:

- It's protecting him.
- It helps him feel safe.
- He likes it.

Isn't it interesting how the same item (the cage) can take on different meanings when considered from another perspective? Help your child change his perspective and look for the good. Talk with him about one of his difficult situations.

---

### A Parent's Cue Card

"I know this current situation is really hard for you, and it's easy to just think about getting out of it. Maybe, like the caged hamster, there is a positive reason for what's happening to you. If you think about this and find one, you will feel so much better. How do you think these circumstances could be helpful for you? How could this experience be useful for you when you are in high school?"

---

You may have to give him a few ideas about some positive reasons:

- It helps me see what is really important.
- It makes me rethink my values.
- It helps me evaluate my actions.
- It allows me to understand and be helpful to others who are going through similar circumstances.
- It helps me be appreciative of what I have.

Help him find the good. It makes the bad easier to handle. This will help him keep his anger in check and encourage him to work toward resolving difficult situations.

We know there is good in a situation, because God is not limited in how he can work. "And we know that in all things God works for the good of those who love him, who have been called according to his purpose" (Rom. 8:28).

We have seen how revenge, control, and resentment can prevent resolution of a problem and how negotiating, shifting perspective, and forgiving can help bring problem situations to resolution. Learning how to seek resolution to problems with others will not come easily to your child, but seeing how the positive steps work will encourage him.

## Recommended Books

Neil Clark Warren. *Make Anger Your Ally.* Colorado Springs: Focus on the Family, 1990.
Susan Heitler. *From Conflict to Resolution.* New York: W. N. Norton & Company, 1990.

# Part 4

# Reducing Your Child's Success in Using Anger

Anger works. It can be an effective tool for the child getting what he wants. Can he change your *no* to *yes* by throwing a tantrum or threatening you? Kids learn quickly what is effective. If he gets what he wants by being angry, he'll continue getting angry. Many parents inadvertently reinforce angry responses in their children by giving in, thereby encouraging more angry responses. Changing the way you respond when your child is angry will help him get his anger under control.

# 22

# Parental Modeling

The way you as a parent deal with your anger becomes a viable option for your child, so work on providing a good example. As a parent, I wish I always modeled positive, healthy behavior. I don't, and neither do you. Nevertheless, our parental example is crucial and we need to work on making it positive.

Recently I met with a family who struggled with their anger. The devastating effects of anger were quite visible and a sense of heartfelt sadness pervaded the room.

## A Poor Model

Dad, a hard-working, generous, caring, and loving father, really wanted the best for his family, but over the years he allowed his anger to ruin his relationships. You see, he becomes quite angry, loud, and very critical when things aren't to his liking. His seventeen-year-old son Anthony, as well as other family members, tried to tell Dad his anger was abusive, but the information fell on deaf ears. I felt for Dad. It's hard to hear that we've failed. He didn't listen to what he most needed to hear.

Anthony resents his Dad's anger. He plans to leave the family as soon as it is legally possible. Now that Anthony is physically big enough not to fear his dad, he says what he thinks to him, and does so with calculated cold-ness. He's become just like his dad.

Because of the damage and discouragement, little could be done. Their only option was to separate on a somewhat positive note—instead of Dad throwing him out or Anthony stomping out and never returning. Distance and time may allow some of their wounds to heal, and the time apart will prevent many angry interactions. Both see this as a workable solution, hoping things will calm down when they aren't together to trigger the anger. Neither one was willing to work on his own anger, but both believed the other one should. Anthony learned well from a powerful example. They are both angry men.

## The "Dirty Dozen" Approaches to Expressing Anger

Because the parents' style of expressing anger often becomes the way their children express anger, it's important to identify, evaluate, and—if needed—change your style. I have a preferred way of com-municating my anger, so do you, and so does your child. Ever wonder how you chose your style? "We know from careful psychological re-search that most people learn to express their anger when they are very young. The learning process is largely characterized by two phe-nomena: modeling and reinforcement."[1]

As a child, you watched how significant people in your life dealt with their anger. You then (subconsciously) "picked" one of those ex-amples to try for yourself. If it worked reasonably well, you adopted it as your "official anger response." Having found an acceptable choice, you stuck with it, adjusting it over time to fit changing circumstances and relationships. Let's examine your "official anger response."

For help in identifying your style, see if you can find your usual re-sponse in the "Dirty Dozen" approaches to anger expression. These twelve common approaches are organized under four destructive styles of managing conflict that were identified by Howard Mark-man, Scott Stanley, and Susan L. Blumberg through more than fif-teen years of research conducted at the University of Denver. The four styles are 1. escalation, 2. withdrawal and avoidance, 3. invalida-tion, and 4. negative interpretations.[2] While their research focuses specifically on couples, the resulting principles can easily be applied to the parent-child relationship. Modeling constructive ways of resolving conflict and dealing with your anger will help your child learn healthy ways to resolve her issues.

As you will see, the solution to an anger problem is to stop doing the negative response (like yelling) and actively pursue a positive response (like enforcing reasonable consequences).

Let's look at the "Dirty Dozen" and see if any of them operate in your home.

### Escalation

Escalation "occurs when partners negatively respond back and forth to each other, continually upping the ante so that conditions get worse and worse. Often negative comments spiral into increasing anger and frustration."[3]

#### 1. OLD YELLER APPROACH

Yell about anything you don't like.

*Anger rule:* It's always appropriate to yell, no matter what the issue or who is involved. You "have the right to get it off your chest."

*Reason approach adopted:* "Gets it out of your system" and lets everyone know exactly how you feel about the issue.

*Problems with approach:* People tune you out, "forcing" you to yell louder and longer to get their attention. Nothing is negotiated or resolved. Resentment builds.

*Changing would require:* Stopping yelling and taking action. Parents often yell because they are unwilling to enforce an appropriate consequence. Think specifically about what you can actually do to get your point across—even if you get no cooperation from others.

#### 2. DIRTY HARRY APPROACH

With this approach, you look for ways to engage in a fight, making sure you always win. *Never* walk away. Squash the opposition.

*Anger rule:* Might makes right. Be the mightiest and get your way!

*Reason approach adopted:* The opposition is squelched, and a victory is achieved.

*Problems with approach:* People get hurt, relationships are ruined, and legal charges are often filed. Additionally, input is lost, and even insignificant issues require maximum energy to ensure a win. Issues are always more important than relationships, resulting in multiple relationships with little depth.

*Changing would require:* Controlling your aggressiveness and giving up the competitive need to win and control. You must also realize that not everything is worth fighting about, so you will need to choose your battles more carefully. Developing verbal skills to talk about issues would be necessary.

### 3. DYNAMITE APPROACH

With this approach, you tolerate little frustration and respond with a big explosion (short fuse with a huge bang!). This causes people to be cautious around you so they don't accidentally do something to set you off.

*Anger rule:* Throw a big fit to get what you want. Explosions settle issues rather than thought, compromise, or good plans.

*Reason approach adopted:* Exploding gets you what you want, and you like the powerful feeling. People give you a lot of space, avoiding anything that might upset you.

*Problems with approach:* Resolution is not attained. You've just intimidated others into silence. People often reach a point where they won't continue to endure this approach. Because issues can't be discussed in a calm manner, the only resolution is to leave the relationship.

*Changing would require:* Taking a time-out and cooling off so your anger doesn't harm those around you. Once you are calm, identify your specific complaint, ask for what you want, focus on solutions, and negotiate an acceptable compromise.

### Withdrawal or Avoidance

Withdrawal or avoidance occurs when a person "shows an unwillingness to get into or stay with important discussions. Withdrawal can be as obvious as getting up and leaving the room or as subtle as 'turning off' or 'shutting down' during an argument. . . . Avoidance reflects the same reluctance to participate in certain discussions, with more emphasis on preventing the conversation from happening in the first place."[4]

### 4. SPEEDY GONZALES APPROACH

This approach gets you out of there! "I'm fine. I'm not angry. I'm history. I'm gone."

*Anger rule:* Avoid, leave, and escape! If you can't physically leave, then check out emotionally. When angry, avoid the feelings and people and keep away from the issues.

*Reason approach adopted:* Avoids confrontation and the need to do something about the situation.

*Problems with approach:* Nothing is resolved and your input is lost. It also consumes a fair amount of energy not to think about something.

*Changing would require:* Courage and a willingness to get involved. You would need to be aware of your feelings and what you want from the situation so you could then share it with the other person.

### 5. MONK'S VOW APPROACH

This approach says give them the silent treatment.

*Anger rule:* Use silence and other withholding techniques to punish and get what you want. Refusing to talk (to those who wish you would) increases your power.

*Reason approach adopted:* Keeping silent when others want you to talk is a powerful way to control circumstances and relationships. By keeping your anger and resentment, you maintain control over others.

*Problems with approach:* Issues aren't identified or resolved, causing anger and frustration to build.

*Changing would require:* A willingness to let go of the power and control gained from the withholding technique. You would also need to develop the skill of speaking clearly and strongly so that your point is heard and considered.

### 6. SUBMARINE APPROACH

If you like to get 'em when they aren't looking, you're using the submarine approach. You do things secretly to others. If found out, you are appropriately apologetic, claiming "accidental circumstances." Everything is below the surface with no direct confrontations.

*Anger rule:* Never be direct or clear with your anger. Get others when they aren't looking.

*Reason approach adopted:* Gives you some "get even" satisfaction while avoiding confrontations and loud arguments.

*Problems with approach:* Issues aren't identified or resolved. This approach erodes the basic trust in a relationship.

*Changing would require:* Your willingness to be clear and straight with others about your anger. Stop submerging and deal with the issues, negotiating a mutually agreed on solution. You may feel frightened, but the amount of risk can be minimized by properly engaging the other person. See chapter 20 for more specifics on engaging.

## Invalidation

Invalidation "is a pattern in which one partner subtly or directly puts down the thoughts, feelings, or character of the other.[5]

### 7. BLAMING (OR FINGER POINTING) APPROACH

Whenever you are angry, blame someone else for the problem. Find someone who is at fault, thereby avoiding any personal responsibility.

*Anger rule:* Always blame others, avoiding any personal responsibility.

*Reason approach adopted:* By shifting the responsibility, you avoid blame or punishment.

*Problems with approach:* In this approach, the focus is on assigning blame, rather than on finding possible solutions. Fighting over who is to blame creates additional problems and hard feelings and doesn't move you closer to solving the problem.

*Changing would require:* Focusing on your part or responsibility and allowing the other person to deal with her part. Shift to a solution orientation.

### 8. BELITTLING APPROACH

With the belittling approach, you make the other person feel stupid, small, and insignificant.

*Anger rule:* Forcefully point out the stupidity and absurdity of their position, actions, and feelings.

*Reason approach adopted:* This approach makes others look bad, increasing your "credibility" and the amount of control exerted over them.

*Problems with approach:* Over time you lose the input of others. Instead of trying to assist you, they eventually put their efforts into finding a way to get out of the relationship.

*Changing would require:* Eliciting the input of others, understanding their point of view, and incorporating their ideas into the solution.

### 9. THE ASSASSIN'S APPROACH

When you use the assassin's approach, you attack the character of the person.

*Anger rule:* Focus on character assassination to take the person out of the conflict.

*Reason approach adopted:* This approach squelches opposition by undermining the other person's character and credibility. If she has a defective character, her opinions are flawed and must be dismissed.

*Problems with approach:* Issues aren't resolved, feelings are hurt, and the relationship is destroyed.

*Changing would require:* A commitment to negotiate the conflict. Focus on solutions, asking for what you want.

### Negative Interpretations

Negative interpretations "occur when one partner consistently believes that the motives of the other are more negative than is really the case."[6]

### 10. JUMPING TO CONCLUSIONS APPROACH

*Anger rule:* Anticipate the negative and guard against it by always being prepared for the worst.

*Reason approach adopted:* Past negative experiences have alerted you to the need to be cautious. This approach limits the amount of hurt, pain, and concern others may cause for you.

*Problems with approach:* Keeps you stuck in a negative and protective stance. It puts others on the defensive, making it harder to resolve issues.

*Changing would require:* Checking out the accuracy of your assumptions and expecting the best from others, not the worst. Don't allow your negative mind-set to interfere with your seeing the good things the other person does.

### 11. ARCHAEOLOGICAL APPROACH

If you use the archaeological approach, you dig up problems from the past and use them to your advantage in the current discussion.

*Anger rule:* Save resentments and "dig" them up at a convenient time. Use the past to confirm current negative perceptions.

*Reason approach adopted:* This approach gives you something to say, adds weight to your side of the argument, and gets it off your chest. If desired, it can also divert the focus from the current situation.

*Problems with approach:* Bringing up old issues clouds the current discussion and interferes with reaching resolution. Two problems are harder to solve than one.

*Changing would require:* Forgetting, forgiving, and letting go of old resentments. You would need to work hard on current issues so they are resolved, not buried.

### 12. HATFIELD AND MCCOY APPROACH

In the Hatfield and McCoy approach anger becomes a lifestyle, always slandering those on the other side. In this approach, sides are chosen and the two factions never reach agreement. Divorced parents may get stuck here, continuing the fight long after the divorce is final.

*Anger rule:* Remain loyal to your side by continuing to fight. Believe everything bad about the person and always question her motives and behavior—even when they are positive.

*Reason approach adopted:* This approach organizes your life, provides a sense of belonging, and offers the hope of revenge.

*Problems with approach:* This feuding never ends and nothing is forgotten. Your goals and energy are focused for you against "the enemy."

*Changing would require:* A willingness to think for yourself and pull yourself out of your "side." You would also need to recognize your mind-set (see chapter 10 for more information), test its accuracy, and stop vilifying the other person.

Do you use any of these approaches? You may have recognized yourself in several of them. Perhaps you have one style when you are just annoyed and another style when you are really peeved.

Describe your approach:


Describe your child's approach:


Would she agree with your description of yourself, and of her?


Now that you have identified your style, consider how well it works. On a scale of 1 to 10, how satisfied are you with it?

| 1 | 2 | 3 | 4 | 5 | 6 | 7 | 8 | 9 | 10 |
|---|---|---|---|---|---|---|---|---|---|
| very dissatisfied | | | | okay | | | very satisfied | | |

If you gave your style a score of 5 or better, you probably won't change your style.


## A Caution

Before leaving this section on modeling, I need to address a statement I frequently hear parents say: "If I had ever said to my dad what my son says to me, he would have knocked me out. I do get in his face and call him names, and sometimes I push him. But he's lucky I don't do to him what my dad did to me."

From your perspective, the statement makes a great deal of sense. You've controlled your temper better than your dad, so your son really does have it easier than you did. You may even feel a sense of accomplishment. While you may have made progress in modeling a less severe form of punishment, your son doesn't share your perspective. He doesn't like the harsh way you treat him. You may say to him, "You should be thankful I only whipped you. If I had said that to my dad, he would have blackened both of my eyes." This won't make him feel grateful. Your harshness will continue to generate hard feelings in your child, just like it did between you and your dad.

## Model Positive Anger Expression

| Do's | Don'ts |
|------|--------|
| • Pay attention to what you model. | • Expect your child to act differently from your example. |
| • If needed, work on providing a better model—that's good modeling! | |
| • Limit the old ineffective behavior and practice the new behavior. | |
| • Focus your efforts *first* on providing a better model for your child. | • Continue to lecture her on why her style isn't acceptable. |
| • Get help if you aren't able to make the needed changes. | |
| • Identify your child's style of anger expression. | |
| • Talk with her about her style of anger expression. | |
| • Support her to evaluate for herself how well her style works for her. | |
| • Notice and support positive changes she makes. | |

 *Parental Plan*

### Don't Be Discouraged

You knew this book would contain a chapter dealing with how you cope with your anger. You knew you would be confronted with the example you set. Many of these kinds of books make you feel guilty about your less than perfect performance. But WAIT! Just because you can't do it perfectly doesn't mean you have to feel tremendously guilty and avoid the topic. Working at it is being a good model. You don't have to act correctly all of the time, you just have to work at it. If your behavior isn't what you want it to be, you can talk to your child about the goals you've set for yourself.

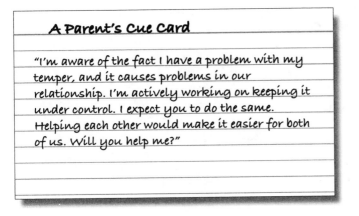

**A Parent's Cue Card**

"I'm aware of the fact I have a problem with my temper, and it causes problems in our relationship. I'm actively working on keeping it under control. I expect you to do the same. Helping each other would make it easier for both of us. Will you help me?"

## Change Inappropriate Responses

Some parents who come to the office seeking help expect their child to change but aren't willing to change themselves. They explain, "That's just the way I am," as a reason for not altering their actions. I understand their thinking because changing can be hard. However, when I suggest to the parents we should allow their child to continue on in his behavior because that's just the way he is, they are not amused. Neither is past failure an acceptable reason not to keep on trying. Change requires two things:

1. Stop the old ineffective behavior.
2. Practice the new behavior.

Change doesn't have to occur all at once. With each new situation, you can stop the old and practice the new. You won't do it perfectly, and neither will your child. But practicing with each new situation gradually shifts the habit. It also helps to keep you motivated if you "go public" with what you are trying to do.

For additional assistance in managing your anger through the A.N.G.E.R. method see chapters 17–21.

Be cautious of focusing on the progress you've made if it prevents you from being responsible for your current behavior. Of course you should feel good about your progress, but if your anger is still harmful or out of control, you can't stop working on it, because it will continue to do major damage to your relationship with your child.

---

### A Parent's Cue Card

"I know my anger has been out of control but I'm
working on it. The thing that bothers me the
most is _____. So instead of doing (old
behavior) I'm going to do (new behavior)."

---

*Get Help*

From time to time, all of us need help. There is nothing wrong in needing or asking for support or direction. Don't let your pride interfere with getting the help you need. Ask for assistance. Find someone who will listen, support you, pray for you, and hold you accountable for your progress. "Two are better than one, because they have a good return for their work: If one falls down, his friend can help him up. But pity the man who falls and has no one to help him up!" (Eccles. 4:9–10).

Consider the possibility of counseling. Yes, it's hard to go for help, often it's expensive, and you don't *have* to do it. However, what is the cost of not dealing with your anger? Can you put a price on your relationship with your children or your spouse? If your anger is destroying your relationships, call your pastor, friend, or counselor and get some help.

If you've tried your best and still have serious concerns about your ability to control your anger, consider an evaluation for medication. Contacting your family doctor is a good place to start. Antidepressants aren't addictive, and you can stop taking them if you don't feel they help. A pill won't take away the problem, but it may give you a needed boost to deal more successfully with your anger. Many people are hesitant to think about medication, but consider the cost of not trying every available option to remedy the serious, possibly permanent, damage that anger can cause in your family.

In the next chapter we'll see how parental decisions can either increase or decrease tension in the home.

## Recommended Books

Ron Potter-Efron, Pat Potter-Efron, and Ronald Potter-Efron. *Letting Go of Anger: The 10 Most Common Anger Styles and What to Do about Them.* Oakland, Calif.: New Harbinger, 1995.

Sal Severe. *How to Behave So Your Children Will Too!* New York: Viking, 2000.

# 23

# Parental Decisions

Your parental decisions impact the way your child expresses his anger. If you reinforce good decisions and don't reinforce his angry behavior, it will become easier for him to make good choices concerning his anger.

## A Child in Charge

Joan is frightened of Jessie, her ten-year-old son, because he is so rude and threatening to her. She is a peacemaker at heart, so she doesn't like negative confrontations. Jessie throws all of his clothes on the floor of his room and leaves soda cans and candy wrappers lying around. When his room starts to smell, Joan tries to get him to clean it up.

"Jessie, there's junk all over your room. Do you think you will have time to clean it today?"

"What are you thinking? You know I'm going to see my friends. Clean it up yourself, woman."

Joan doesn't want to cause a blowup so she says, "Okay, maybe you will have time to get to it over the weekend."

"Whatever."

What happened in this brief interaction? Joan made a request and then withdrew it when Jessie was rude to her. Jessie learned to be rude because it works! If he says, "Oh Mom, no thanks. I really don't want to pick up my room," Joan would still be on his case to get the job done. But when he's rude and aggressive, the request/demand to clean his room disappears. If you found a way of getting out of work, wouldn't you use it at least once in a while? This aggression works for Jessie, so he will stick with it until it no longer works.

 ## *Parental Plan*

### *Examine How Your Decisions Impact Your Child's Actions*

It's easy to focus on your child's behavior and miss the fact that your behavior influences his. Think back on the time of the last explosion. What occurred prior to your child losing it? What did you do? The point of these questions is not to make you feel guilty, but to point out that you have a great deal of power. Controlling what you do will greatly influence what he does.

James (fourteen years old) wants to go to the school dance, but his grades were terrible (4 Fs and 2 Ds), and he routinely cuts one or two classes per day. His mom, Monica, told him, "You can't go to the dance. You've not earned it and I'm tired of your disrespect. Your attitude stinks. You cannot go. That is the end of this discussion."

The discussion may have been over, but the battle had just begun. James really wanted to go because he had already received a yes from one of the cutest girls in the seventh grade class. He really wasn't worried about getting permission. He thought to himself, "Mom's given in before and she'll probably do it again. I just need to bug her enough and she will let me go."

James's bugging campaign was successful because on Friday Monica said to James, "Go to the dance! Just get out of my face and out of the house!" James did feel a little guilty about pushing his mom to that point, but it was very important for him to go, and she would eventually get over it.

This was a difficult situation. After we talked, Monica understood that she was reinforcing James's bugging when she gave in to him. We increased her support, helped her avoid the times he bugged her, and talked with James about his inappropriate actions. These helped her make it through a couple of rough times, which built her confidence in making good decisions for James. When bugging her and being angry didn't get him what he wanted, he began to control himself more.

### *Take an Active Role in Your Child's Decisions*

A child is not a small adult. He lacks experience, maturity, and patience to make all of his decisions by himself. Expecting him to direct his own life apart from parental guidance will result in many bad decisions. He needs your direction and thoughtful input.

#### AVOID INAPPROPRIATELY EMPOWERING THE CHILD

Parents inappropriately empower their child by allowing him to make his own decisions without parental direction and input. If your child has considerable power, he will use it to get what he wants. If you limit his power, he won't be able to control you.

Children need to learn how to make decisions for themselves. When your child is young, allow him to make only specific decisions. You may let him decide the time of his bath, not whether he takes one. You may give him a choice of which coat to wear, not whether he wears one. With your guidance, you can gradually allow your child more freedom in making choices.

Some parents hand over their power to their child, indirectly because they're too busy or too tired to notice the decisions their child is making; or directly by not parenting and by giving their child full control over his life: "Do what you want to do, just don't bother me."

#### DON'T REINFORCE ANGRY OR AGGRESSIVE BEHAVIOR

If your child learns that aggression works, he'll continue to use it. If it stops working, he'll look for other ways of coping.

Carol Tavris addresses this issue of reinforcement and how it teaches children to adopt an angry, aggressive style of coping.

> In distressed families, Patterson finds (by close observation of literally thousands of family exchanges), children progress steadily from learning to be disobedient to learning to be physically assaultive. A three-step process may occur hundreds of times each day: The child is at-

**A Parent's Cue Card**

"I know I've allowed you to make most of your decisions, and in many areas you've shown yourself to be very mature. However in the specific area of dating (or whatever area you want to reinvolve yourself), I want us to talk more about what is okay. This can be a difficult area. If we talk more about it, I think you'll be happier with the outcome. Let's set up a time to

talk. When we get together, I'd like to hear your ideas and thoughts about figuring out whom to date."

tacked, or criticized, or yelled at by an exasperated parent or sibling; the child responds aggressively; the child's aggression is rewarded when the attacker withdraws. Thus the child learns to use manipulative and coercive tactics (such as whining, yelling, and temper tantrums) as a substitute social skill.[1]

To summarize this information:

Child is attacked—He responds aggressively—People back off

Because the child likes it when people back off, his aggressive behavior is rewarded. Finding a response that produces the desired result, the child stops looking for others that could work. Acting aggressively becomes his first choice in dealing with situations. He hones this skill, applying it to a variety of circumstances and geographical locations. If it works at home, will it work at school? Remember, though, once something is learned, it can be unlearned by changing the outcome.

### Exert Parental Control

You must work through disagreements with your spouse so you can present a united front to your child and retain parental control. Reaching agreement may be difficult, especially when parents focus solely on one important (but different) aspect of the problem.

#### DON'T GIVE AWAY YOUR PARENTAL POWER

If your child has more power than you, his parents, he will use it to his advantage.

If you saw a speed limit sign saying "Speed Limit 40 or 65," what speed would you drive? Similarly if you and your spouse aren't in agreement, your child can choose which parental expectation to meet. By not being in agreement, you leave a loophole that most children will use.

Two adults should certainly be stronger than one child, regardless of the child's age or size. If your child frequently gets his way over your objection, you probably have a power leak. A child simply cannot have more strength than two adults unless one (or both) is sharing power with the child. Enough power can be siphoned from the parents for the child to exert control. If you've teamed up with your child against your spouse, expect your child to use this power for his own benefit.

#### SPOUSES WORKING TOGETHER

Working together allows you and your spouse to exert your parental control and hold your child accountable for his decisions and for the way he expresses his anger.

Bill and Betty couldn't agree on what to do with their thirteen-year-old daughter, Ebony.

Bill focused on the positive things she did and minimized the importance of her disobedience. He talked with her instead of giving meaningful consequences. He thought Betty was too negative and always looked for a way to be critical of Ebony.

Betty loved Ebony but believed she manipulated Bill and "got away with murder." Betty attempted to open Bill's eyes by pointing out how Ebony did exactly as she wanted, ignoring their parental expectations.

The more Bill excused Ebony (because Betty was too negative), the more Betty pointed out how Ebony was being defiant (because Bill was being manipulated).

This typical cycle occurs when parents aren't working together. Note that each parent is trying to balance out the other's response, creating more frustration for the other spouse. Each time through this cycle the tension increases, creating more parental division. To correct this, Mom and Dad need to reach agreement on the rule and the consequence for breaking the rule, otherwise they won't be able to hold Ebony accountable for her actions.

If you as parents work together and reach a compromise for the expectations you both support, you eliminate the loophole. Be assured your child will check to see if you two are really working together. Once he knows he would have to deal with both of you, he will likely comply.

Winning, control, and power can become focal points in the parent-child relationship. Here are my rules concerning power struggles:

- Pick your battles. Every battle isn't worth fighting.
- Win or don't play. If the battle is important and it is one you can win, you must win. If it isn't important or you can't win, don't play. Playing and losing diminishes your power.
- Win because it's important for your child, not for your ego. If you win for your ego, you teach your child to fight for his ego, not for the principle.

### Politely Make Requests, Expecting Compliance

The three-step process of reinforcing aggression (parent attacks, child counterattacks, parent removes demand) has two parental pieces that can be changed. Politely asking for what you want, rather than attacking your child, is more likely to result in a positive response. The second point of intervention that is under your control is whether you withdraw your request. Holding firm on your expectation disrupts the pattern and stops reinforcing your child's angry response.

---

### A Parent's Cue Card

"It seems like we are always yelling at each other. I don't like that, because it makes me feel bad. I don't expect a lot from you but I do need you to help out once in a while. From here on out, I'm going to ask you politely to help me out, rather than yell at you. I'd appreciate it if you would also respond politely and do what I ask. I'll give you a few minutes to get started, and then I'll

---

come check on it. If you can't do what I asked in a reasonable time frame, I may be open to negotiating the time, but you need to talk with me about it. Don't just blow me off; I need to have you do what I ask."

---

*Say Yes or No*

Say yes as much as you can. When you say no, stick with it. Your parental decisions reinforce either positive anger expression or aggressive anger expression.

Here are the guidelines I offer parents:

- Think about the request before you answer. Take more time if needed.
- Say yes as much as you can when asked nicely. This reinforces your child's asking in a positive manner.

- If you are going to say yes after he bugs you a lot, say yes right away and avoid the bugging.
- If you say no, stick with it no matter how much he bugs you or threatens you.

*DON'T CHANGE YOUR NO TO YES*

If your no becomes a yes after your child has acted aggressively, you've rewarded his aggression. If you say no, stick with it. Your child will observe what caused you to change your no to yes and will in the future repeat that behavior. As a parent, you've reinforced those actions.

To understand what happened, let's get technical for just a few moments. B. F. Skinner believed that the occurrence of a behavior is influenced by the positive and negative consequences that follow the behavior. A positive consequence increases the frequency of a behavior, while a negative consequence decreases the frequency of a behavior. In other words, there is a connection or a bond between a behavior and its consequences. The stronger the positive bond, the more likely it is that the behavior will reoccur.

### A Parent's Cue Card

"I've noticed when you don't like my answer, you bug me until I change my mind. This really bothers me and makes me mad at you. You get to do what you want, but I'm not happy about it and then I give you a hard time. I don't necessarily expect you to believe it, but I'm changing the way I act. I'm going to try to say yes as much as I can. But if I say no, I'm going to stick with it. I wanted you to be aware of the change. Do you have any questions?"

*DON'T BECOME PASSIVE*

Once your child discovers he can manipulate you through the use of threats or angry outbursts, he will continue to use them until they no longer work. If you are being threatened, make a plan that takes away the power of the behavior and keeps everyone safe.

Boys are likely to use verbal and physical intimidation. If your son dislikes your answer, he will get in your face and call you bad names. If that doesn't work, he may escalate to shoving, hitting, or other abusive behavior. He will push until you're scared enough to give him what he wants.

Girls may use intimidation but are more likely to use threats: never speaking to you, never forgiving you, doing drugs, getting pregnant, running away, or committing suicide. Some of these threats are every bit as frightening as physical intimidation.

Claiming "child abuse" is the other card a child may play to get his way. If parents remain firm or attempt to control their child by physical means (restraint or spanking), the child threatens to report them to social services. Parents who have been reported for child abuse, regardless of the outcome, often feel that all of their parental power has been stripped away. What little control they previously had is gone. (See the next section for how to handle such situations.)

### Make a Plan

What would your child do if you ignored his usual threat? Typically he thinks, *If that threat didn't work, a bigger one will.* So if threatening to run away doesn't work, a suicide threat ought to do the job. These are dangerous waters, so you need a well-thought-out plan that addresses both aspects of a threat: removing the power from the threat and ensuring safety. Threats work because of the power in the fear. If the fear is removed, so is the power. Identifying clearly why you are frightened allows you then to brainstorm ideas for dealing with those fears.

In my book *Haven't We Gone through This Before?* I've outlined a safety plan for dealing with these situations.

1. Assess the situation.
    Identify your fears.
    Are the fears realistic?
    Identify your strengths and your ability to deal with the situation.
2. Make planned, conscious decisions.
    Decide if things will get better or worse if left alone.

>Determine the point at which you will no longer respond to the child's threats.

>Determine with your spouse how you will respond to each escalation of your child's threatening behavior.

3. Have a safety net in place.

>Prearrange support people who will commit to helping you (friends, grandparents, other relatives, pastor, church people, counselor, probation officers, police). If you see a blowup coming, have the support people on hand before the confrontation to keep things from escalating.

>Check on places where your child can go to settle down for a few days if needed (friend's or relative's house, shelter care for adolescents, hospital—will your insurance cover this?).

The following deals with the four major threat categories: verbal threats, physical threats, running away, and self-abuse.

*A Verbal Threat.* Implied or clearly stated and nasty.

- *The power of the threat* is that it *scares* you or *hurts* you so much you let the child have his way.
- *Remove the power* by calling him on the minor threats, not allowing them to escalate into big ones; acknowledging that you are scared or hurt but telling your child that it won't stop you from dealing with the situation; holding your child accountable with consequences you can enforce.
- *Keep safe* by involving others. Isolation and secrecy add to the child's power and increase the probability of things escalating; tell your spouse; call the police; deal with the threats and other relational issues through counseling.

*A Physical Threat.* From something minor like a push to something major like a weapon.

- *The power of the threat* is fear that he will do what he said.
- *Remove the power* by calling him on the minor threats, not allowing them to escalate into big ones; holding him accountable

with consequences you can enforce; removing him from the home for a time-out, allowing him to think about what he did; letting him know you will involve the police and the court system if he persists in using physical violence; following through on calling the police and pressing charges.

- *Keep safe* by avoiding these situations until you have the backup from the authorities or police to deal safely with the concerns; not escalating the situation by pushing him back, for example; developing a specific plan for limiting violence.

*Runaway Threat.* Threatening to leave or actually leaving for an extended period.

- *The power of the threat* is your fear of losing him and what might happen to him if he runs away, so you let him have his way.
- *Remove the power* by telling him that running away from problems doesn't solve them; holding him accountable with consequences you can enforce; letting him know what you will do if he runs: call the police, talk with all of his friends' parents, press charges against anyone who is harboring him.
- *Keep safe* by limiting his ability to run; dealing with the concerns he has that are causing him to run away; empowering him in positive ways to deal with his concerns rather than run away from them.

*Threat of Harming Self.* May be a suicidal gesture or a serious suicide attempt.

- *The power of the threat* is your fear of his actually harming or killing himself.
- *Remove the power* by telling him that hurting or killing himself isn't the answer to his problems; being clear with him that you won't give in because of his threats to harm himself; having him evaluated by a mental health professional; taking him to the hospital.
- *Keep safe* by removing guns, knives, and large bottles of pills (overdosing on Tylenol is especially harmful as it causes liver damage); getting a written and verbal contract or promise that

he won't hurt himself; being with him at all times until the crisis is over.

Refusing to be intimidated by your child's threats takes courage and determination.

Paying attention to your decisions, using your parental power to reinforce your child's positive responses, and sticking with your "no," can be a challenge. However, with some focused effort you can use your parental decisions to greatly influence the way your child expresses his anger. If you find yourself struggling in this area, join a parent support group and talk to your pastor, your child's school counselor, or a counselor in your community.

## Recommended Books

Foster Cline and Jim Fay. *Parenting Teens with Love and Logic*. Colorado Springs: Piñon Press, 1992.

Richard Berry. *Haven't We Gone through This Before? Breaking Out of Those Parent-Child Ruts*. Grand Rapids: Revell, 1996.

# 24

# Parental Attention

---

Focusing parental attention and large blocks of time on angry misbehavior or poor choices actually rewards those behaviors because your child likes, wants, and needs your attention. Focusing your attention on your child's positive actions, while minimizing the attention given to inappropriate actions, encourages your child to control her anger and make better decisions.

## Negative Attention

Let's get acquainted with Amy, who is eleven years old and in the fifth grade. She's a bright, precocious child with facial expressions that can kill. Her cute little nose, shoulder-length, auburn hair, and expressive eyes immediately caught my attention. Amy is the oldest of three children and lives with her biological parents, Randy and Roberta. Amy's younger siblings are Amber (seven years old) and Laura (four years old).

Amy was brought in for counseling because she was driving her parents absolutely crazy with her lying. Randy said, "She lies about everything, even things that would be better served by the truth. We can't believe a word that comes out of her mouth. We've tried everything to make her stop, but she won't. She's really good at it. She will look you straight in the eye and tell you she didn't do something when you have just caught her in the very act of doing it. If we don't get this fixed now, how is she going to be when she reaches the teenage years? She always seems so angry. But when you ask her what's bothering her, she doesn't say anything."

Randy and Roberta are both high school teachers with good parenting skills. They love all of their daughters but are approaching a crisis point that will negatively impact the entire family if they don't reach some type of resolution with Amy.

After meeting with the entire family for about fifteen minutes, I decided to talk with Randy and Roberta without the children. I wanted more information about Amy's lying. Talking about it in front of her would reward it by spending time on it and focusing on her, so I had all of the children sit in the lobby.

With just the parents present, I said, "Tell me about the last time you caught Amy in a lie." They proceeded to tell the story. It turns out that they tried unsuccessfully for about three and a half hours to get Amy to tell them the truth. What did they get out of it? Three and a half hours of frustration. What did Amy get out of it? Three and a half hours of her parents' undivided attention. Granted, it was negative attention, but attention nevertheless.

 ## *Parental Plan*

### *Listen to Concerns*

You can listen to your child's concerns or you can watch her angry actions. Amy said she tried to talk with her parents about how she couldn't do anything right. She felt like the "bad kid" and certainly couldn't compete with the perfect child, Amber. When that didn't work very well, she started lying. This probably wasn't a conscious choice on Amy's part, but she just slid into doing what got the most attention. In addition, it gave her a way of showing her anger. When your child persists in negative behavior, it could be a way of communicating her anger, a bid for attention, or a way to appear cool to her friends. Remember, the way you define a problem determines possible solutions. If your child is persisting in negative behavior because of anger, help her talk about why she's angry. If it's to get attention, give her attention for positive behavior. If it's to be liked by other kids, help her feel good about herself and teach her positive social skills.

### Applaud Positive Effort

I frequently hear teens say about their parents: "They never see it when I do something good. They only see the bad things. It would be nice if just once they would say something about the good things I do." As parents we need to recognize and reward effort. Your child may have poor grades or have trouble controlling her angry outbursts. Obviously you can't say to her, "Nice work on those Fs." But you can say to her, "I've noticed you've been working on bringing up those Fs." It may take a while before you can be satisfied with the product, but you can always be pleased with effort in a positive direction. Give your attention to behaviors you wish to see more often.

---

### A Parent's Cue Card

"I saw that before you became angry and cussed you were really trying to control yourself. You almost made it through the whole situation without saying anything bad. Keep trying."

---

### Minimize Time Focused on Negative Behaviors

I think of attention as food, and we know that what we feed will grow. Our motto as parents should be: Starve negative angry actions; feed positive actions.

We know that Randy and Roberta "fed" Amy's lying, causing it to grow and become a bigger problem. Understandably, they didn't mean to do that, but motivation isn't a factor when dealing with attention. If you feed something, giving it attention, it grows. So how would they stop feeding Amy's lying? Minimize the amount of attention it receives.

Unlike the American judicial system, parenting does not require the accused to be present at the trial and conviction stage in order to impose a sentence. The "trial and conviction" stage is where Amy extracts large amounts of attention from her parents. Eliminating Amy's participation in this phase would shorten the whole process by about three and one half hours, greatly reducing the amount of attention given to her behavior. Sentencing requires very little time. The judge simply indicates to the guilty party the consequence of her actions. This is done in a nonemotional, matter-of-fact kind of way.

To effectively impose a sentence, parents must go through the trial and conviction phase on their own. They must weigh the evidence. To minimize the risk of falsely accusing your child, the evidence may include the following: a history of the negative behavior, a motive, an opportunity, ruling out other suspects, and both parents being convinced of guilt.

If you cover these safeguards and both parents believe the child did it, you are on solid ground. If you can't be sure enough to be comfortable giving a consequence, express your concern to all of the children, being careful not to accuse anyone. Let go of the situation and move on. If the guilty party didn't learn her lesson, you will have another opportunity to discipline her when she does it again.

### A Parent's Cue Card

"In the past we've spent a lot of time arguing and fussing over whether you did this or that. It takes quite a bit of time to do that and causes a great deal of angry feelings. We are shifting how we handle such situations. If we are sure you misbehaved, we won't be arguing about it, we'll just give you a reasonable consequence. We know there's a chance we might be punishing

*you unjustly, so we'll be cautious about that.*
*Our relationship is important so we don't want to*
*continue the present plan of arguing and*
*fighting."*

### Remove the Audience

Don't have discipline conversations with your child when an audience is present. By removing the audience, you've:

*Greatly reduced the amount of attention paid to a particular behavior.* Five minutes' worth of attention paid to negative behavior isn't bad. But if you do this in the context of an audience or classroom of twenty, you've now given one hundred minutes' worth of attention to that behavior. It now makes sense why the class clown role is a difficult one to leave. It is well fed!

*Made it easier for your child to compromise without losing face.* Some children are very sensitive to what their peers think of them. If you try to have a conversation in front of her peers, she may have to be "cool," which limits her flexibility. Pull her aside and talk about the situation.

It's easy to spend large amounts of time trying to get your child to see or admit to the error of her ways. Parents, out of frustration, often increase the number of words, hoping something they say will trigger a positive response from their child. Haven't you already communicated to your child what you want her to know? Repeating it several times won't help her to get it. Instead of giving your child all that negative attention, determine with your spouse a reasonable consequence and impose it. With practice, you can become very adept at attaching your attention to behaviors you like.

## Recommended Books

John Gray. *Children Are from Heaven: Positive Parenting Skills for Raising Co-operative, Confident, and Compassionate Children.* New York: HarperCollins, 1999.

James C. Dobson. *Parenting Isn't for Cowards: Dealing Confidently with the Frustrations of Child-Rearing.* Pamona, Calif.: Word, 1987.

# 25

## Parental Vagueness

If you aren't clear and consistent in presenting your expectations and enforcing the rules, your children will assume you don't mean what you say. They will then continue to express their anger inappropriately, ignoring your wishes.

### Mixed Messages

Gwen grew up in a home where children definitely were to be seen and not heard. She wasn't allowed to express her opinion in any adult conversation. This really bothered her, and she vowed never to restrain her child from expressing his opinion. This vow was certainly fulfilled and was the reason for Gwen's bringing her fifteen-year-old son, Chris, to counseling. He was in the habit of calling his mother every filthy name that came to his mind. Chris got the message at an early age that he had the right always to say anything to anyone. Gwen wanted to give Chris permission to speak up but she intended for him to speak respectfully. In her desire to encourage him to speak freely, she failed to instill in him the need to speak with respect.

Gwen needed to be clear and include detail in what she wanted Chris to do. That's easy enough to say. Why do some parents have such a difficult time doing it?

| Parents may be vague because: | To remedy this, parents can: |
| --- | --- |
| They don't know it's better to be clear, detailed, and firm. | Understand that clear limits are helpful to their child. Being clear, detailed, and firm provides the child with direction, security, and a way of evaluating how he's performing. It's easier for him to please you if he knows what you want. |
| Fear prevents them from taking a firm stand. They don't want to make things worse. | Deal with the fear. Being frightened of what their child may do can stop parents from giving him clear, firm expectations. Imagine for a moment that you are no longer frightened. With the fear gone, what would you do to deal with these circumstances? Is that a good plan? Should you allow the fear to deter you from a good plan? Talk with others about your idea and get support to be firm. |
| They aren't sure where they stand or what they believe, or they aren't in agreement with each other. | Take time to develop a clear position on the issue that both parents can support. |
| They don't like taking a firm stand. | Learn to be more assertive. They can read, take a class, practice, find a parent support group in their community. |
| They don't communicate well. They have clear and firm expectations but they just don't communicate them clearly. | Work on communication. They can do things that make the communication clearer, asking for feedback, writing down the rules and expectations, having the child tell them what he heard. |
| They don't know what to do, so it's hard to communicate a clear message. | Get some assistance to know what to do! There are many good parenting books. Attend parenting classes, go to counseling, develop a parent support group in their neighborhood. |

 *Parental Plan*

*Clarify the Message*

*Be specific in what you say to your child.* Conveying confusing, mixed, or inaccurate messages to your child makes it very difficult for him to meet your expectations. Most parents have specific ideas they want their children to hear, understand, and follow. In some families this parental message is several paragraphs long, but the child is only willing to listen to three or four sentences. This time discrepancy creates communication problems. Think of the one sentence you would like to say that will powerfully influence your child's thinking and behavior. As soon as you know what that sentence is, tell it to her very slowly and clearly.

When I asked Gwen to do this, she said, "I can't do it in one sentence." Being supportive, I sent her to the waiting room with a clipboard and a sheet of paper and asked her not to return until she had her one sentence!

Twenty-five minutes later she returned with this sentence. She looked Chris in the eye and said, "Chris, you're a bright, handsome, talented young man who will ruin your chances for success in school, jobs, and relationships unless you begin right now to control your temper and your mouth. Your opinion is important, but sometimes you need to keep it to yourself."

Even though it was two sentences, Gwen sent an extremely powerful and clear message to her son. It was a moment of concern, contact, and care. It was a holy moment that clearly impacted both of them.

After the session was over and they left, I thought about the clarity and power in Gwen's message. It was so different from the other messages Chris had received from his mother. I wasn't sure how Chris would respond, but Gwen did her part by giving her son a message on which he could focus his thoughts.

What's your sentence to your angry kid? You get only one, so make it a good one.

*Clearly Present Expectations, Rewards, and Consequences*

If you give mixed messages, how will your children know what to do? A mixed message is one in which the different parts of the message are inconsistent with each other. This makes it hard for your child to understand and comply with your expectations. Consider what occurs when the message parts don't match:

*Verbal and nonverbal.* When you tell your child you are serious about a rule (verbal part), your face should look serious (nonverbal part). It will likely confuse your child if you have a pleasant look on your face while using a firm tone of voice or vice versa.

*Actual words and the intent of the message.* When the situation is important but you are using words that are tentative and iffy, your child may miss the significance of the rule or consequence.

*Expectation and consequence.* One way children know about the significance of an issue is the seriousness of the accompanying consequence. If the penalty for breaking the most serious rule in the house is no television for thirty minutes, your child won't understand how strongly you feel about this particular rule. On the other hand, if you ground your child for a month for an innocent accident, he also receives a confusing message about the importance of that action.

*Words and actions.* If you tell your child one thing but you do another, you've given him a mixed message. Which message—the verbal one or the action one—do you think he'll follow? The way you act becomes a viable option for the way your child acts.

---

### A Parent's Cue Card

"Sometimes we give you directions and explain expectations that may not be clear. We then become upset when our expectations aren't met. Your mother and I need to have you do the things we ask you to do. If you don't do your part, our family will definitely have more tension. To make things even more clear, we're going to write down our expectations and the accompanying

---

Gwen and I talked about how she could reinforce her clear message. Gwen decided on the following: "Chris, I'm most concerned about your

consequences. We will have that list to you by
Friday. It would be helpful for us if you'd ask
questions if you don't understand."

ability to control the words you use when you become angry. We will treat each other with respect and not call each other names. If you call me any names, you will be grounded for two days from the phone, friends, family, stereo, television, and Nintendo. Basically you're isolated to think about what you've done and how you can stop yourself from doing it again. You can go to work and school, and you may come out of your room to eat and use the bathroom. But other than those activities, you will be in your room. I know this may or may not help you change how you act when you're angry. That will be up to you. Do you have any questions?"

### Enforce Consequences

Increasing the certainty of consequences has a bigger impact on your child's decisions than does increasing the severity of the consequences. Parents often become harsh out of frustration, relying on the severity of the punishment to change their child's behavior. Obviously the consequence must be meaningful (speeding fines aren't twenty-five cents), but the certainty and swiftness of the penalty's occurring is crucial in helping your child make good decisions. Consistency in connecting consequences to choices will have more impact on your child's behavior than your harshness. Part of the reason we speed is because we aren't stopped all of the time. Imagine for a moment if your speedometer were connected to the police station computer. If every time you went over the speed limit the computer automatically sent out a fine to your address, there would be considerably less speeding! The same holds true for our children and the consistency of consequences. "When the sentence for a crime is not quickly carried out, the hearts of the people are filled with schemes to do wrong" (Eccles. 8:11).

If on Tuesday you severely punish your child for angrily slamming his door but do nothing on Thursday when he does it again, you're giving your child a very confusing message about your expectations and the importance of controlling his anger. It would be better to give him a consequence each time he slammed the door. If the reasonable consequence doesn't help him to stop slamming his door, you can remove the door for a brief period of time. A door is really hard to slam if it isn't there.

Even though your child probably won't believe you, I still recommend that parents tell their child of any changes in the way they will interact with him.

---

### A Parent's Cue Card

"In the past your father and I have sometimes come down on you pretty hard for your swearing. That didn't seem to work, so now we've decided to charge you a fine of a quarter for each cuss word we hear you say. We're not going to hassle you, but each and every time you swear—whether you're angry or not—you will owe a quarter to the jar. If the jar ever reaches five dollars, we will empty it and give the money to your sister's adopted child in Africa."

---

One of the most important rules of disciplining children is consistency. As we have seen, inconsistency and vagueness send mixed messages and children quickly assume you don't mean what you say. Being precise about consequences and following through with them take energy but pay off in your child's improved behavior.

## Recommended Books

Ron Taffel. *Why Parents Disagree: How Women and Men Parent Differently and How We Can Work Together*. New York: William Morrow, 1994.
Cynthia Ulrich Tobias. *"You Can't Make Me": But I Can Be Persuaded*. Colorado Springs: WaterBrook Press, 1999.

# 26

## Parental Consequences

You can't make your child control her temper, but you can hold her accountable for what she does when she's angry. If her temper outbursts cost her nothing, why should she try to control herself? When your child has to deal with the consequences of her actions, she will be motivated to control herself.

### Lack of Control

Becky, a seventeen-year-old senior, was referred for counseling by her grandparents, Mike and Melissa, because of their concerns about her temper tantrums. Nothing seemed to stop her from destroying her room when she was upset. She had even kicked holes in her bedroom wall.

Mike and Melissa agreed to be Becky's guardians for her senior year when her parents were transferred out of the country. They knew she was an angry child, but they were quite surprised to see how she acted out her anger. At first, they were somewhat understanding, but as the number of holes in the walls began to multiply, they became angry that she was destroying their home.

Like many grandparents who take on the responsibility of raising their grandchildren, Mike and Melissa didn't know how to control Becky. We talked about a variety of interventions, including anger management techniques, exercise, talking, relaxation, and writing down her feelings. We finally talked about consequences.

"Mike, when Becky kicks a hole in the wall, what do you do?"

"Well, we've tried a variety of things. At first, we talked with her and asked her not to do that again. I think you can see that didn't work. Then we had her pay for the damage, but she doesn't have a job, so she owes us for the last two holes we had fixed. Then we began grounding her for a week."

Becky jumped into the conversation, "Grandpa, you can do whatever you want to do to me, but it isn't going to matter. I will do what I'm going to do no matter what!"

You know what? I believed her. I'm seeing more children who absolutely don't care what's done to them. Parents can't make them change their mind.

"Do what you want to me. It doesn't matter. I'm going to do what I want to do anyway."

While this is scary, it's really nothing new. People—adults and kids—have always had the ability to decide for themselves what they will and will not do. The police officer doesn't make you stop speeding. He simply gives you a ticket that serves as data to help you make the right decision in the future. Similarly, your job as a parent isn't to force your child to make the right decisions but to assist her, through the use of consequences, to make the best possible choices. It's up to her to decide if she wants to change.

 *Parental Plan*

*Your Discipline Program*

When parents think through and develop a discipline program for their children, they have gone a long way in having an impact on their children's behavior. As we have seen, children respond to consistency and fairness. Consider the following as you develop your discipline plan.

While listening to a talk show about children, I heard the guest make this statement: "Rules without relationship equals rebellion." This doesn't mean that you have to be "best friends," but it does mean that your child needs to be sure that you love her, care about her, and make decisions with her best interests in mind.

Relationships require time. Are you spending time with your child? Do you know what's happening in your child's life? Dr. John Gottman researches the elements of happy marriages. He believes couples develop and maintain their love by being aware of what's occurring in their spouse's life. Adapting his "Love Map Questionnaire"[1] to fit children, how many of these ten sentences can you complete? If you can't complete all of them, use them as questions to discuss with your child.

1. My child's best friends are
2. The stresses my child currently faces are
3. People who've been irritating my child recently are
4. Some of my child's life dreams are
5. My child's basic philosophy of life is
6. My child's favorite ice cream is
7. My child's favorite song or musical group is
8. My child's three favorite movies are
9. If my child could go anywhere, she/he would go to
10. My child is the most proud of this accomplishment

### *TEACH YOUR CHILD*

If there are specific things you want your child to know, you must teach them to her. You don't allow your small child to touch a hot burner on the stove and then discuss the different options. You instruct her with specific direction what to do and what not to do. As she matures, it's her job to determine if that instruction works for her. She may keep it, change it, or discard it, but until she's old enough to decide for herself, she needs to have clear parental direction.

As parents, what have you recently been teaching your child? If you can't answer the question, you may want to consider taking a more conscious and focused approach to the specific information you want your child to have.

### MODEL APPROPRIATE BEHAVIOR

What you do becomes an option for your children to copy. "Talking the talk" isn't enough, you must "walk the walk." If your child hears what she is to do and sees what she is to do, she's more likely to follow your instruction. I know this is a difficult one, because I don't always act the way I want my children to act. Check out chapter 22 specifically for how parents model anger. Here's a bit of encouragement: Children don't expect us to be perfect! Just don't pretend you are, and keep working on areas that need improvement. Isn't that what you really want from them?

### DEVELOP EMPATHY

If your child learns that only her wishes and feelings are important, she'll have trouble getting along with others. Yes, what she wants is important, and what others want is also important. Assist your child in understanding and appreciating others' feelings. Get her involved in team sports, group projects, and other teamwork activities, such as playing in a band, so she learns how to interact with others. Here are other ways to teach empathy:

- When you watch television shows, ask your child how she thinks one of the characters feels when something happens— either good or bad.
- Talk with her about how you feel.
- Ask her what kind of a day her teacher(s) had.
- Point out the importance of an individual's functioning as part of a larger group by asking her how she might get along without her nose or her heart. (Everybody has an important part to play, even though sometimes it doesn't feel like it.)

### DEVELOP AND USE EFFECTIVE CONSEQUENCES

Consequences can assist your child in making good decisions. But if you don't work on your relationship with your child, teach her needed information, model appropriate behavior, or help your child develop empathy, don't expect the use of consequences to produce the desired results.

As you can see, the effective use of consequences is just one component in the overall discipline process. There's no guarantee that applying just the right consequence to a situation will produce the right response from your child. However, when used properly, consequences help your child "come to her senses," control herself, and choose wisely. Let's consider a few key concepts:

*Natural consequences* are outcomes that naturally accompany an act. If you hit your thumb with a hammer, you naturally feel pain. Natural consequences are wonderful motivators to change. The prodigal son didn't change his mind because of a persuasive letter he received from his dad. He came "to his senses" because he was hungry and there was plenty of food at home!

Some parents interfere with natural consequences and then complain their child still makes poor decisions. Paying your daughter's speeding ticket would be a good example of interference. If you pay the ticket, she learns that speeding is free, which doesn't cause her to slow down.

*Logical consequences* are connected to an action and are usually imposed by a parent or authority figure. If the officer stops you because you are driving while intoxicated, he doesn't allow you to continue driving. If your daughter talks on the phone and keeps it tied up too long, it makes sense to restrict her from the phone.

*Enforceable consequences* are the only effective consequences. A consequence you can't enforce isn't a consequence. Trying to enforce a consequence that requires cooperation from your child won't be effective. Telling your teenager she can't use the phone when you aren't home—short of removing all of the phones and the phone service—isn't a consequence you can enforce. It also sets her up to sneak and lie to you about her actions. Instead, tell her she can't use the phone after 6:00 P.M. when you are home to monitor her compliance. You can enforce that and it is a meaningful consequence.

*Sureness of consequence.* The certainty of the consequence is more influential in changing behavior than the seriousness of the consequence. I will drive slower if I know that every time I speed I will receive a five-dollar ticket. A fifty-dollar ticket won't have the same impact if I get it only once out of every twenty-five times I speed.

*Time-limited consequences.* While you may want to ground her for the rest of her life, it isn't a good idea. It won't work and it punishes you more than it does your child. It's usually better to go with a shorter rather than a longer consequence. Then you have the consequence available to use again. Many kids become too discouraged and give up trying if the consequence is imposed for too long a time. If your child has school problems, reward and impose consequences daily rather than weekly. That way if he has a bad Monday, he still has motivation to make Tuesday better.

*The magic consequence.* You may have a favorite consequence you use for everything. The only difference in your punishment is how long it lasts. Nothing works forever. Try some new ones—some lenient and others more stringent.

*Time-off consequences for good behavior.* Sometimes it's a good idea to reduce the punishment if your child has handled it with a good attitude and hasn't pushed it. Other times it's best to stick with the length and severity of the consequence so it makes the point. It's okay to cut your child some slack the first time or two. But if you're continually dealing with the same infraction, stick with the consequence and don't allow time off for good behavior.

### Present Rules, Monitor Behavior, Enforce Consequences

Because I have numerous traffic signs in my office, I often use the speed limit as an example of how effective rules and consequences work. The City of Cheyenne doesn't merely hope people drive a safe speed. To ensure safe driving and to minimize traffic accidents, the city: 1. presents expectations—there are speed limit signs posted, 2. monitors compliance—police have radar equipment to accurately measure a driver's speed, and 3. enforces the rule—judges impose consequences if the expectations are violated.

If you want consequences to have the maximum influence on your child's actions, you should use the same three components:

1. *Present expectations.* Tell your child clearly and specifically what you expect. Write it down and post it. Both parents need to be committed to the expectations.
2. *Monitor compliance.* Check to see if your child is doing what you expect. Compare her behavior with the stated rule.

3. *Enforce the rule with consequences.* Enforce reasonable consequences for violations. Remember, the certainty of consequences is more important than the seriousness of the consequences. Reward for compliance. Rewarding your child when she makes good decisions is more effective than punishing her when she makes wrong choices.

Parents who don't use these three components in their discipline and then react harshly and unpredictably create aggressiveness in their children as Carol Tavris indicates:

> Parents of aggressive boys use a great deal of punishment (shouting, scolding, spanking), yet they fail to make the punishment contingent on the child's behavior. They do not state clear rules, require compliance, praise good behavior, or consistently punish violations. Instead they threaten, scold, nag, bluster, and "natter" at the child, but, Patterson adds, "they seldom follow through on their threats." So the child continues to misbehave. At infrequent and unpredictable intervals the parents explode and verbally or physically assault the child. This pattern of parental behavior has been repeatedly linked to children's aggressiveness in elementary school.[2]

Some couples do quite well presenting the rules but then never check to see if they are being followed. Some parents do the first two pieces very well but then collapse when it comes to giving meaningful consequences. How are you doing in these areas? If you have a weak link, where is it?

| Weak Link | Remedy |
|---|---|
| Presenting the rules | • Discuss with your spouse the specific rules you need.<br>• Update the current set of rules. They need to be revised as children mature.<br>• Reduce the number of rules.<br>• Write down the rules and post them.<br>• Clarify which parent is in charge of presenting which rules.<br>• Have a family conference to clarify the rules.<br>• Develop a written contract (outlining expectations, rewards, and consequences), which is signed by parents and child. |

| Weak Link | Remedy |
|---|---|
| Monitoring the behavior | • Specify who is in charge of monitoring which behavior.<br>• Determine how behavior will be monitored.<br>• Take turns following up on the expectations and behavior.<br>• Schedule events so additional effort isn't required to supervise. |
| Enforcing the conse-<br>quences | • Allow natural consequences to do their work. Don't interfere or rescue your child from them.<br>• Make sure you and your spouse agree on the consequences so you both support them.<br>• Choose consequences that require a minimal amount of your effort or supervision.<br>• Reduce the length of the consequences so you don't have to enforce the consequence over a long period.<br>• Write down the consequence (time frame, parameters) so you don't forget what you imposed. |

Some parents have significant fears that hinder presenting and monitoring rules and enforcing consequences. These usually include the concern that they:

*Don't want to make things worse.* If you don't enforce rules, won't things also get worse?

*Don't want to make their child mad or upset.* The child will be mad and upset, but that doesn't mean your relationship is over.

*Don't want their child not to like them.* Parenting isn't a popularity contest. You will need to make decisions that aren't popular.

### Make Consequences Effective

Paul Simon sang the song "Fifty Ways to Leave Your Lover." I can't sing or write lyrics, and I'm only half as creative. So I've written "Twenty-five Ways to Foul Up Perfectly Good Consequences."

| Problem | Remedy |
|---|---|
| 1. Benefits of wrongdoing are greater than consequence for wrongdoing. | 1. Increase consequence within reasonable limits. |
| 2. Enforcement of consequences is uncertain. | 2. Monitor consequences more closely to ensure certainty. |

| Problem | Remedy |
|---|---|
| 3. Consequence is too far removed in time from the infraction. | 3. Work at having consequences closely follow infraction to reinforce cause-effect relationship. |
| 4. Consequence is not enforceable. | 4. Change consequence to an enforceable one. |
| 5. Consequence requires your child's cooperation. | 5. Use consequence that doesn't require cooperation of the child. |
| 6. Consequence is applied for too long a time period. | 6. Set a reasonable time frame so your point is made, but not so long as to only build resentment. |
| 7. Consequence is compounded beyond reasonable limit. | 7. Cool down before imposing consequence and don't increase consequence because you are angry. |
| 8. Consequence isn't related to infraction. | 8. Use consequence related to infraction if possible (if she talks too long on the phone, restrict her phone time). |
| 9. Parent uses only one consequence. | 9. Vary consequences. Don't ground for everything. |
| 10. Consequence was imposed when you were angry. | 10. Wait until cool to impose consequence. |
| 11. You're caught in a power struggle that you and your child both want to win. | 11. Walk away while you can; don't play that game. |
| 12. Parent inadvertently reinforces misbehavior rather than obedience. | 12. Make sure your attention is focused on actions you wish to see increased in frequency. Minimize the amount of time you spend disciplining. |
| 13. Parents disagree on presentation, monitoring, or enforcing of rules. | 13. Work out an agreement with your spouse. Blend perspectives; don't try to eliminate one view. |
| 14. Child works parents against each other. | 14. Stand united. Don't make decisions without discussing it with your spouse, communicate more, don't undermine. |
| 15. Parental guilt influences use and severity of consequences. | 15. Recognize the effects of your guilt. Don't allow it to be a major factor in how you make decisions. |
| 16. Parental rescuing interferes with natural consequences. | 16. Use natural consequences and shift to a supportive role to help the child deal with the consequence. |

| Problem | Remedy |
|---|---|
| 17. High parental tolerance level (child can get away with too much before parent intervenes). | 17. Don't wait until things are at a crisis point to intervene—great patience isn't necessarily a virtue. |
| 18. Low parental tolerance level (everything is a major problem). | 18. Don't get upset over minor things. Think about what behavior is most important. |
| 19. Parent is uncomfortable with being the "bad guy" or "the heavy" and avoids disciplinary situations. | 19. Realize that sometimes you have to take a stand because of the future implications it has for your child. Get support. |
| 20. Parent doesn't want to risk alienating the child because they are "best friends." | 20. You aren't supposed to be best friends at this point in life. As a parent your job is to guide. |
| 21. Parent doesn't have power to enforce consequences. | 21. Check for power leaks—how do you give your power away? Use your strengths and find community help. |
| 22. Parental history of abuse in family of origin. | 22. Be firm and clear in expectations and consequences. Guard against being physical. |
| 23. Parent blames others and protects child. | 23. Hold child accountable for her actions. That is how she learns to change her behavior. |
| 24. Inconsistent enforcement of rules (parental mood becomes the basis of enforcement). | 24. Be as consistent as you can be. Modify rules so that you can consistently enforce them. |
| 25. Parent substitutes other behaviors for consequences. For example, he yells and threatens only. | 25. Stop talking and start acting. Use consequences so you don't have to nag or lecture. |

Similar to the message on the Crest toothpaste box, consequences have been shown to be an effective teaching method that can be of significant value when used as directed in a conscientiously applied program of discipline and regular parental care! Use them wisely as they can be of great assistance in helping your child make good decisions.

# Recommended Books

Foster Cline and Jim Fay. *Parenting with Love and Logic: Teaching Children Responsibility*. Colorado Springs: Piñon Press, 1990.

Noni Cohen-Sandler and Michelle Silver. *I'm Not Mad, I Just Hate You!* New York: Penguin, 1999.

So why is he so angry, and what can you do about it? Now that you've observed your child and thought about the principles in this book, you have a clearer idea of why he's angry. You now know several things you can do to help.

Dealing with anger can be hard, but you know your child better than anyone in the world, and you love him more than anyone else. Because of your knowledge, special relationship, and love, you can have a tremendous influence on him and his behavior. In fact no one is in a better position than you to pray for him, help him understand, listen to him, support him, teach him, provide a good example for him, give him skills for managing his life, emotions, and anger, and hold him accountable.

At times it will be difficult, but you can do it, and it will be worth it—for both of you!

# Helping Your Child Deal with Life Experiences

## Abuse

| Generates Anger Because: | Parental Plan | Encourage Your Child To: |
|---|---|---|
| • Safety is compromised.<br>• Pain is inflicted.<br>• Fear is heightened. | *Provide a safe environment.*<br><br>• Ensure safety. No progress can be made until your child is physically safe from the abuser.<br>• Take reasonable precautions (night light, lock doors . . .), but avoid going overboard as this may frighten the child.<br>• Contain your fear and deal with it, not allowing it to spill over to your child. | • Be honest about fears. Don't pretend to be brave.<br>• Say what would help him/her feel safe. |
| • Child became a victim with little or no power to stop the abuse. | *Hold abuser responsible for his/her actions.*<br><br>• If the parent is the abuser, he must take responsibility for his actions by admitting he was wrong, apologizing, and taking necessary steps to make sure incident doesn't reoccur.<br>• Apologize and make necessary amends. | • Accept that the abuser did something wrong and must be held accountable.<br>• Accept an apology.<br>• Be cautious about interacting with the abuser. Stay where it is safe. |

- Child was warned not to tell.
- She was probably repeatedly told it was her fault the abuse occurred.
- Power is abused.

- Reassure your child that telling was the right thing to do.

- Feel good about speaking up.

*Empower your child.*

- Help her see she already took the first step of reclaiming her life by telling and dealing with the situation.
- Talk with her about how she's changed since the event. She's bigger, stronger, wiser . . .

- Identify her strengths and resources that would prevent future abuse.

- Trust is broken.
- She often feels guilty as though she were the cause of the abuse.

*Address the emotions connected to the abuse.*

- Help your child identify the emotions that are connected to the abusive situation: anger, rage, shame, fear, sadness, guilt.
- Check back with your child at new developmental milestones to minimize the impact of the abuse.

- Talk about feelings and identify trouble spots.
- Deal with feelings and not ignore them.
- Be aware that coping with the abuse once won't resolve the issue forever. She may have to determine how she feels about the abuse at various stages of her life.

- Relationships are strained or broken.

*Help your child build a positive life that isn't centered on the abuse.*

- Work at developing a positive relationship.
- Build trust.
- Spend time in positive activities.

- Leave the door open to have a positive relationship with a parent who was the abuser.
- Be cautious in interacting with the abuser until the trust is reestablished.
- Not develop an identity around the abuse.
- Not let the abuse interfere with positive activities.

## Divorce

| Generates Anger Because: | Parental Plan | Encourage Your Child To: |
|---|---|---|
| • There is nothing the child can do about it. It's an adult decision. (Ironically, children often feel responsible for the divorce.) | *Provide appropriate information to help your child understand.*<br>• Tell child about the divorce only when it is absolutely certain.<br>• Provide pertinent information regarding changes, moves, school, contact with the other parent, location of favorite toys/bed/belongings.<br>• Reassure child he didn't cause the divorce.<br>• Encourage child to ask questions. | • Ask questions.<br>• Share his ideas and input.<br>• Talk about his feelings and concerns.<br>• Ask for what he wants. |
| • He has many difficult adjustments to make—personal, emotional, financial. | *Minimize changes when possible.*<br>• Don't move or change schools, keep the children together, continue doing the activities they enjoy.<br>• Find a workable routine and stick with it.<br>• Help child differentiate between areas he must accept and those he can do something about. | • Learn the routine and stick with it.<br>• Do something about the things he can control; accept those things he can't change.<br>• Talk about the adjustments.<br>• Ask for help. |
| • He loses a parent or parental contact in some form. | *Maximize the time and connection with each parent.*<br>• Children benefit from a relationship with both mom and dad.<br>• Make regular and predictable contact with child.<br>• Celebrate birthdays, holidays, and special events.<br>• Don't use visitation as a weapon.<br>• Periodically reassess the visitation plan as child's needs change. | • Contact parents in ways he can (phone, letter, visits).<br>• Take time to be with a parent—instead of always being with friends.<br>• Make the best of the time he does have with each parent.<br>• Ask for special times with a parent if desired. |

- He is pulled in both directions and can't make one parent happy without hurting the other one. It causes loyalty problems, especially if one parent expects 100 percent loyalty. (Even if parents don't demand allegiance, children fear betraying a parent.)

- Some parents continue to fight and litigate long after the divorce is final (longer litigation creates more mental health problems, especially for the child).

- Some parents make the child into a confidant, a junior parent, or pseudo-spouse. (This creates jealousy and adjustment problems when that parent begins to date.)

*Avoid putting child in situations where he must choose sides.*

- Don't use child as a pawn, snitch, spy, or message carrier.
- Encourage child to be honest, not slanting his conversations with either parent to avoid hurting the parent's feelings.
- Parents should make the custody/visitation decisions.
- Don't entice or manipulate the child to want to live with you by offering large gifts, special privileges, lenient rules, or extravagant vacations.

*Resolve differences with ex-spouse as quickly as possible.*

- Resolve legal issues as quickly as possible, preferably without involving child in court process.
- Don't pump child for useable information about the other parent. Keep him out of your fights.
- Don't try to control or punish the ex-spouse.
- Focus energy on things you can control.
- Keep negative thoughts to yourself about the other parent.
- Reach for the goal of resolution, not exact fairness for each parent.

*Keep parent/child boundaries clear. Don't make child your confidant.*

- Retain reasonable rules and expectations. Don't make him a junior parent.
- Find adult support and direction for your emotional needs.
- Deal with your loss, guilt, and anger.
- Invest your time and energy in building your new life.
- Nurture yourself, pray, read.

- Be honest with both parents about how he feels. Avoid trying to say only what the parent wants to hear.
- Ask parents not to expect him to choose sides.
- Avoid laying guilt trips on parents.

- Ask parents not to expect information about the other parent from him.
- Ask each parent not to talk negatively about the other one.
- Not threaten to go live with the other parent when he doesn't get his way.

- Focus on his adjustments and allow parents to do the same.
- Be a child, not the "little man or woman" of the house.

## Blended Family

| Generates Anger Because: | Parental Plan | Encourage Your Child To: |
|---|---|---|
| • Your child loses hope her biological parents will reunite. With the new marriage, the loss becomes permanent. She may not be ready to move on to a new family unit. | *Deal with your divorce before you date. Ask yourself, Why didn't my marriage work?* <br>• Take your time to grieve the losses associated with the divorce. <br>• Share your feelings and listen, listen, listen to your children. | • Talk, share feelings and struggles. <br>• Identify specific adjustment concerns. |
| • Child can't meet all the expectations placed on her by parents and stepparents. | *Be realistic in your stepfamily expectations.* <br>• Don't expect instant love and caring. <br>• Read stepfamily books, and be patient. | • Ask clearly and consistently for what she wants. <br>• Give the new people in the family a chance. |
| • She must live with changes and losses: less contact with one parent, fewer financial resources, and less emotional support. If she had to move or change schools, she has lost friends. | *Minimize changes and additional losses when possible.* <br>• If you must move, try to keep your children in the same school. <br>• Maintain usual activities when possible. <br>• Provide substitute roles or jobs when practical. | • Grieve. Deal with the losses, and don't avoid the pain through drugs, sex, or alcohol. <br>• Talk about her anger rather than act on it. <br>• Seek new roles and ways she can contribute to the family. |
| • Relationships may be significantly different with her parent. | *Spend special individual time with your biological children.* <br>• Schedule a regular time and keep it a priority. <br>• Don't include the stepparent in your individual time. | • Ask for time or attention. <br>• Not to act up to get attention. <br>• Make time with the parent a priority. |
| • Loyalty conflicts occur. Can she like and get along with the new stepparent and still be loyal to her biological parent? | *Avoid putting your child in a situation where she must choose sides.* <br>• Don't bad-mouth the other parent or stepparent (no matter how deserving). <br>• Don't tell your child, "You don't have to listen to or obey your stepparent." <br>• Encourage her to have a positive relationship with her stepparent. | • Ask parents not to put her in the middle. <br>• Be honest with both parents concerning feelings and thoughts. |

- There are authority and discipline problems. Does the stepparent have the right to discipline her? Are expectations and discipline consistent between the biological children and the stepchildren?

*Clarify parental rules and ruling system.*

- Parent and stepparent need to clarify, agree upon, and apply reasonable rules, expectations, and consequences to all the children in the home.
- Initially the biological parent makes the bulk of the discipline decisions, allowing the stepparent time to develop a positive relationship.
- Inform the children of your expectations regarding the stepparent's authority and jurisdiction.

- Follow the rules.
- Don't argue technicalities.
- Be respectful.
- Work at building the family, not tearing it down.
- Take time to get to know the new stepparent.

- She lacks personal power to achieve her desires.

*Seek input from the children.*

- Get information from all your children about how they would like the family to interact and what they want their family to be like.
- Help your child distinguish between those things she can do something about and those she must accept.

- Ask for what she needs.
- Focus on the things she can do!
- Do the things she can do.
- Accept the things she can't change.

## Parental Favoritism

| Generates Anger Because: | Parental Plan | Encourage Your Child To: |
|---|---|---|
| • It's not fair! The favored one receives the best the parent has to offer, while he receives the leftovers. | *Listen to and examine any claims of favoritism.*<br><br>• Make sure your affection, resources, and attention are equitably distributed. (It doesn't have to be exact, just reasonable.) | • Talk with you about his concerns rather than act on his anger by doing mean things to the favored one.<br>• Be appreciative of what he receives. |
| • The parent doesn't understand him. Parents reportedly listen to the star, but don't listen to him. | • Validate and understand your child's perceptions without becoming defensive. | • Calmly and respectfully talk about his concerns at times when you aren't angry or trying to get out of something. |

- The parent isn't doing anything to correct the situation.

*Deal with your child's concerns, letting him know you are taking him seriously.*

- Develop a plan to address the concerns of both the favored child and his siblings.

- He can't do anything to correct the situation.

*Develop a consistent structure in the home so that everyone is judged and rewarded according to the same expectations.*

- Don't get caught up in the negative cycle by giving more to the favored child because of the negative treatment he received from his angry siblings.
- Call the siblings on their inappropriate behavior. Getting even isn't okay.

- The nonfavored siblings believe they can't do anything to become a favored child.

*Affirm your love.*

- Show your love to all your children.
- Indicate ways the nonfavored siblings could also gain your approval and blessing.

- The favored child reports bad things about him to the parent.

*Hold the star accountable for his actions.*

- Don't automatically believe everything the star tells you. Check it out.
- Hold the favored child accountable.

- Be patient and give parents an opportunity to correct the situation.
- Don't become sarcastic.

- Be sure his own behavior is appropriate.
- Give you time to deal with the problem by keeping out of the situation.

- Ask what he can do to feel closer to the parent.
- Ask for what he wants.
- Avoid revenge as a way of dealing with the problem.

- Talk about the situation with the parent and not try to deal with it himself.

## Parental Abandonment

| Generates Anger Because: | Parental Plan | Encourage Your Child To: |
|---|---|---|
| • Your child doesn't understand why the parent left.<br>• She wants contact with the absent parent (A.P.).<br>• Directly confronting the A.P. may push him even further away. | *Provide pertinent information regarding the parent's absence.*<br><br>• If available, provide the address so your child can contact the A.P. | • Deal with her loss rather than avoid it or pretend it doesn't matter.<br>• Ask questions.<br>• Decide if she wants to contact the A.P.<br>• Determine what she wants to communicate.<br>• Write a letter when she's ready to deal with either a positive or negative outcome. |

- She feels like she is missing out—her friends have a dad and a mom.

- The absent parent makes promises he doesn't keep.

- She wants to know the missing parent and what he's like in order to shape her sense of self-identity.
- She thinks she did something wrong that caused the parent to leave.
- She wants the A.P.'s approval.

*Don't overcompensate for the absent parent's lack of involvement.*

- Assist your child to clarify why she's upset and what she can do to make things better.

*Empathize with your child but don't be overly negative.*

- Help your child evaluate whether the promises can be trusted.
- Encourage your child to adopt a "wait and see" attitude rather than going through the emotional roller coaster of great excitement and then great disappointment.

*Support your child to reach resolution concerning the absent parent.*

- Check to see if your child feels guilty. Reassure her that she wasn't the cause of the parent's departure.
- Wonder with your child what will happen if she never receives the A.P.'s approval.

- Acknowledge her loss and the accompanying feelings and what she is going to do about the situation.

- Determine how she feels about the A.P.

- Talk with you about the parent's leaving.
- Think about the kind of person she really is, hopefully reaching the conclusion that the absent parent is missing out on a relationship with a terrific kid!
- Think about why she needs the absent parent's acceptance.
- Think about how she will cope if she never gets that acceptance.

## Losses

| Generate Anger Because: | Parental Plan | Encourage Your Child To: |
|---|---|---|
| • He misses what has been lost.<br>• He begins to realize he isn't invincible—bad things do happen to him.<br>• He feels guilty or responsible about what he did or should have done that might have prevented the loss.<br>• He feels helpless to make things better. | *Support him to accept the reality of the loss.*<br><br>• Encourage your child to deal with his emotions, not avoid them through drugs, alcohol, sex, television, video games.<br>• Empathize. | • Grieve his loss and expect the accompanying emotions. Don't try to avoid them.<br>• Identify and deal with one emotion or situation at a time. |
| • His life has been changed and he must deal with it.<br>• The loss creates his first sense of immortality. | *Help him to adjust to the loss and accompanying changes.*<br><br>• Listen, listen, listen.<br>• Assist him to make sense out of the loss.<br>• Assist your child to make the needed adjustments.<br>• Highlight his strengths and his ability to cope.<br>• Help him differentiate between areas he must accept and areas he can do something about. | • Take charge of areas that he can influence.<br>• See if some good can come out of this difficult situation. |
| • It's difficult to move on without the deceased or the important aspects of life that were lost. | *Help him move on, investing time and energy into new endeavors.*<br><br>• Help him understand the importance and fragile nature of life.<br>• Assist him to "seize the moment" and reprioritize issues in his life.<br>• Give him permission to move on. | • Incorporate this experience into his life and his view of life.<br>• Say good-bye. |

# Parental Alcoholism or Drug Use

| Generates Anger Because: | Parental Plan | Encourage Your Child To: |
|---|---|---|
| *Specifically regarding the drinking parent:*<br><br>• Parental expectations may vary from day to day.<br>• Parental behavior is unpredictable—large mood swings and erratic behavior.<br>• The drinker can't be counted on to attend ball games, concerts, or other activities.<br>• The drinker may be very hard to please.<br>• The drinker makes promises he doesn't keep.<br>• The child can't stop the parent from drinking. He may feel blamed or responsible for the parent's drinking.<br>• The child is frustrated with the lack of a close relationship with that parent. | *Parental plan for the using parent:*<br><br>• Honestly and openly examine how your usage impacts you and your family.<br>• Don't minimize the impact of your usage.<br>• Understand that to stop using requires lifestyle changes, not just discontinuing the usage.<br>• Choose to stop drinking and set a date to stop.<br>• Go public with your decision to quit.<br>• Develop a plan to quit—use countering and environmental control techniques.<br>• Increase your support to stay sober.<br>• Keep your promises and reconnect with your family. | • Do a good job and feel good about it, even if the drinking parent doesn't approve.<br>• Not use the parental drinking as an excuse to drink or do other things he wants to do.<br>• Understand that the drinking parent must choose to stop.<br>• Offer support for the using parent not to drink.<br>• Offer to spend time with the using parent to help their relationship.<br>• Deal with the losses and disappointments directly. Be sad, angry, and disappointed about the situation.<br>• Don't take on a negative mind-set that there is nothing he can do about difficult situations in his life. |
| *Specifically regarding the family:*<br><br>• Using parent doesn't make amends for his poor choices.<br>• The home is not a secure, stable environment.<br>• There is little family fun.<br>• It's not okay to talk about feelings, the only emotion expressed is anger.<br>• Issues aren't resolved; they're swept under the rug. | *Parental plan for the non-using parent:*<br><br>• Don't soften the consequences of drinking for the using parent.<br>• Provide structure and help your family members focus on their responsibilities—not on the user's responsibilities.<br>• Initiate and take time for family fun.<br>• Encourage your children to identify and talk about their feelings.<br>• Deal with issues instead of avoiding them.<br>• Develop a plan and work toward resolution of issues. | • Stop excusing poor parental choices.<br>• Understand that it isn't his responsibility to stop the parent from using.<br>• Be accountable for his responsibilities.<br>• Join in the family fun.<br>• Identify his feelings and begin to talk about them instead of pushing them down and ignoring them.<br>• Be willing to talk about issues, offering his input and committing to resolving them. |

## Parental Overindulgence

| Stopping Overindulgence Generates Anger Because: | Parental Plan | Encourage Your Child To: |
| --- | --- | --- |
| • He likes getting everything he wants. | *Deal with the reasons why you feel compelled to give him too much.*<br><br>• Identify the specifics that cause you to give too much.<br>• Separate your issues from your child's concerns.<br>• Deal with your guilt and sympathy. | • Realize it's unrealistic to get everything he wants.<br>• Deal with his feelings regarding his life situations instead of expecting special treatment because of them. |
| • He believes he's entitled to whatever he wants. His mind-set says he should get what he wants without working for it. | *Decide to stop the overindulgence.*<br><br>• Talk with your spouse and determine together how the overindulgence is harming your child.<br>• Decide when you are going to change how you treat him. | • Understand the difference between "entitlement" and "earning what you get."<br>• Explore how his mind-set influences his perceptions and actions. |
| • He doesn't like operating on the "earn your way" system as it's harder than the "entitlement" plan. | *With your spouse develop reasonable and agreed upon expectations, rewards, and consequences.*<br><br>• Develop a written plan of what you expect. | • Begin to accept the change.<br>• Talk with you about the expectations, rewards, and consequences.<br>• Deal with the changes in a positive way, minimizing the amount of trouble he may incur. |
| • He doesn't like the changes, and you didn't even consult with him before making the decision. | *Advise your child of the change and be prepared to be tested.*<br><br>• Involve those who can support you to be firm.<br>• Contact those your child may turn to when he wishes to avoid consequences. They need also to be firm and not rescue him from his deserved consequences. | • Develop new ways of getting what he wants.<br>• Stop pouting, whining, threatening, manipulating. |

- Initially he doesn't perform well and is upset about how little he earns.

*Give him what he earns, reinforcing cause and effect.*

- Emphasize cause-and-effect connection.
- Reinforce effort.
- Don't give in to poor performance or manipulation.

- Work at the expectations instead of fighting against them.
- Refine behaviors that get him what he wants.
- Feel good about the effort he's exerted.

- He's only interested in how he feels and what he gets.

*Teach the importance of empathy for others.*

- Understanding how others feel makes it easier to share and be considerate.

- Empathize with others.
- Look at situations from others' perspectives.

# Helping Your Child Manage Anger

## A.N.G.E.R Tips for Parents

### Assess Feelings
### Ephesians 4:26

| Child's Responsibility | Parents' Responsibility | Negative Outcome | Positive Outcome |
|---|---|---|---|
| *Goal:* Identify and use feelings beneath anger.<br>Q: *How do I feel?*<br>*Action:* Stop what he's doing.<br>• Honestly identify his feelings concerning situation—not just his anger.<br>• Use the feelings to develop an action plan consistent with biblical/parental principles. | • Help child identify his feelings by giving feedback, asking questions, explaining your feelings.<br>• Help him see the connection between his feelings, the specific event, and his actions. | • Child acted only on his anger.<br>• He denied feelings, forcing them to be dealt with indirectly.<br>• He blamed others for causing him to have certain feelings. | • Child had awareness of his feelings and their influence on his behavior.<br>• He used awareness to plan positive response. |

## Neutralize Anger
### James 1:19–20; Psalm 103:8

| Child's Responsibility | Parents' Responsibility | Negative Outcome | Positive Outcome |
|---|---|---|---|
| *Goal:* Neutralize strong emotions so child doesn't immediately act on them.<br>Q: *How can I cool down?*<br>*Action:* Delay responding until cool and in control.<br>• Call a time-out, count, write, draw, talk.<br>• Identify triggers that cause great anger.<br>• Do things that calm her down. | • Positive modeling.<br>• Encourage time-outs.<br>• Help child discover things that calm her down.<br>• Set guidelines for angry behavior.<br>• Enforce consequences: She must repair damage, replace items. | • Emotions, not thought, dictated response.<br>• She offended more people, making it harder to reach a solution.<br>• The situation escalated to a higher problem level. | • Thought dictated response rather than emotions.<br>• Child is prepared to deal positively with people and situation. |

## Gauge Anger
### Proverbs 29:11; Amos 1:11

| Child's Responsibility | Parents' Responsibility | Negative Outcome | Positive Outcome |
|---|---|---|---|
| *Goal:* Determine appropriate amount of anger relative to goal and significance of event.<br>Q: *How angry should I be?*<br>*Action:* Think about consequences from last time he blew up.<br>• Choose his anger level. | • Offer guidance, perspective, personal successes and failures.<br>• Give direction to help him stay calm.<br>• When appropriate, physically contain him, call police. | • Amount of anger not matched with goal and importance of event.<br>• Overreacted or underreacted, causing people to miss his point. | • Made a good match of anger with goal and importance of event, allowing people to see his point. |

## Engage the Correct Person
### Matthew 5:22–24; 18:15–17

| Child's Responsibility | Parents' Responsibility | Negative Outcome | Positive Outcome |
|---|---|---|---|
| *Goal:* Choose appropriate time, place, and circumstance to talk with the right person about the correct issue.<br>Q: *Who am I mad at, and why?*<br>*Action:* Determine correct person and issue.<br>• Clarify what she needs—use "I" messages. | • Model appropriate way of approaching and talking to people.<br>• Give feedback on where the child is directing her anger.<br>• Help child determine her needs. | • If problem solving is attempted with wrong person or about wrong issue, there is minimal or ineffective resolution. | • Child talked with right person about right issue, so problem solving can proceed. |

## Resolve the Situation
### Matthew 18:15

| Child's Responsibility | Parents' Responsibility | Negative Outcome | Positive Outcome |
|---|---|---|---|
| *Goal:* Reach resolution and move on.<br>Q: *What can I do to make this better?*<br>*Action:* Do what she can to make improvements, regardless of what other person does.<br>• Ask for what he wants, negotiate, focus on his actions, shift his perspective, forgive, find something good in the situation.<br>• Accept what he can't change and move on. | • Model positive negotiation skills.<br>• Ask questions about situation to help him clarify his position and to identify his responsibility.<br>• Support him in developing a plan or creating other workable solutions.<br>• Help him grieve and move on. | • Didn't resolve issue, causing ongoing trouble.<br>• Didn't resolve relationship concerns.<br>• Kept energy tied up in negative interaction. | • Resolved the issue.<br>• Mended the relationship so it can continue in a positive direction.<br>• Freed up energy that can now be used in other situations. |

# Notes

## Chapter 2 Divorce

1. Mitchell A. Baris and Carla B. Garrity, *Children of Divorce: A Developmental Approach to Residence and Visitation* (DeKalb, Ill.: Psytec Corporation, 1988), 8–10.

2. Lise Bisnaire, Philip Firestone, and David Rynard, "Factors Associated with Academic Achievement in Children Following Parental Separation," *American Journal of Orthopsychiatry* 60, no. 1 (January 1990), 75.

3. Ibid.

4. N. Kalter, "Long-term Effects of Divorce on Children: A Developmental Vulnerability Model," *American Journal of Orthopsychiatry* 57, no. 4 (October 1987), 597.

5. Baris and Garrity, *Children of Divorce,* 4.

6. Ibid.

7. www.divorcecentral.com/parent/par_ans.html, p. 3.

8. Baris and Garrity, *Children of Divorce,* 5.

## Chapter 3 Blended Family

1. Emily Visher and John Visher, *Stepfamilies: A Guide to Working with Stepparents and Stepchildren* (New York: Brunner/Mazel, 1979), 164.

2. www.askdrgayle.com/mhsf.html

3. Tom and Adrienne Frydenger, *Stepfamily Problems: How to Solve Them* (Grand Rapids: Revell, 1991), 177.

4. www.askdrgayle.com/mhsf.html

## Chapter 6 Losses

1. Janice Wood Wetzel, *Clinical Handbook of Depression* (New York: Gardner Press, 1984), 302.

2. J. William Worden, *Grief Counseling and Grief Therapy: A Handbook for the Mental Health Practitioner* (New York: Springer Publishing, 1991).

## Chapter 7 Parental Alcoholism or Drug Use

1. James Prochaska, John Norcross, and Carlo Diclemente, *Changing for Good* (New York: Avon, 1994), 176.

2. Ibid, 30.

## Chapter 8 Parental Overindulgence

1. Prochaska et al., *Changing for Good,* 134.

## Chapter 10 Mind-sets

1. Ross Green, *The Explosive Child* (New York: HarperCollins, 1998), 12.

## Chapter 14 Solution Problems

1. Stephen R. Covey, *The Seven Habits of Highly Effective People* (New York: Simon & Schuster, 1989), 83.

## Chapter 15 Focus Problems

1. Larry Fisher, "New Directions in ADHD" workshop, 2501 Cypress Creek Road, Cedar Park, Tex. 78613; 1-800-272-4641; web site: www.rage-behavior.com

2. For the complete list of the fifty tips, see http://www3.sympatico.ca/frankk/50class.htm

3. *Mental Health: A Report of the Surgeon General* at www.surgeongeneral.gov/library/mentalhealth/chapter3/sec4.html.

4. Ibid.

5. American Psychiatric Association, *Diagnostic and Statistical Manual of Mental Disorders,* 4th ed. (Washington, D.C., 1994), 78–85.

6. http://www.chadd.org/doe/doe-par.htm

## Chapter 17 Assess Feelings

1. Neil Clark Warren, *Make Anger Your Ally* (Colorado Springs: Focus on the Family, 1990), 3.

2. Ibid., 79.

## Chapter 18 Neutralize Emotions

1. Carol Tavris, *Anger: The Misunderstood Emotion* (New York: Simon & Schuster, 1989), 159.

2. Marsha M. Linehan, workshop material at http://faculty.washington.edu/linehan

## Chapter 19 Gauge Anger

1. Tavris, *Anger,* 151–52.

## Chapter 21 Resolve the Situation

1. John Gottman, *The Seven Principles for Making Marriage Work* (New York: Crown, 1999), 161.

## Chapter 22 Parental Modeling

1. Warren, *Make Anger Your Ally,* 4–5.
2. Howard Markman, Scott Stanley, and Susan L. Blumberg, *Fighting for Your Marriage* (San Francisco: Jossey-Bass, 1994), 13.
3. Ibid., 14.
4. Ibid., 20.
5. Ibid., 18.
6. Ibid., 25.

## Chapter 23 Parental Decisions

1. Tavris, *Anger,* 307–8.

## Chapter 26 Parental Consequences

1. Gottman, *Seven Principles,* 50–51.
2. Tavris, *Anger,* 308.

**Dr. Richard L. Berry** is a full-time marriage and family therapist with Youth Alternatives, where he receives numerous referrals from the courts, schools, community agencies, and parents concerning angry kids. He resides in Cheyenne, Wyoming.